WHAT EVER HAPPENED TO VATICAN II?

What Ever Happened to Vatican II?

Michael M. Winter

Sheed & Ward
London

ISBN 0–7220–9720–4

Published in Great Britain in 1985 by
Sheed & Ward Limited,
2, Creechurch Lane,
London, EC3A 5AQ

Book production Bill Ireson

Filmset by Waveney Typesetters, Norwich, Norfolk
Printed and bound by
A. Wheaton & Co. Ltd., Exeter, Devon

Contents

Acknowledgements

The quotations from the texts of Vatican II are taken fro
the edition of W. M. Abbott, *The Documents of Vatican I*
New York, 1966.

Parts of Chapters Four and Five appeared originally in *T.
Month*, and I am grateful to the editor for permission
reproduce them here.

Introduction

Twenty years have elapsed since the Second Vatican Council concluded its deliberations (8 December 1965), but we have not yet seen the results which might reasonably have been expected from it. It is argued that half a century elapsed before the reforms of the Council of Trent became effective. ·That is perfectly true, but we are now living in a society where social change is so rapid that twenty years in this period accomplishes the changes that required fifty years in the sixteenth century. Admittedly there have been some changes in Church life, of which the most obvious is the celebration of mass in English with the celebrant facing the congregation. But even in the liturgy the extent of change has been more apparent than real. For the most part we have contented ourselves with cosmetic alterations which usually amount to no more than optimising the performance of old structures inherited from pre-Conciliar days and not infrequently from the Middle Ages.

In the twenty year period which should have been one of progress, we have not been able to arrest the general decline which has afflicted all Churches, certainly in Great Britain (which is the area within which I limit my study). This fact is so widely accepted that I will not devote more space to it than is necessary to indicate the sort of evidence which has been brought forward during the last decade. Although practically every book and article which is published agrees with this general judgment of debility, it is not easy to define the criteria by which a Church may be judged to have succeeded or failed. Its operational objectives are too diffuse to be measured exhaustively. It is rather like an Art school. It is successful if it produces good artists; but what is a "good" artist, how many should it produce and how much benefit does it confer on society? The difficulty of devising a

satisfactory yardstick yields to the temptation of saying that
the operation is impossible and therefore might as well be
omitted. This is very dangerous and could induce the Church
members to live in a fools' paradise, refusing to consider the
possibility of their own shortcomings. Other walks of life
have their own harsh indicators of success or failure, even
where precise measurement is unattainable. Armies suffer
defeat, political parties lose elections, and commercial enterprises go bankrupt. For a Church we must try to discuss the
point of practical ineffectuality. A Church might go beyond
this point, without its members having noticed that it had
ceased to be serviceable. What is important is to try to
ascertain this point of practical ineffectuality, where a Church
ceases to hold the loyalty of large numbers of those born into
it, makes few converts, and exercises little influence on
society around it. Unfortunately, Churches are treated with
exceptional courtesy. If the clergy are still being paid, and if
the routine services are still being enacted, then it may not be
easy to discern when ineffectuality has occurred. In searching
for the indicators, something more comprehensive than
statistics must be found. Let us consider a few qualitative
indicators.

A small but significant straw in the wind is the fact that
Anthony Sampson no longer expounds religion as one of the
elements in the life of the nation. In the first edition of his
Anatomy of Britain, there was a chapter on the Churches,
alongside the universities, the stock exchange and other
institutions which shaped the pattern of public life. That was
in 1962. Twenty years later, *The Changing Anatomy of Britain*
contains no such chapter. Its omission is significant. Thirty
years ago, the government would consult the Churches
officially when certain types of social legislation were being
contemplated (the law affecting gambling, for instance), but
when the Warnock Committee was assembling evidence
with a view to legislation on genetic engineering, there was
no formal consultation with the Churches, although a
number of the Committee happened to be committed
Christians. In Cambridge, in the year 1985, for the first time
in the university's history, not one of the heads of colleges is
a cleric.

These are a few indicators, selected at random, to show the

areas from which religious influence is receding. Within the Churches themselves, their decline in members tells its own tale. Basic statistics of Church affiliation and practice are available in published sources; however, the different denominations do not employ the same criteria, and some carry out the operation more accurately than others. With these reservations, the conspectus of the last twenty years is as follows:

By the 1970s the Church of England's Easter communicants had diminished from 2,348,000 (in 1956) to 1,510,000 (in 1973). The Non-conformists have been declining for a number of years and their active membership was: Methodists 601,000 (in 1974); Baptists 263,000 (in 1971); and United Reformed Church 192,000 (in 1974).[1] Catholics have shown a similar diminution in number and practice, one indicator of which is the attendance at Sunday mass. Once a year, on a particular Sunday in October, the mass attendance is counted. Unfortunately, the *Catholic Directory* is too shy to publish the results, but they can be found in other sources. In 1962 there were 2,092,667 regular mass-goers, but they had contracted to 1,831,550 in 1973. The significance of those figures depends to some extent upon the estimate of the total number of Catholics (since in our Church the regular Sunday mass attendance is regarded as a serious obligation). There is no agreement on the exact figure. The pioneer of Catholic demography in this nation, A. E. C. W. Spencer, put it at a little over 7,000,000 in 1971.[2] Dr M. Hornsby-Smith concluded that it was approximately 6,000,000 in 1979.[3] Of all the figures collected or estimated by the Catholics, that of conversions is the most accurately recorded. Before Vatican II the annual total was between 10,000 and 12,000; ten years after the Council it seemed to have levelled off at a little over 5,000. The Catholic Directories for the appropriate years indicate that there were 5,352 conversions in 1973, 5,225 in 1975 and 5,034 in 1976.

After 1980 the same trends continued. The Church of England's Easter communicants have declined by 3.3 per cent between 1980 and 1982.[4] The Methodists counted 487,972 members in 1981, Baptists were 221,766 adult members in 1983, and United Reformed Church members numbered 150,000 in 1981.[5] Among the Catholics, conversions numbered 5,783 in 1980, 5,731 in 1981 and 5,401 in

1982. The survey of Dr Hornsby-Smith, *Roman Catholic Opinion*, showed that the rate of matrimonial breakdown among Catholics was almost identical with that of the rest of the nation.[6] This is sad, but significant in a Church which attaches so much importance to the permanence of the marriage bond.

I will not devote further space to evidence of religious decline because the facts are agreed so widely by all writers on the subject.

It is significant, and reinforces the conviction about the enfeebled state of religion, that these indicators of debility among the mainstream Churches have taken place during a period when it is becoming clear that the world's major problems are basically religious. If we accept that the human race is seriously menaced by the danger of nuclear warfare, by the population explosion in relation to food production, by the unequal distribution of wealth, and the possible breakdown of the international banking system, then it will be equally clear that these are moral matters. Ultimately their resolution is a matter of the motives behind the decisions. Our technology is capable of producing sufficient food and the other components of a satisfactory life-style for the whole of the world's present population. The distribution of these benefits is the problem, and the priorities implied in the choices bring us directly to moral considerations, which is equivalent to regarding them as religious questions.[7]

The challenge facing Christians is fantastic. Really noble spirits have perceived it, and risen to the demands of the situaton. From the time of the worker priests in the 1940s to the Liberation theologians of the 1970s, dynamic personalities have sought to make the Church's mission relevant to society's needs. As will become apparent in the course of this book, the Church's inertia has tended to marginalise these initiatives instead of taking them into the mainstream of its life, largely by denying them the appropriate institutional framework. There is also the psychological inertia which militates against radical re-thinking and radical reform. Once again the profound thinkers have perceived what is needed and have not hesitated to say so. One representative example is the speech of the Jesuit General Fr Arrupe in the debate on Scheme 13 of the Vatical Council:

It is necessary that a Christian community should not enclose
itself in a ghetto, but live in the midst of ordinary life. Thence it
is necessary *to re-think all the pastoral methods*, and to bear in mind
the inadequacy of every theoretical solution, which remains in
the speculative realm without passing on to the level of practical
realities.[8]

In spite of that kind of insight, we in England have had little
more than cosmetic adaptation since the Council. The
paradox is heart-breaking. The quality of the conciliar
documents is so good, that it is unbelievable that the results
have been so poor.

In the course of this book there will be numerous instances
to show just how superficial have been the attempts to
implement the Conciliar decrees. For the moment one brief
example will suffice. In the response to the Council a dozen
or so episcopal commissions were established in 1967,
dealing with such matters as ecumenism, the laity, liturgy,
and priestly formation. Basically they were fact-finding
committees nominated by the Bishops' Conference, which
could be called upon to supply expert advice and information
when the bishops might call for it in the course of their work.
They bear a superficial resemblance to the British parliamentary or royal commissions which take evidence before new
legislation is introduced to Parliament. They have the same
weaknesses as those parliamentary commissions in that their
findings may be quietly shelved,[9] and the added weakness
that their deliberations are not normally published. Furthermore, they lack that refinement of a mature society, namely
the publication of the minority report. It would not be unfair
to categorise their work as the systematic evasion of radical
reform while giving the appearance of serious activity. One
humorist described it as re-arranging the deck-chairs on
board the Titanic. Ironically it has not been the bishops' commissions, but parallel organisations, with more independence
of episcopal control, which have produced the really valuable
work in the last twenty years. The activities of the CIIR
(Catholic Institute for International Relations) have been far
more effective than those of the commission on Justice and
Peace; similarly, the ARCIC (Anglo-Roman Catholic International Committee) committee has been of more service to
inter-Church affairs than the ecumenical commission.

What the Church needs in Great Britain, as well as elsewhere, is a reform of structures. This was perceived by the theologian M. J. Congar in the early 1950s, and it is still true today.[10]. His fundamental study about true and false reform in the Church is unsurpassed and his conclusions are as valid now as when he first enunciated them. At other times in its tumultuous history the Church stood in need of moral reform, or doctrinal reform in the face of heresy. Neither of those dangers confront us now. What is required is something more pedestrian, but absolutely necessary, and that is a reform of structures. Many of the institutions and the apparatus which served useful purposes in the past are now not merely useless, but constitute barriers to spiritual progress, as will become apparant in subsequent parts of this book.

Spiritually the Church shows remarkable signs of dynamism. Books about prayer by writers like Michel Quoist and Carlo Caretto, which are translated into all the main languages, are purchased in their thousands. The prayer life of the Church is dynamic. Since the Council we have shaken off the old inhibitions about using methods of prayer which other Churches have found helpful. The charismatic movement flourishes, and so does every other form of group prayer such as those who pray together in silence like the Quakers. The divine office is at last accessible to the laity, thanks to its being published in English.

Another sign of vitality is the sense of responsibility for social justice which is now widespread among Catholics. Organisations like CAFOD (Catholic Fund for Overseas Development) are flourishing, and this is both symptom and cause of a new awareness among believers that we must make use of our Christian convictions to influence the political and social life of the nation. The Catholic community as a whole has taken to heart Burke's dictum that "if wickedness is to triumph, it is only necessary for good men to do nothing". In all manner of organisations one sees Catholics working alongside other Christians: in Amnesty International, the peace movements, and countless other bodies which strive to bring justice into the workings of our society.

A further sign of spiritual dynamism is the number and

quality of the personalities who have emerged from within the Catholic Church offering inspiring ideas to the whole nation, like Lady Jackson, and Dr Schumacher. Many more could be named, but I will confine myself to those lately dead so as not to embarrass the living by praising them.

In spite of all these signs of encouragement, the Church as a whole manifests much lethargy and irrelevance. There is an unmistakable block which effectively inhibits the dynamism of the Council from transforming the community as a whole, despite the excellent theology of its Decrees and the signs of vitality which I have indicated in the preceding paragraphs. This block is nothing other than the persistence of obsolete structures and institutions. Expressing the situation in biblical terms, one can perceive it as a perfect illustration of the parable of the new wine in old wineskins. The new wine of the Vatical Council is too powerful for the skins inherited from the Middle Ages. It will become apparent in the course of this book that those institutions have been shattered and have lost their self-confidence. It is undeniable that the wine is being spilt, and the anguish which is felt by so many people as they contemplate this wastage is the reason why I have written this book to mark the twentieth anniversary of the Council.

Although Catholics repose great confidence in the workings of General Councils, their ultimate success cannot be taken for granted. Infallibility applies only to doctrinal definitions, but reforming Councils have no corresponding guarantee of achieving their results. The most striking example is that of the Fifth Lateran Council which took place during the pontificates of Popes Julius II and Leo X. Its working sessions lasted intermittently from May 1512 until March 1517, but it was almost totally ineffectual. As far as the reform of the Church was concerned, it might as well not have been held. Half a century later the Council of Trent occupied itself with the same reforms and was successful. The difference between the two was not a question of authority (both were General Councils), but the attitude of the entire Church was decisive. At the time of Lateran V the Church as a whole was not seriously concerned with moral reform, but at Trent, in the aftermath of Protestantism, the generality of the laity and clergy saw clearly the need for reform and had the will to achieve it. The decisive factor was the attitude and determination of the Church as a whole. In our own day it is pertinent to ask in all seriousness, how strong among us now is the will to reform the Church in obedience to the decisions of Vatican II? It is conceivable that they might remain merely an achievement on paper, and have no more effect on the Church's life than did the decisions of the Fifth Lateran Council.

Clearly there must be some intermediate steps between the documents of a General Council and their practical realisation in the life of the layman and the communities in which he lives and works. Psychologically, some sort of lift-off is needed. The Church in Latin America has given us a superb example of how this can be done. In 1968 the bishops of Latin America met in the Colombian city of Medellin, and after exhaustive deliberations produced practical guidelines for implementing Vatican II in the context of South America. The best known principle enunciated at that meeting was the preferential option for the poor.

In the last century the English Catholic community experienced something of a lift-off, or at least the opportunity to realise it, when the hierarchy was restored in 1850. The Vatican set up the normal system of diocesan bishops, to replace the former Vicars Apostolic. In effect, this iniative gave the bishops more autonomy and hence greater efficiency in organising the apostolate for a rapidly increasing number of Catholics. Shortly after 1850, four provincial synods were held, thanks to which the Church in this nation received all the apparatus of what was considered to be the "normal" Catholicism of mainland Europe. The limitations of this operation need not detain us now, but its effect has been to inhibit any further attempt at "lift-off", as if the efforts of the 1850s had left us exhausted and disinclined to do any further re-thinking, and still less any further re-organisation. It is rather like the psychological paralysis which afflicts British industry. Having led the world in the Industrial Revolution, we have shown a disinclination amounting to an inability to do any further fundamental re-organisation or planning. Basically the management of industry and the organisation of the Trades Unions possess the same pattern and the same presuppositions as they did in the latter part of the last century.

In the two decades since the Council there have been a number of events which could have provided the lift-off for the radical implementation of the Council's theology. They were the creation of the National Conference of Priests in 1969, the Liverpool Pastoral Congress in 1980, the establishment of new episcopal commissions in 1983, and the publication of the new Code of Canon Law in the same year. All of them have failed in that respect, and it will become apparent in different parts of this book that not one of them has been utilised to its full potential as a means of restructuring our institutions in such a way that the Council's insights can be applied at the practical level so as to transform the life of our community.

Two of these events warrant detailed analysis (the National Conference of Priests, and the Liverpool Congress), so I will deal with them in separate chapters (Three and Four), when I have set the scene with preliminary chapters on Mission, and Ecumenism (Chapters One and Two). The other two (the Commissions and the New Code) require less extensive treatment, and since they illustrate the principle that structural change is needed, I will include them here in the Introduction.

In 1967 a series of advisory bodies was created, whose members were to supply expert knowledge and information (on matters like liturgy or social justice) if and when the Bishops' Conference should require it. It was assumed that the systematic collection of such information would be particularly important in the aftermath of Vatican II, when the English Catholic community would be implementing the Council's decisions.

Their terms of reference were basically unsatisfactory. The members of the Commissions were all nominees of the bishops, and no other organisation (lay or clerical) had the right to insert their own representatives. They did not have the right to initiate research. If they were invited to find information and present reports the results of their efforts remained vulnerable. If the facts proved displeasing to the Bishops' Conference the matter could be shelved quietly. If the experts, who had expended much time and energy on the research, wished to publish the results themselves, they could be blocked effectively because the bishops claimed to possess the copyright on information which they had commissioned.

For sixteen years these bodies remained under-used and under-valued, until 1983 when they were re-organised. The former groups were re-shuffled, re-named and re-appeared in the form of six Departments, six Bodies[11] and eight Agencies. The Departments are concerned with such areas as Christian Doctrine and Formation, Social Responsibility, and International Affairs. The Bodies comprise the National Conference of Priests, the National Board of Catholic Women, the Canon Law Society, etc. Finally, the Agencies include the Catholic Youth Service Council, the Catholic Missionary Council, the Catholic Child Welfare Council and others. The Bodies elect their own chairmen and have a bishop as liaison officer for contact with the hierarchy. The others are presided over by a bishop.

Apart from tighter episcopal control, it is not clear how the new organisations will differ in their working from the former Commissions which they have replaced. The document which promulgated their inception sounds optimistic, but it may prove to be ill-founded. For instance, we read that:

> New opportunities for partnership and responsibility are being offered in the changes set out . . . The new structures will draw other ministries into effective co-operation with the bishops in at least eight new ways. (Paragraph 32.)

Among the eight new ways, the most exciting are that "there will be formal consultative status accorded to national bodies representing priests, religious and laity". And "the expert lay voice will make a more direct impact in the reformed committee and should enhance their intrinsic authority". (Paragraphs 32 Sections (a) and (c).) These are brave words. They read like an optimistic commercial advertisement, but nothing specific is said about how the aspirations are to be translated into practice. Later in the report Paragraph 62 indicates clearly who has the responsibility:

> When a committee wishes to report to the Conference as a whole or to seek a decision by the Conference, it will submit its point with a memorandum to the Standing Committee of the Conference. It should not undertake such action without the knowledge of the department's chairman.

This is hardly the language for encouraging the laity in a sense of initiative and responsibility; it shows that there are three levels of veto to be negotiated for an idea to be accepted, and no indication as to how it might be carried out in practice.

It would be unreasonable to expect dramatic progress in the short time which has elapsed since the reorganisation of the new Departments, but there is little in their constitution to suggest that they will be any more effective than their predecessors.

The final event which could have given us the post-conciliar lift-off was the appearance of the new Code of Canon Law in 1983. I will discuss its provisions in succeeding chapters, but for the moment I ask the reader to suspend judgement and prepare his mind for the realisation that this too has proved to be another disappointed hope. The fundamental structures, institutions and procedures which must be changed if the Council's theology is to influence our mission, will be seen to remain unreformed in the rules of the new Code. Thus we reach the sorry conclusion that all the opportunities of the last twenty years in Great Britain have failed to create the kind of opening which would allow the Vatican Council's decisions to transform our apostolate from the status of a holding operation to that of a genuine mission.

It will be apparent from the previous pages that the modernising operations carried out within the British Catholic community have penetrated no deeper than cosmetic alterations. In this we have not been alone. Other parts of the Church have been responsible for comparable trivialisations. For example, the reduction of the number of Minor Orders from four to two. In antiquity these minor orders of Porter, Reader, Exorcist and Acolyte, did have a functional purpose in the liturgy, in spite of the fact that they were an imitation of the Roman ladder of promotion for administrators, known as the *cursus honorum*. By the twentieth century it was apparent that they no longer possessed any importance. If the Church is anxious to divest itself of everything that is irrelevant, then it would have been logical to abolish them all. However, since they did no harm, it might have been justifiable to retain them for the sake of history. To have reduced the number from four to two fell neatly between two stools.

However, this reluctance to undertake fundamental reforms is not confined to the Catholic Church; it afflicts many other organisations, whose hesitations provide useful parallels to our own vacillations. The University of Cambridge presented a perfect comparison in the nineteenth century. A variety of factors conspired to urge reform upon the indolent university, and its authorities became alarmed lest Parliament should force it upon them. In order to stave off such a danger, which would have entailed radical reorganisation, they sought to undertake just enough reforming to satisfy their critics. To this end the university undertook a mass of trivialised activities, such as endless committees of enquiry, circulating vast quantities of memoranda, and they mistook it for creative innovation. In 1849 the Senate approved a provision which would exempt the students of classics from a preliminary examination in mathematics; but they did not manage to free them entirely. In the same year there was a bold suggestion that there should be an entrance examination for all students who wished to enter the university. After much discussion, it was rejected in the Senate by a vote of 29 to 11. A sympathetic writer has noted "such incidents as this, and the failure completely to remove the mathematical fetters from the classics Tripos, suggest that the university was not quite so capable of self-reform as it thought itself to be".[12] With small measures they felt themselves mightily satisfied, but they had evaded the far-reaching issues. At that time all Fellowships were held by bachelors, who had to resign upon marriage. A change of that arrangement was never envisaged. In the end, Parliament had to compel the university to accept realistic reforms which it had been incapable of undertaking on its own.

The motives which govern these reluctances are well understood now by sociologists: it is a widespread phenomenon. The reluctance of the British army in the 1930s to abandon cavalry in favour of tanks is yet another example. The resistance to reform was well known though before the sociologists analysed its causes. In sixteenth-century Italy, Machiavelli summed it up in an accurate (if inelegant) observation: "Innovation will always be opposed by those who have done well out of the old system". At times the resistance to change assumes tragic proportions, and it was one of the causes which led to the crucifixion of Jesus. His popularity posed a threat to the *status quo*. Admittedly, the Jews were living as subject people under the power of the Roman Empire, but the temple was intact, and its priests were doing quite well; hence the anxiety (John 11:47):

> The chief priests and the Pharisees gathered the council and said, "What are we to do? For this man performs many signs. If we let him go on thus, every one will believe in him, and the Romans will come and destroy both our holy place and our nation".

In spite of the lost opportunities of the last two decades, hope has not been extinguished. One change has taken place which is irreversible. It is not in the area of institutions, but belongs to the realm of attitudes, and I refer to the arrival of free speech in the Church. It emerged during the course of the Vatican Council. (It seems strange now to reflect that the first session took place in secret.) It is based upon the simple fact that the laity cannot be coerced in any way, and therefore they cannot be silenced. The clergy have benefited indirectly from the changed climate of opinion. Fifteen years ago, Fr Herbert McCabe was sacked from his post as editor of *New Blackfriars*, but later reinstated. Did we realise the significance of the second part of that drama? The power of free speech to change attitudes and thence institutions in incalculable, and that is why totalitarian political systems are so insistent about censorship of newspapers, television, radio, books and even of the theatre.

The sense of urgency which inspires the writing of this book arises out of the sadness which I have felt at seeing so many good people leave the Church because they feel that it is irrelevant to their lives. I will discuss in detail the causes of their departure in later chapters, but the fact of their going challenges the survivors to re-think our policies at a fundamental level. Inevitably this entails criticism of the existing methods of work, and reflects indirectly upon their proponents who still repose confidence in the old system. It is my intention to criticise only policies and not persons. It is also my plan never to present criticism without offering a creative alternative. Fortunately, it follows from what I stated in the preceding paragraph that the Church as a whole is now habituated to the critical discussion of policies without a neurotic obsession lest those in office should take offence.

CHAPTER ONE

The Church's Mission

Earlier in this century, Archbishop Temple was asked whether the Church existed primarily for those within, or outside its ranks. He replied that it existed first of all for those outside. This question and its answer were reflected a generation later at the time of the Second Vatical Council. Bishop Butler records the disquiet which he felt when he heard Cardinal Ottaviani state that the Church's principal task was the safeguarding of tradition. It appeared quite obvious to Bishop Butler that the Church's primary task was that of mission, and that conservation of past traditions was subordinate to evangelisation.[1]

Observations such as the three opinions noted above do not arise out of a vacuum, they are the consequences of the speakers' ecclesiology. They reflect certain attitudes to the nature of the Church, and to be more precise, they imply different models of the Church. On reflection, it is clear that all descriptions of the nature of the Church imply certain presuppositions. Only recently has the role of these pre-suppositions been studied clearly, and for this we are indebted to the American Jesuit, Fr Avery Dulles.[2] His theory can best be explained by describing the first model which he analyses, and applying it to the theological study of the Church. It is the model of the Church as an Institution. According to this model, the Church is analysed and studied as if it resembled closely the political reality of the nation state. It is a model which pays great attention to the competence of the organisation to make its own laws, and create the structures to make them effective throughout the society. It is a model which came to prominence in the late Middle Ages as a result of the Church's long disputes with the Holy Roman Empire, and as a consequence of the Canon lawyer's influence in the life and organisation of the Church.

After the Reformation it received a further impetus from the need to justify the institutions of the Catholic Church in the face of opposition from the new Churches sprung from the Reform. The classical exposition of this ecclesiology came from Cardinal Bellarmine; it influenced all studies on the Church in the post-Reformation period, and generated the concept of the Church as a "perfect necessary society". This means that the Church is like the State in that it has within its control all that is needed to achieve its own working objectives. For example, the Church conducts its own schools and seminaries to educate the laity and clergy, and it does not require the assent of the civil power to make its own laws. The ultimate refinement of this pattern of thought was to insist that the Church was indirectly superior to the State because its objectives were intrinsically superior to those of the State.

A reading of the statement about the Church in the First Vatican Council makes it clear that this was the underlying model which is implied in the document, although it is not stated explicity. The decree *Pastor Aeternus* of Vatican I is a truncated document because the Franco-Prussian war necessitated a premature closing of the Council. What was produced was a six-page statement which divided its material between one sentence on the Church in general, two sentences on the episcopal office, and the rest on the papacy. It deals at length with the position of Peter among the apostles, Peter's primacy, its transmission to the Bishops of Rome, the nature of his jurisdiction over the Church, and finally the limits within which the Pope is infallible.[3]

It is pointless to speculate on how Vatican I might have completed its decree on the Church if the Council had been at work for a few more years. Although it did not explicitly exclude other models, the model of the Institution is clearly its presupposition, and indeed the only one.

Although it has received considerable adverse criticism in recent years, the model of the Institution has undeniable advantages provided that they are not cultivated in isolation from what other models can supply. As the Church is a community, some measure of visible institutionalisation is inevitable, and indeed desirable. This model provides an adequate framework for it. By emphasising the visibility of the Church, it reinforces the believers' experience of self-identity, continuity with the past, and communion with a recognisable world-wide organisation.

Its disadvantages are in part caused by the way in which people misunderstand it. The text books which were currently used in the seminaries up to the 1960s gave scarcely any attention to other models and thus presented a distorted ecclesiology. Its intrinsic limitations were summarised by the Belgian Bishop de Smedt in the Second Vatican Council, with the now famous observation that it leads to Clericalism, Juridicism, and Triumphalism.[4] Clericalism is an attitude which derives from viewing the Church as a pyramid in which authority travels down from its apex (the papacy), through the Curia, the bishops, and the parish priests, in such a way that the laity come to be regarded as purely passive recipients of commands from above. The effective neglect of the laity becomes all the more shocking when one reflects that it would be possible to conceive of a Church without clergy (like the Quakers), but impossible without lay-people. Juridicism came naturally out of this matrix, and almost unconsciously presented people with a pattern of religious observance which consisted in the exact implementation of detailed regulations. Even the sacraments were surrounded by the most detailed rules about how they should be received. Fortunately the Church has outgrown these limitations, but it is instructive to look back thirty years to the complications about Holy Communion, for example. The recipient was required to fast from food and drink from midnight, forbidden to receive the sacrament with his hand, and often advised not to touch it with his teeth. Conscientious penitents would accuse themselves in Confession of having perhaps swallowed toothpaste beforehand. The obverse of this phenomenon was Triumphalism, in which the visible Church rejoiced in visible success. Spiritual progress was described in metaphors drawn from military history (particularly the victories), which were completely at variance with the unassuming profile of the "little flock" of the gospels. Even moral pronouncements were presented in a most extraordinary tone, as a couple of examples from the 1930s will show:

As We gaze out upon the world from the watchtower of this

Apostolic See . . . We consider it our duty . . . to raise our voice in warning . . . The Catholic Church . . . standing erect amidst this moral devastation, raises her voice in sign of her divine mission . . .[5]

The content of that document does not concern the present book, but the tone of the pronouncement cannot be accounted for except as an example of the triumphalism which was an almost inevitable by-product of this model of the Church.

The use of the Institution as model for the Church tends, almost unconsciously, to undervalue the laity, to maintain the existing Church structures as ends in themselves, and inhibit true mission which must involve change. This is the best explanation of why it was that the missionary endeavours of the 1940s and 1950s seemed inevitably to come into collision with the Church authorities. As is well known, in the Second World War the French Catholics, during the period of the Occupation, displayed a remarkable enthusiasm to re-christianise their nation. The movement was epitomised in the book *France Pagan*, by the Abbé Godin,[6] and resulted in numerous experiments in evangelisation. The most regrettable confrontation was the suppression of the worker-priest movement in the early 1950s by the Vatican, although it has the backing of the six French Cardinals. Ten years later the concept of the worker priest was approved by Vatican II,[7] but the initial hostility of the Roman Curia can be accounted for as a consequence of their having the institutional model as the implicit basis of their understanding of the Church.

Roughly a hundred years after the First Vatican Council, when the Second Vatican Council was giving its attention to the nature of the Church, the theological scene had changed. Theologians had developed other models of the Church and about half-a dozen of these were explained in the decree *Lumen Gentium*, which was Vatican II's pronouncement on the nature of the Church. Among these models, that which received the most extensive treatment was that of the Church considered as the People of God.[8] This theme had been studied thoroughly by theologians in the period before the Council, and its classical exposition is perhaps to be found in a well-known book by L. Cerfaux.[9] Although it sounds like an informal description, the phrase "People of God" is a technical term taken from the Old Testament. It goes back to the assembly of the Israelites by Moses at the foot of Mount Sinai, and more particularly to the understanding of that event as presented in the Book of Deuteronomy. Through no merits of their own the descendants of Abraham had been chosen by God as the only nation which would receive the revelation of the true God. The relationship between them and their God was sealed in the contract or covenant concluded on Mount Sinai. This meant that the gifts and privileges from God would be predictable, so that the people could count upon them, without detracting from their gratuitous character. From then onwards their knowledge of God was increased by the teaching of the prophets and by God's interventions in history shaping their destiny and educating their religious consciousness.

Before the Babylonian exile in the sixth century, they were given the promise of a new Covenant and a second figure like Moses who would be the intermediary in its establishment. The New Testament writers depict all these events as taking place in the mission of Christ. In particular, St Paul presents the early history of the Jerusalem Christians as the re-living of the Sinai experience and the establishment of the new Covenant. The twelve apostles represented the twelve tribes, and the eucharist at the Last Supper is recounted in terms which make it clear that the evangelists and St Paul wished to describe it as an exact parallel of the sacrifice with which Moses ratified the first Covenant on Mount Sinai. After the Resurrection the infant community received the Holy Spirit on the feast of Pentecost in a context which was reminiscent of the Israelites receiving the Law, when Moses descended from Mount Sinai. Thereafter the Christian Church is the vehicle for God's revelation to the human race, and it is the channel for His gifts, notably the benefits of Christ's redeeming sacrifice. Within the framework of a close parallel with the first Covenant on Mount Sinai there are, of course, differences because of the perfection of the second and permanent Covenant, the most obvious of which was that the relationship with God which was enshrined in the Covenant was thenceforth destined for the whole human race, and not just one nation.

I have described this model of the People of God at some

length (although it is well known now) because Vatican II devoted more space to it than to the other models, and because the concept of the Mystical Body of Christ can best be understood within the context of the People of God.

When the Catholic Church was developing its ecclesiology in a direction which moved away from the exclusive preoccupation with the Institution, it was the model of the Body of Christ which first came to the fore. Pope Pius XII gave considerable encouragement to this line of investigation by his encyclical letter on The Mystical Body of Christ in 1943. As is well known, this theological model comes from St Paul. He speaks of it in nearly all his letters, and towards the end of his life, when his theological thinking had reached its most mature phase, it is the most prominent vehicle for his doctrine of the Church. To some extent it replaced the model of the People of God, and that was due principally to the fact that the gentile Christians were rapidly outnumbering the erstwhile Jews. It is clear that the gentile converts would not be so familiar with the Old Testament books, and the finer points of the People of God would be lost upon them. The model of the Body of Christ was as accessible to them as to the Jewish converts and it tended to dominate the ecclesiology of the infant Church. The advantages of this model are that it indicates clearly the unity of the Church, the interdependence of all the members, and the central place of Christ. It also indicates, at least by implication, but very forcibly, that the bounds of unity are invisible, as are the channels of grace. Other images of the Church, employed by the same conciliar document, like the Sheepfold, the Building, the Bride of Christ, confirm these characteristics of the Church.

The mysterious nature of the Church is indicated in the very first paragraph of *Lumen Gentium* which employs the model of Sacrament. The exact words are important, so I will quote them verbatim: "By her relationship with Christ, the Church is a kind of sacrament, or sign of intimate union with God, and of the unity of all mankind".[10] The model has this much in common with the well-known seven sacraments, that it is a visible phenomenon indicating the presence of invisible grace. It enables the believer to perceive and co-operate with the transmission of grace, but it does not encapsulate the process. God's gifts remain unlimited, and unconstrained in human institutions, although their operation is to some extent disclosed for the benefit of the recipients.

It is impossible to overemphasise the importance of these models which have been used by Vatican II to explain the nature of the Church. Hierarchy and visible authority have not been forgotten. In fact they receive lengthy treatment,[11] but it is clear that these functions are surbordinate to the nature of the Church and are not ends in themselves. The influence of other models can be seen clearly where authority in the Church is described as "service".[12] The biblical models enable us to study the nature of the Church without making unnecessary distinctions between laity and clergy, and without stressing unduly the factor of authority, which is, after all, merely subservient to the Church's unity and mission. The Institution model carried with it the danger of overlooking the laity's active role in the Church. Thanks to its employing other models, Vatican II devoted a whole chapter to the laity in *Lumen Gentium*, and stated explicitly that they share in the threefold functions of Christ, namely the priestly, kingly and prophetic roles.[13] Since these models deal with the relationships between the believers, with God, and with the unconverted world, they are the proper preparation for an analysis of the Church's mission which is the central theme of this chapter.

The Church's mission can be traced back to Jesus himself. The preparation of his disciples culminated in the command to teach all nations (Matthew 28:19). Some years were to elapse before the first pagan (Cornelius the centurion) entered the infant Church, and the gentile mission did not make notable progress until after the conversion of St Paul. The reason for the delay was twofold: it was difficult for the erstwhile Jews to break with the habits of past exclusiveness, and it was a reasonable expectation to hope that the Jewish nation as a whole would accept Jesus as the Messiah, and join the new community.

Throughout its history the Church has been faithful to the duty of extending the message of Christ to all nations, more or less as soon as they became accessible, thanks to geographical discoveries or favourable political circumstances. St Augustine's mission to England in the sixth century, so movingly described by Bede, is an example of the latter, and the conversion of the Spanish American empire illustrates the former. When Catholics have found themselves in a minority position in any nation they have usually tried to share their religious convictions with those who seemed to be bereft of all religion, and even with those who were not. The latter case has presented some dilemmas in the period since ecumenism has been taken seriously, but before that it did not.

The missionary outlook of the English Catholics was depicted, not unfairly I think, in the television presentation of *Brideshead Revisited*. We were given Evelyn Waugh's vision of what Catholicism looked like in the 1930s. We saw there the perfect image of a Church which was faithful to a limited ecclesiastical mission, but something was clearly absent. The Catholics depicted in it observed the feasts, kept the fasts, obeyed the rules, but clearly they did not liberate themselves to the fullness of life, although in the end some of them made the correct decisions. Leaving the world of fiction for that of reality, we gain another view of the English missionary outlook in the life of one of Waugh's friends, namely Ronald Knox. He was a man of undoubted intelligence and integrity, who like Newman a century earlier entered the Roman communion for motives which could be described as the quest for a satisfactory ecclesiastical pedigree. It is my opinion that those considerations count for little in today's world. People of equal integrity have been more impressed by the statement that "By their fruits you shall know them". They are looking for a community whose way of life produces the values of God's kingdom, rather than those of the *Brideshead* believers whose credentials were nevertheless impeccable, at any rate within a limited frame of reference.

If there is something lacking in the apostolate described in the preceding paragraph, we should look back to Christ, and see what his mission consisted of. In the simplest terms we can say that Christ preached about the Kingdom of God.[14] It is a well-known phrase, which together with equivalent expressions like Kingdom of Heaven, occurs approximately 70 times in the gospels. It continues to appear in practically all the New Testament writings, but as the gentile population came to outnumber the erstwhile Jews it receded somewhat on account of its strongly Old Testament overtones.

By now it is a truism to observe that Kingdom does not mean territory or any sort of geographical entity. It is a somewhat infelicitous translation of a Hebrew/Aramaic word for which a better English equivalent is "reign". There again the equivalence is not exact, since it does not mean the duration of a monarch's time in office, but the fact of his control of the affairs of his subjects. Perhaps a better translation of the semitic original would be "rule", as in the English expression "the rule of law".

The notion of Kingdom was the subject of many parables and other sayings in the teaching of Jesus. One series of texts shows that the Kingdom will come to its perfection at the end of time, when Christ returns in glory for the general judgment of mankind. Other texts, which are not in contradiction to the former, indicate that the Kingdom is present, in an incomplete sense, already, that is to say from the time that Jesus began to preach. As far as human conduct is concerned, it is a state achieved by living in righteousness, peace, and joy in the Holy Spirit (Romans 14:17). It presupposes submission to the rule of God. It requires a moral revolution in those who submit themselves to the reign of God. They may be required to give up riches (Matthew 19:23), or abandon family ties (Matthew 19:12).

Collectively its operation is mysterious and unperceived in the normal political sense (Mark 4:11), yet this Kingdom will influence the whole of society so that others will benefit from its strength, as is indicated in the well-known parables of the mustard seed and the leaven in the dough.

This profound concept is not easy to define, and indeed it would impoverish it if it were encapsulated within legalistic categories. Without limiting its dynamism unduly, the Kingdom can fairly be described as the situation among men when the will of God prevails, or to be a little more precise, when the saving act of the Father is accomplished through Jesus.[15] This holds true even when the righteous did not recognise that it was Christ whom they had served in the persons of the poor and the suffering.[16]

When one develops the implications of the service of Christ by those who did not recognise him at the time, I

think that it is not unreasonable to discern the extension of
the Kingdom in such situations as Amnesty International
securing the release of a pagan from a Muslim prison, or the
rejection of materialistic standards by Buddhists in search of
spiritual enlightenment.

We are now in a position to analyse the relationship
between Church and Kingdom, and in doing so, to draw
together the various threads of this chapter which have not
yet been integrated.

Negatively it must be pointed out that the Church and the
Kingdom are not identical, nor are they equivalent terms. At
times they overlap, and their spheres of operation may be so
close that they interpenetrate, as in the promise to Peter of
the Keys of the Kingdom: "You are Peter, and on this rock I
will build my Church, and the powers of death shall not
prevail against it. I will give you the keys of the kingdom of
heaven". (Matthew 16:18,19.) The Kingdom is a wider,
more diffuse, and richer notion than that of Church. It is
inaccurate to make a simple equivalance between them, and
the point is worth mentioning because before the Council so
many text books on ecclesiology used the terms interchange-
ably.

The simplest way of describing the relationship positively
is to say that the Church is the visible instrument or agency
which brings about the arrival of the Kingdom of God. This
is precisely how the Vatican Council envisaged it:

> The Church, consequently, equipped with the gifts of her
> Founder and faithfully guarding his precepts of charity, humility,
> and self-sacrifice, receives the mission to proclaim and establish
> among all peoples the kingdom of Christ and of God.[17]

If we take the establishment of the Kingdom as the general
task of the Church's mission, then everything else falls into
position coherently. Clearly it does justice to the straight-
foward evangelisation by which the gospel is announced to
non-believers in the hope that they will accept it with faith,
and enter the visible ranks of the Church by baptism. It also
includes the more delicate matter of the migration of sincere
people into the Catholic Church, though not from the
starting point of non-belief. It is also a formula which

satisfies the Church's concern for the spiritual welfare of those within its own ranks. From one point of view conversion, and entry into the Church, are merely the preliminaries. Once they are established as members of the visible Church the faithful must develop an ever-deepening love of God, so that it influences the whole of their lives. It would be confusing to describe this precisely as a mission, but it is clearly an aspect of the advance of the Kingdom when the believers deepen their convictions and lead an ever richer spiritual life.

In fact the relationship of Church and Kingdom as I have described it answers the dilemmas latent in the opinions of Temple, Ottaviani and Butler which I mentioned at the start of the chapter. Temple was presented with the question as to whether the Church existed for those inside or outside its ranks, to which one must reply that he had been asked the wrong question. In working for the Kingdom the Church serves those who are outside and also those who are inside its ranks. The dilemma is artificial. In the same way, Bishop Butler's concern for mission is fully safeguarded while Ottaviani's desire to protect tradition is not lost sight of. The preservation of the past is the concern of the Church, provided that it is seen as part of the service of the Kingdom, and not a fossilisation of past glories.

This vision of the interrelation between Church and Kingdom also gives a satisfactory account of the Church's desire to promote moral progress in areas where the recipients of this progress will not be members of the visible community. The works of charity and justice which are promoted by the Church throughout the world are too numerous to list. Clearly there is no wish to limit their scope just to Catholics (famine relief, for example). Unless we regard such activities as extensions of the Kingdom, there would be a danger of viewing them as marginal to the Church's life, which would be an unwarrantable down-grading of their importance.

The concept of sacrament or symbol is important in this context. When the Vatican Council applied the notion to the Church in general, it was not quite the same as the restricted use which is reserved to the special group of seven. It stresses the role of a visible organisation achieving and enshrining various spiritual values, and making the process accessible to human perception. Without this medium there is a danger that the workings of God's grace could seem unreal to the average person, because they cannot be grasped in any simple way. The believer lives by faith, and puts his trust in realities which cannot be seen; nevertheless it is important that some manifestation of their operation should be disclosed to him. This is one aspect of the system of the seven sacraments, and it also applies to the Church as a whole. Being the vehicle for the mysterious operations of God, it enables the world to see something of how God's power acts in the lives of believers, and even outside the ranks of the Christians. It is reassuring to be able to point out in the visible Church the kind of thing which is happening invisibly elsewhere among mankind.

In this perspective I think it is no exaggeration to describe as an advance of the Kingdom the situation when a drug addict repents and begins to lead a morally disciplined life, although he might not join the Church; when, for example, the Samaritans persuade a man not to commit suicide, or when Oxfam persuades people to donate money for starving refugees. Activities of this kind are clearly fulfilling the will of God. They would be even more pleasing to God if they were accompanied by explicit recognition of the love and power of God, so that they could be explicit manifestations of faith. In this sense the activities which take place within the believing community, are more deliberate and articulate forms of co-operation with the will of God. Thus they are visible signs of the activity which goes on elsewhere among people who might understand God's will only partly, and accomplish it without recognising Christ.

Another advantage of treating the Church as the instrument for advancing the Kingdom is that it smoothes out potential difficulties between Churches. In a de-christianised nation like Great Britain, where all the Churches are trying to bring back the gospel to peoples' lives, there is always the latent danger that they will be competing with one another in a process which looks like a high pressure recruitment drive. Since we cannot halt the process of evangelisation until all Christian Churches have been reunited into full communion, some interim solution must be found. If the self-augmentation of the Churches is their first objective, then competition and rivalry are almost inevitable. However, if each Church strives to advance the cause of the Kingdom of God, it is possible for them all to regard each other as collaborators and allies.

CHAPTER TWO

Ecumenical Standstill

The previous chapter's description of the Church's mission leads naturally to a consideration of the relationship between different Churches. It would be seriously misleading to suppose that any one Church could announce the gospel in this nation without taking account of the efforts of other Churches.

The beginnings of ecumenism were virtually ignored by the Catholic Church, and when some Catholics on the Continent took an interest in the matter in the 1930s, it was scarcely noticed by the English Catholic community (except for the translation into English of Fr Congar's first major work, *Divided Christendom*).[1] The attitude of most of the clergy and laity was not one of hostility, but one of aloofness, lack of interest, and incomprehension. This was compounded by the attitude of the Irish, with whom the majority of English Catholics had some blood ties, and who regarded English non-Catholic religious bodies as simply alien and outside their area of concern. A powerful contributory factor in the Catholic incomprehension of other Churches was the poor state of theology which underpinned the catechetical formation of children. The full extent of the shortcomings of that pedagogy need not detain us in this chapter, but it is instructive to quote one question and answer from the standard catechism which was in general use up to the time of the Council.[2] Question 178 asked: "How do we expose ourselves to the danger of losing our Faith?", and the answer was: "We expose ourselves to the danger of losing our Faith by neglecting our spiritual duties, reading bad books, going to non-Catholic schools, and taking part in the prayers and services of a false religion". It was universally taught that all other Christian denominations came under the designation of a false religion. Catholics who plucked up their courage and attended marriages in other churches for social reasons were not infrequently assailed by overwhelming feelings of guilt.

To the community which prided itself on the lack of contamination by the prayers and services of false religions, the message of Vatican II came as a predictable shock. There is a certain element of serenity in the observation that: "This sacred Synod is gratified to note that participation by the Catholic faithful in ecumenical work is growing daily. It commends this work to bishops everywhere in the world for their skilful promotion and prudent guidance."[3] The serene gratification of the synodal fathers would have been somewhat disillustioned if they had realised how badly the English Catholic community had been prepared for this message.

Having received official approval by the Council, the small number of devoted ecumenists whose efforts had been constantly frustrated in the past, now assumed the initiative. In the last twenty years there has been a great deal of positive progress, to such an extent that it is difficult to envisage just how narrow-minded were the attitudes before the Council. Possibly the most important advance has been in the area of prayer. The details are well known, so the matter will not require a lengthy exposition. There is no barrier now to prevent Catholics praying with other Christians in liturgical services, informal meetings, school assemblies and similar occasions. We are happy to employ forms of prayer which had been popularised by other churches, like the spontaneous prayer of the charismatic movement, or the shared silent contemplation usually associated with the Quakers. Many people have realised that in this exercise the denominational boundaries do not constitute a barrier, and countless groups of Christians meet regularly all over the country to pray together in a variety of forms.

Prayer together has been complemented by a variety of study groups and more formal classes for theology and biblical study. The examples of joint charitable work and social action are virtually beyond counting. One well-known example is the long-standing co-operation between the Anglican and Catholic bishops in Liverpool in trying to cope with the city's desperate economic and social problems. On a more diffuse plane one can observe the activities of bodies like Christian CND whose local branches unite members of all churches, in a moral crusade in which denominational allegiances present no barrier to progress. Other areas of ecumenical progress which are more expressive are in the sharing of buildings and institutions. A number of inter-Church schools are now functioning, and the sharing of churches is widespread. It varies from diocese to diocese according to the attitude of the local bishops and the density of the Catholic population. In East Anglia, a region where the density of Catholic population is low, this arrangement has been of the utmost value. In numerous villages where the number of Catholics does not warrant the building of a church, the Catholics celebrate mass in the Anglican church, at a time on a Sunday morning when its regular worshippers are not using it. In addition to the practical utility of this arrangement, the psychological effects on the two communities is considerable. It also indicates to society in general that the different Churches are no longer in competition with each other, but are collaborators.

Over and above these practical exercises there has been a great deal of serious theological dialogue, of which the best known meetings have been those of the Anglican–Roman Catholic International Commission. In 1966 the Anglican and Roman Catholic authorities agreed to set up the mechanism for serious dialogue about the doctrine of the eucharist, ministry and ordination, and the nature and exercise of Church authority. Half a dozen documents were published representing the conclusions of the international joint working party, and these were referred back to the parent Churches for consideration. When they had taken cognisance of the reception which had been accorded to those statements, they published the final report in 1982.[4]

The first doctrinal matter to be studied, and one which had caused so much dissension in the past was the doctrine of the eucharist. The first report on it was published in 1971, and in the final paragraph the commission was able to report:

> We believe that we have achieved substantial agreement on the doctrine of the eucharist. Although we are all conditioned by the traditional ways in which we have expressed and practised our eucharastic faith, we are convinced that if there are any remaining points of disagreement they can be resolved on the principles here established. We acknowledge a variety of

theological approaches within both our communions. But we have seen it as our task to find a way of advancing together beyond the doctrinal disagreements of the past. (p. 16)

It lies outside the scope of this book to set out in detail just what those points of agreement were. It is significant that they could speak so confidently of having achieved that much unity.

In 1973 the same commission published its conclusions on the matter of ordination and ministry. Although they did not claim to have solved all the difficulties, they achieved a significant measure of agreement in which they claimed that both the Churches would recognise their own faith. (p. 29). Clearly the encyclical of Pope Leo XIII in 1896 denying the validity of Anglican Orders had been a problem for them, but they concluded on an optimistic note:

> Nevertheless we consider that our consensus on questions where agreement is indispensible for unity, offers a positive contribution to the reconciliation of our churches and of their ministries. (p. 38)

It says much for the realism and optimism of the commission that they did not evade the serious issues, but tackled the central question of the papacy in their next round of talks, which concerned the general area of authority in the Church. In 1976 they published their first report on the subject of authority, and prefaced it with the observations that:

> Our consensus covers a very wide area; though we have not been able to resolve some of the difficulties of Anglicans concerning Roman Catholic belief relating to the office of the bishops of Rome, we hope and trust that our analysis has placed these problems in a proper perspective. (p. 49)

The extent of their consensus became apparent in the remarkable paragraph about the Pope's role in relation to Church unity. I will quote it in full:

> If God's will for the unity in love and truth of the whole Christian community is to be fulfilled, this general pattern of the

complementary primatial and conciliar aspects of the *episcope* serving the *koinonia* of the churches needs to be realised at the universal level. The only see which makes any claim to universal primacy and which has exercised and still exercises such *episcope* is the see of Rome, the city where Peter and Paul died. It seems appropriate that in any future union a universal primacy such as has been described should be held by that see. (p. 64)

Five years later, they identified four areas which still constituted difficulties, but which did not invalidate the remarkable statement of unity which had been agreed in 1976. The difficulties were specified as:

The interpretation of the Petrine texts, the meaning of the language of "divine right", the affirmation of papal infallibility, and the nature of the jurisdiction ascribed to the bishop of Rome as universal primate. (p. 81)

At the end of the Final Report, the participants were cautiously optimistic:

Our agreement still needs to be tested, but in 1981 it has become abundantly clear that, under the Holy Spirit our Churches have grown closer together in faith and charity. There are high expectations that significant initiatives will be boldly undertaken to deepen our reconciliation and lead us forward in the quest for the full communion to which we have been committed, in obedience to God, from the beginning of our dialogue. (p. 99)

To some extent, that statement marks the high-water mark of twenty years' ecumenism in Britain. It is symbolic of many things, namely of a sincere willingness of different Christians to work in collaboration and an important acknowledgment by the Catholics that God's grace operates authentically outside the boundaries of the Roman communion. To some readers it may seem superfluous to mention such a notion, but among most Catholics, before Vatican II, it was almost unthinkable.

In spite of these real achievements, ecumenism has almost come to a standstill. We have "taken up the slack", and there is no discernible sign of further progress. The high expectations of the ARCIC report have not so far shown signs of being fulfilled. There is a danger of evading further difficulties by contenting ourselves with a range of activities which display impeccable good taste. Two examples of this are the Pope's visit to Canterbury Cathedral in 1982, and the gesture of the Anglicans in Liverpool a decade earlier. When the Catholic cathedral was about to be consecrated the Chapter of the Anglican cathedral commissioned the composer Matthias to compose the organ music (named Invocations) for the occasion. I do not criticise these charming gestures in themselves, but I fear greatly that they are the substitutes for sacrifices. The Vatican Council indicated clearly that we must be prepared to set our own house in order, before we offer ourselves for union with other Churches:

> Their primary duty is to make an honest and careful appraisal of whatever needs to be renewed and achieved in the Catholic household itself, in order that its life may bear witness more loyally and luminously to the teachings and ordinances which have been handed down from Christ through the apostles. [5]

With the exception of the Methodists, who at the request of the Anglicans, were prepared to take episcopal government into their system, none of the Churches have shown themselves willing to make real sacrifices for the cause of ecumenism. There has been a great deal of dialogue. Obvious paths of co-operation, like working and praying together, have been taken up but no real sacrifices have been made.

This is regrettable, because it offers an area of ecumenical progress which does not involve doctrinal compromise, about which all Churches have hesitations as a matter of sensitivity to the authentic traditions of their Churches.

In spite of the Pope's visit in 1982, the Catholic Church in this country has still not joined the British Council of Churches. For some Catholics it would represent a sacrifice of past attitudes of exclusiveness, but clearly nothing vital is at stake in the realm of doctrine. A similar kind of sacrifice, in a totally different area would be, for example, if the Catholics withdrew our clergy and territorial claims inside the church of the Holy Sepulchre in Jerusalem and other "shared" sanctuaries. It would be an unambigous gesture of good will towards the Orthodox Church which would speak more eloquently than a great volume of theological dialogue. Emotionally it would entail a great wrench because the Franciscans have been there since the time of the Crusades, but in addition to ecumenical considerations it would proclaim to the world that our service of God does not depend upon bricks and mortar. In the worst possible scenario that one could envisage, the Catholic pilgrims might be excluded from the church of the Holy Sepulchre, but this would be a relatively small sacrifice in comparison with the gesture of generosity towards the Orthodox Church.

On the English scene there is ample scope for this kind of activity. I speak with some diffidence about the opportunities open to Anglicans, but it could not fail to benefit the cause of ecumenical progress if they were to relinquish the privileges of Establishment, withdraw their bishops from the House of Lords, and free themselves of the Prime Minister's power over episcopal appointments.

I speak with less diffidence when I consider the sacrifices which the Catholic Church might offer to the cause of ecumenism. The work of the Roman Curia offers ample scope for pruning, in such a way as to reassure other Churches. It is arguable that the stumbling block to Church unity is not the acceptance of the papacy as a safeguard to world-wide communion, but the power of the Curia which is seen as a threat to the traditional responsibilities of bishops. The dialogue between the Lutherans and Catholics in the United States spoke very perceptively on this matter, and deserves to be better known in this country.[6] Envisaging the long-term goal of unity, and the problem posed by the present manner in which the papacy conducts its affairs, they declared that three principles should be observed: legitimate diversity, collegiality, and subsidiarity. The first of these is self-evident. For the second, they invoked explicitly what had been agreed at Vatican II:

Collegial responsibility for the unity of the Church, as emphasized by Vatican II, is of the utmost importance in protecting those values which excessive centralization of authority would tend to stifle. No one person or administrative staff, however dedicated, learned or experienced, can grasp all the subtleties and complexities of situations in a world-wide church, whose many communities live and bear witness in the variegated contexts of several continents and many nations.

The invocation of the principle of subsidiarity pointed in just the same direction:

> What can properly be decided and done in smaller units of ecclesiastical life ought not to be referred to church leaders who have wider responsibilities.[7]

The words about subsidiarity echo almost perfectly the principle as it has been taught in Catholic circles. In the public statements of the Catholic Church it was first enunciated by Pope Pius XI in the context of governments nationalising economic enterprises which worked perfectly well in private hands, and whose absorption by the state would tend to increase the power of the government and lessen the freedom of the citizens. In the encyclical letter *Quadragesimo Anno*, the Pope expressed the principle thus:

> Just as it is wrong to withdraw from the individual and commit to the community at large what private enterprise and endeavour can accomplish, so it is likewise unjust and a gravely harmful disturbance of right order to turn over to a greater society of higher rank functions and services which can be performed by lesser bodies on a lower plane.

In the same context the principle was affirmed again by Pope John XXIII in his encyclical *Mater et Magistra*, and it was repeated again by Vatican II.[8]

In spite of its consistent use in economic matters, Catholic theologians have been reticent in making the obvious application to the Roman Curia. This was done by the Lutheran–Catholic Dialogue referred to already, and they expressed straightforwardly what many Catholics had felt for a long time:

> Nevertheless, for Lutherans as well as for many Roman Catholics, the present mode of operation of the papacy and the Roman Curia leaves much to be desired.[9]

It is obvious that the Papacy requires some kind of administrative staff so that the Pope can keep in contact with a world-wide Church. No-one would deny the usefulness of a functional bureaucracy of this kind. What is genuinely feared by other Churches is the danger that this bureaucracy might take over the kind of decision-making activities which have traditionally belonged to the bishops. The value of a symbolic gesture in this area would be incalculable, and would be all the more significant because it is clear that it would represent a real sacrifice. Bearing in mind the need to make gestures which demonstrate unselfishness, but do not compromise doctrine, the most obvious part of the Roman Curia which could be sacrificed would seem to be the diplomatic service. In the Middle Ages, when the Pope was the secular ruler of that part of Italy known as the Papal States, it was natural for him to appoint ambassadors to other nations. With the loss of the Papal States in 1870 they should normally have been disbanded, along with the other departments of the civil service which had administered the Pope's territory. However, by a strange quirk of history, which is a perfect illustration of Parkinson's Law, they were converted into Apostolic Delegates and became the Pope's ambassadors, not to the nations, but to the Catholic community in those nations. Since that time there has been the establishment of the other group, known as Papal Nuncios, who are, strictly speaking, ambassadors from the Pope to the government. What is really anomalous is not the causes which produced such a system, but the historical accidents which retained it in existence. By 1984, these diplomats to Church and State numbered 124. If their role was abolished as a gesture of ecumenical goodwill, the communication between the Papacy and the local Catholic community could be assured adequately by the local Bishops' Conferences, who could equally well communicate with their respective governments whenever it should be necessary.

I have described these ecumenical sacrifices at some length because they would seem to provide a creative solution to the impasse which has been reached in so many areas of inter-Church dialogue. It is hard to overestimate their value as symbolic gestures, and equally difficult to see why they should be resisted, granted that no doctrinal principle is at stake.

Other areas of ecumenical activity which would require sacrifices, are not quite as straightforward as those indicated in the previous section. Inter-Church marriages are still not provided for satisfactorily. Before the Council the Catholic Church insisted that the non-Catholic party should sign a written promise to have all the children brought up as Catholics, and the liturgical ceremony was deliberately bleak, as if to symbolise the Church's displeasure. Things have improved a little since then. In many parts of the world the Catholics are a minority group in the population. In Great Britain we are about 10 per cent, and it follows that out of every ten men that the average marriageable woman meets, only one of them will be a Catholic. Sometimes the religious factor will enter in as an element of deliberate choice in the selection of a spouse, but we must recognise that the majority of marriages in a nation like ours will be between a Catholic and a spouse belonging to another Church, or of no religious allegiance at all. Instead of lamenting such a situation we must arrange our laws and institutions to assist such marriages in every possible way and ensure that the children will acquire a positive religion.

The simplest means would be for the Catholic Church to allow the ceremony to take place in any church without any special permission being required. Even the mildest of dispensations carries with it the implications of disapproval which cannot fail to be hurtful to Christians of other Churches. Furthermore, the decisions about the christening and religious upbringing of children should be left entirely to the judgement of the parents. Theoretically one can envisage a situation where a Catholic and a non-Catholic are equally committed to their Churches, and who both feel that children should be baptised and introduced to religion at an early age. Granted that both parents have equal rights over all their children, that situation admits of no antecedent theoretical solution. Like many of the most important moral choices in life there is literally no "blueprint". In the interests of ecumenism, and the spiritual welfare of those families, the Catholic Church should educate its own members, and leave the practical decisions to the responsible judgement of both parents.

The final area of ecumenism which I will touch on in this

chapter is that of the Catholic attitude to Anglican ordinations. In 1896 Pope Leo XIII declared that they were invalid. The time has come to re-open the matter and examine it afresh. It is conceivable that the Church might arrive at the same conclusion, but all the same a re-examination of the matter would be valuable for ecumenical relations. In the first place, it would exonerate the Catholics from the accusation of intransigence. Secondly, it could make amends for the manner in which the first enquiry was conducted. It is not generally realised that the investigations which led up to the condemnation of 1896 excluded the Anglicans from participation. No Anglican was invited to present evidence to the commission. As a result, the process and its decision have the overtones of a trial in which the accused has been condemned unheard and *in absentia*. Without offering any observations about the theological content of the nineteenth-century enquiry and one which might be envisaged now, I simply state that a re-opening of the matter would be a minimal gesture of sincerity towards the Anglicans.

The relationship between the Catholic Church's mission, and its relationship with other Churches is complicated. I suggest that the most satisfactory orientation is for the Church to look upon the establishment of the Kingdom as its operational goal. With this orientation, other problems will not vanish, but we will be in a reasonable position to cope with them.

CHAPTER THREE

The Clergy React

As soon as the Council concluded its deliberations, the clergy and laity began the task of assimilating its message. I will describe the clergy's reaction first, because a recognisable forum emerged quite soon after the Council, thanks to which it has been possible to discern what the majority of priests were thinking. This forum is the National Conference of Priests, which elects four representatives from each diocese in England and Wales, for an annual meeting of four days' duration. It has the added advantage that its deliberations and resolutions are published each year.

The National Conference of Priests had an unusual beginning. Two English bishops were present at Chur in Switzerland in 1969 for the European meeting of priests and bishops. It was the notorious occasion when the bishops were literally shouted down by the priests. One side effect was the realisation by the two English bishops that they did not know what their priests were thinking on any important issue. Accordingly, they persuaded their fellow bishops to call a meeting of priests for the summer of 1970. Four priests were elected from each diocese, producing 76 elected representatives, and a small number of the planning committee (who had been nominated by the hierarchy) were present too. Like income tax it was envisaged as a once-only operation; but of its self-perpetuation I will say more later.

We assembled at Wood Hall in Yorkshire on the first day of June, and it began like a bad retreat. After some meandering debates a young priest from Wales rose to his feet and appealed to his brothers to stop fussing about domestic details and take a courageous leap into the real problems of twentieth-century Britain. This brought the whole meeting to life. Group consciousness formed quickly and we scrapped the original agenda, elected our own chairman, and embarked upon a wide-ranging examination of all aspects of the Church's work. The sense of urgency was fantastic. Debates went on until about ten o'clock at night, and the drafting committee and planning groups were hard at work till after midnight.

Our aspirations were put into the form of a specific resolution which stated that our aim should be: "To have a vision of the evangelisation of England and Wales. To spread the faith throughout those countries and *not* to have the preservation of Church structures as our top priority." In the course of the week, 40 resolutions were accepted, some of them dealing with crucial matters like the need for more and smaller dioceses, the up-grading of the status of curates, and the need for some form of due process to reconcile priests and their superiors if there was conflict. (All too often the clergy can be victimised by their removal from important work simply by an administrative decision.) The meeting at Wood Hall also recommended that the exercise should be repeated, and indeed put on a permanent basis. It is significant that this resolution was accepted almost unanimously; there was only one vote against it. To achieve this the conference elected a committee and empowered them to meet the bishops and request the permanent establishment of the conference.

Accordingly, that committee met with the standing committee of the Bishops' Conference on 18 June. Among them were three archbishops, none of whom is still in office. It was an extraordinary encounter, because most of the bishops could scarcely conceal their resentment at having to discuss pastoral matters with an elected group of priests. They were non-committal about the content of the 40 resolutions but agreed that a second meeting should take place the following year.

The second meeting of the NCP was at Liverpool in 1971. It gave birth to the greatest number of resolutions of any of its meetings, 56 in all. They were of uneven quality, but some of them stressed the urgent need for a pastoral strategy, based upon proper planning, including statistical research. As a result of these aspirations two working parties were set up in conjunction with the hierarchy to investigate the priorities for a properly planned apostolate. The most important achievement of that conference was the elaboration of a constitution which was a *sine qua non* if we were to have the bishops' approval for permanent status. After the meeting there was the usual reporting-back by the committee to the standing committee of the Bishops' Conference. At a meeting in September of that year the bishops approved the constitution and agreed to the permanent existence of the Conference.

Since then, meetings have been held each year, usually in September and regularly now in Newman College, Birmingham. As the years went by, more or less the same resolutions came forward again and again, without really achieving anything. The working parties published their reports, but they were shelved, as I will show in the next section. After eight years a great deal of apathy was apparent among the clergy. The crucial meeting was the eighth one, which took place in 1977. Those who still had faith in the conference and who came to its preliminary meetings had by now developed a collective attitude of outward-looking missionary orientation. It was in this frame of mind that we urged the summoning of a National Pastoral Congress, and the request was agreed to by the bishops. In a sense, that was the supreme achievement of the NCP.

From the standpoint of 1984, it can be seen that the NCP did not in fact provide the lift-off for Vatican II to transform the Church's apostolate in this country. The mass of resolutions can be divided into three categories. There were inevitably a large number which could not be filtered off, which were little more than optative aspirations: "Wouldn't it be wonderful if we all prayed more and worked harder in our parishes." The second category were serious calls for pastoral planning, including theological and sociological investigation. Most of these were in some sense handed on to the Liverpool Congress of 1980, and were effectively shelved as I will show in Chapter Four. The only subject which has not been quietly forgotten or buried in some way or other is that of ordaining married men! The request for the ordination of convert clergy was agreed by the first conference at Wood Hall,[1] and was eventually agreed to by the bishops at their autumn meeting in 1983. Other than that, the lengthy series of meetings and the prodigious labours devoted to them, have produced virtually nothing.

As noted above, there was a considerable amount of apathy by the time of the eighth meeting in 1977. The missionary elan of the Wood Hall meeting had been lost. The bishops have poured so much cold water on the priests' aspirations that the enthusiasm has been quenched for the most part. All of this is extremely serious. At the time of writing there are all too many signs that the clergy are a demoralised body, racked with uncertainties and receiving little creative leadership from the authorities. There is a limit to the amount of discouragement which the priests can absorb. In order to evade the radical reforms asked for by some of the resolutions of the NCP the bishops have shelved all but the most innocuous resolutions (like in-service training for priests). This has caused widespread disillusionment, causing many to lose interest in the NCP. For others, it has been one of the causes which has driven them out of the ministry. Lest this seem to be an exaggeration, let me remind my readers that in 1978 when I was still on the committee of the NCP, two of our small number resigned; not just from the NCP but from the priesthood. One of them was the chairman.

The way in which the missionary enthusiasm of the NCP was extinguished can be seen most clearly by examining the reports of the working parties. In summary, it is not unfair to say that the most valuable resolutions were taken up by the working parties, analysed, emasculated, shelved temporarily and then consigned to oblivion. Some of them were taken up in a different form at the Liverpool Pastoral Congress, but were neutered by similar methods.

In November 1971, after the second reunion of the NCP, the bishops agreed to set up two joint working parties, whose members were drawn from the members of the NCP and from the hierarchy. The first produced the report entitled "Co-responsibility in the Church" in the spring of 1972. Today it is simply forgotten, but that is a great pity since the working party addressed itself to really serious problems among the clergy. The first of these was the difficult relationship between parish priest and curate, for which the NCP has said "equality of status between parish priest and curate requires legal recognition" (Resolution 18 of the Second Conference). "There should be real consultation with the clergy themselves about the deployment of priests" (Resolution 19). "All non-episcopal positions in the diocese should be submitted for review after a set period" (Resolution 22). "All diocesan priests should have a fixed and equal salary" (Resolution 43).

Clearly all of these are important questions which had caused anxiety among the clergy because they concerned the morale of the priests and seriously affected their work. The treatment of these matters in the ensuing pages can best be characterised by what the Americans call "pussy-footing".

The desire for equality of status between parish priest and curate received cold comfort. "Whilst respecting their particular roles we may say that parish priest and assistant share responsibility for the care of souls in a parish."[2] The thread then gets lost in a verbose quotation from Vatican II. Readers in 1985 will not have to be reminded that the power of the parish priest is still as strong as in pre-conciliar days and the curate counts for no more than he did then. As for consultation before moving a priest, we read the qualified request: "We recommend that wherever possible a priest should be consulted before being asked to take up a new appointment."[3] After twelve years this has not been enshrined in any sort of juridical statement or undertaking by the hierarchy. It depends simply upon the goodwill of the individual bishop. If he is a considerate man the priests will be as well treated as before the Council, and if he is not, then they have no safeguard.

Paragraph 23 tells us that: "Maturity and mutual trust are called for. Effective co-operation in priestly ministry is nowadays dependent upon an understanding of the sharing or real responsibility in an hierarchical structure." There is no indication of how this is to be achieved, and in the intervening years nothing practical has been done to promote it.

Paragraph 25 did indeed recommend in-service training, and these courses have been set up extensively. They do not disturb anything or anybody. By contrast, the potentially emotive subject of salaries met with the ever-so-cautious disavowal that: "The working party does not feel able to recommend a fixed equal income."[4]

The final recommendations of the report carry within

them the seeds of their ultimate oblivion, expressing vague generalisations and evading anything precise:

> We believe that the speedy implementation of our proposals will do much to promote the conditions in which a healthy and zealous co-responsibility may grow and flourish . . . The bishops and priests who have made up this Joint working party trust that their collaboration in preparing this report will be of help and encouragement to all those who share their life and ministry in the service of God's people.[5]

Thus with simpering platitudes did the report consign to effective oblivion the aspirations of the NCP. Readers at the present time will be well able to judge how little of those hopes have been translated realistically into the day-to-day work of the Church.

The second working party which was set up by the bishops and the NCP in November 1971 produced its report, entitled "The Church 2000", which was published in 1972. It addressed itself to the preparation of a national pastoral strategy for England and Wales, but failed lamentably. The first page gets off to a bad start:

> First of all in our discussion we had to meet the problem of the meaning of words . . . "Pastoral" is a word which is much more familiar to the clergy than to anyone else. It is a word which covers all the ways in which we serve people. But does it mainly apply to the spiritual care of Catholics by their bishops and priests? Or is it to the whole Church serving the whole of society? Since we found ourselves unable to define the term with sufficient accuracy to satisfy everyone . . . (Paragraphs 2 and 3)

Worse was to follow. The document is devoid of comprehensive, accurate statistics. It lacks clear theological thinking. The introduction ranges over the whole field of theology, liturgy, personal piety and spiritual development in the idiom of truisms and platitudes. Nowhere does it state precisely what are the operational goals of the Church's mission nor is there a realisation that pastoral strategy means devising the kind of structures which are appropriate for the attainment of those goals.

Practically every page indicates the trivialised level of its generalisations, and a few examples will make it clear that I am not exaggerating. On page 2, we read:

> We trust that this interim report will succeed in showing in general terms where the Church should be going and what it should be attempting to achieve. Conscious of an ever-deepening sense of purpose in the Church we are confident that it stands on the brink of a new era in its life of service. (Paragraph 8.)

> Ecumenism is an activity of love, and love does not consist simply in looking at each other but looking together in the same direction. Yet in spite of our looking together in the same direction we still have to acknowledge our lack of full unity and be humbly aware that this remains the great bar to a complete pastoral strategy. We must work more closely together. (Paragraph 24.)

At times the sentiments expressed are grandiose in their aspirations, as for example on the training of priests:

> Priests must be trained for leadership in the society of the future, bearing in mind the Christian view of leadership in and through service to others. They will be trained in all that is necessary to provide a lead in a living liturgy and guidance in prayer. The qualities which make good leaders are to be looked for and encouraged. These qualities include that of obedience, but also the ability to initiate—with all its consequent problems of mistakes and failure . . . Priests will need to be trained, not simply to speak and to listen, but also to recognise where and to whom they should be speaking and listening. (Paragraph 190.)

There is no suggestion of what methods might be employed to achieve these aspirations. The seminary system does not appear to have been affected significantly, as will be seen later in this book.

The aspirations of this working party endured the same fate as those in "Co-responsibility in the Church". Some of them reappeared in the business of the Liverpool Congress, and shared the fate of that exercise. The rest have been lost in a quiet oblivion. The causes of their demise are not difficult to find. There was no practical provision for carrying them into effect. After the publication of their reports the working parties were disbanded. There was no mechanism to enquire whether their recommendations had been implemented. By implication the responsibility for decisions and action rested with the Bishops' Conference, and in the absence of another permanent forum, like a National Pastoral Council, that body is answerable to no-one, least of all to the working parties who drew up the documents. In short, the absence of suitable institutions or structures has meant inevitably that nothing of any significance has emerged from the working parties of the NCP in such a way as to change the life of the Church.

CHAPTER FOUR

The Laity Assimilate The Council

SECTION ONE: MISSION AND SPIRITUALITY

The collective experience of the lay people over the last twenty years is probably the most authentic record of how the Council has been experienced in the Church, because if any section of our community is entitled to regard itself as the epitome of Catholicism it is the laity. They have been taken seriously since the time of Pius XI in the 1930s, and may be said to have come of age since Vatican II. They have not always enjoyed such explicit recognition of their status in the Church. In fact, the present felicitous situation is the result of a thousand years of erratic evolution from a starting point which was diametrically different from the result which we now witness.

In the ninth and tenth centuries the Church crystallised its attitude to the spiritual life in such a way that the cloister was acknowledged as virtually the only place for the committed Christian. A well-known mediaevalist has expressed it succinctly in the context of the monastic reform associated with St. Odo of Cluny.

For the great mass of mankind which was enslaved by concupiscence there seemed to be little hope. The only safe way to salvation lay through repentance, conversion, and entry into the monastic life. The monks were the Pentecostal Church created and renewed by the Holy Spirit. If they utterly renounced the world and were faithful to their calling, they were already living in paradise: the great silence which engulfed the cloister was a participation in the eternal silence of God; and the monk was united to God through the practice of unbroken prayer. This conviction that the restored Benedictine life was the only authentic fulfilment of the Christian vocation was at the heart of the appeal Cluny made to the society of its time. [1]

This attitude was to influence the Church for centuries to come. The secular clergy were modelled on the monks, and even the parish churches imitated the architectural features of monastic chapels, with choir screens concealing remote sanctuaries.

It was taken for granted that the monastic pattern was normal for aspirants to the spiritual life, in rather the same way that university education is now regarded as normal in our nation, for anyone who would take intellectual formation seriously. The first moves to impart spirituality to lay people were the third orders of the friars, and their ethos was to try and extend the monastic régime as far as possible into ordinary life, even extending to such details as encouraging them to wear a habit. Far from acknowledging their authentic status in a Church called to holiness, they attempted to make those lay people into pale reflections of the inhabitants of the friaries and cloisters.

St François de Sales made the decisive breakthrough in the seventeenth century. His famous book, *The Introduction to the Devout Life*, marked an all-important turning point. Its influence is so well known that I will not delay here to expound its message in detail. I wish simply to draw the reader's attention to the fact that the message of this book implied that a lay person leading a normal wage-earning and family life could aspire to holiness in that context. The institutionalised expressions of this conviction took the form of confraternities or sodalities. These were groups of lay people who undertook specific programmes of daily prayer and regular meetings in addition to the statutory Sunday mass. Undoubtedly they led many people to a closer love of God, but their piety was not connected to the Church's official liturgy, and they had little or no concern with political life, or social problems.

A change in the pattern of lay people's organisations came after the First World War, with the establishment of movements like the Legion of Mary and the Young Christian Workers. The latter embodied fully the ideas of Pius XI encouraging lay people to share actively in the Church's mission, not just as auxiliaries of the clergy, but assuming responsibility in view of the experience of secular society and the competence which sprang from that fact. The YCW movement organised its members into small cells of six or ten youths under a lay leader of the same age range as his team. The pedagogical method of See Judge Act is self-explanatory. They apply it in their meetings first of all to the gospel enquiry and then to what is called the social enquiry. It is a method of facilitating their comprehension of their environment in relation to the gospel, and encouraging them to apply it to ordinary life. One issue with which the movement concerned itself a few years ago was that of changing the law so that young workers would have longer holidays than had hitherto been the case. In this organisation the priest acts as an animator, not as the controller of the operation. It marked the first important step in the movement of lay people to share in the Church's mission not just as the recipients of commands from the clergy, but in the role of decision makers, assuming responsibility themselves.

In a Church like ours, which is so hierarchically structured, the safeguarding of lay initiative is not easy. As will be seen later in this book, the powers of a parish priest are so extensive that he can place the veto on practically anything that his curates or parishioners might want, it if happens to be against his wishes. It has therefore been necessary to insist upon developing the sense of responsibility in lay people, if we are to expect them to give their best endeavours to the Church's apostolate. If they do not feel trusted, if they are not involved in the decision-making, and if their decisions cannot be carried into effect, then they will take their skills and talents elsewhere. In the period between the end of the Second World War and the opening of the Council, Karl Rahner wrote about it on several occasions.[2]

Unfortunately, this principle has been accepted only partially in England. The episcopal commissions which were created after the Council treated the lay members purely on a consultative basis, and as the next section in this chapter will show, the whole vast operation of the Liverpool Pastoral Congress gave the laity ample scope to talk but decision-making was effectively withheld from them.

On the positive side, it is a pleasure to note that a number of important organisations like CAFOD and the Catholic Institute for International Relations are effectively in the control of lay people and work with admirable efficiency.

It is reassuring to record, but not really surprising, that the Vatican Council explicitly re-affirmed all the important elements of the laity's participation in the Church's mission. These observations have been made so frequently since the Council that I will not delay long in elaborating upon them. The vocation of lay people to holiness as part of the whole Church's call thereto, is stated in the decree on the Church.[3] Their share in the apostolate is affirmed several times; and this is not surprising.[4] The competence of the laity to exercise real responsibility was spoken of so little in the past that it is worth quoting the exact words of the Council on this matter. The passages occur in a section about lay organisations:

> As long as the proper relationship is kept to Church authorities, the laity have the right to found and run such organisations and to join those already existing . . . For in the Church there are many apostolic undertakings which are established by the free choice of the laity and regulated by their prudent judgement.[5]

The right to free speech was also vindicated,[6] although this is an area where the clergy are more likely to be inhibited than the lay people, since promotion inside the ecclesiastical apparatus could be denied to them if they had the reputation of being troublesome critics.

This long development which has affirmed the lay person's role in the Church has produced uneven results in the post-Conciliar Church. If the institutions are favourable, and if the clergy are enlightened, then the results are truly edifying, but if these two conditions are not fulfilled, then there is stagnation and frustration. This is particularly true at parish level. If the bishop and the parish priest are both enlightened men, then remarkable results can be achieved. Throughout the length and breadth of England parishes can be found where the Church's apostolate and prayer life is thriving. As subsequent chapters will show, this kind of success is achieved in spite of the parish system, and not because of it. It requires of the priest immense dynamism, but if this is lacking and if the parish organisation is left to its own intrinsic momentum, then the pattern of life will be scarcely different from the pre-Conciliar period.

The prayer life of the laity has benefited not only from the direct Conciliar decisions but indirectly too from the more confident atmosphere generated by the ecumenical movement. The adoption of the vernacular and the restructuring of the divine office has made the official prayer of the Church accessible to lay people, and it is reassuring to perceive how many of them are taking it up. The charismatic movement has had a profound effect upon the lives of many people, whose prayers beforehand were little more than pedestrian. This movement has illustrated the ecumenical dimension. Catholics now are no longer shy about adopting methods of prayers which other Churches have found helpful. It may seem superfluous to mention this in the post-Conciliar era, but memories are short and it is worth pointing out that as late as the 1940s Catholics would subconsciously, or quite deliberately, avoid systems of prayer which seemed to reflect the spirituality of other Christian bodies. A case in point is the Quakers' habit of praying together in silence, which many Catholic groups have now adopted with great profit.

The prayer life of the Church has also been enriched by the resources of contemplative monasteries. The number of people who seek creative silence in religious houses has increased significantly since the Council. This is a perfect example of the way in which the appropriate structure will be conducive to a satisfactory end-product. For example, the Abbey of Quarr on the Isle of Wight used to receive about thirty men each year in its guest house in the pre-war period. Since the Council their numbers have increased to something like 500 who stay there for up to a week at a time, and a further 500 who visit the monastery for a day. All these guests are serious seekers of spiritual guidance, who make private retreats, pray with the community, share their silence, and receive spiritual guidance from individual monks.

Spirituality is exceedingly difficult to quantify or measure, but there are reliable signs of the deep maturing of the prayer life of many lay people since the Council. All comparisons are odious, and I would not attempt to draw any distinctions between the present practice, and older methods of prayer. It is however reassuring, and important to record, that the Catholic community in this nation has benefited greatly from the Council in this area of prayer and interior piety.

Before the Council began, some clergy and laity in England considered the whole exercise to be superfluous. They could not see that anything substantial needed alteration. Liturgical reform was considered to be the hobby of cranks, and ecumenism was the preserve of a fringe which was disloyal. After the First Session had opened, and the nature of some of the proposals percolated back to England through the press, gradually it became apparent that the unthinkable was about to happen. The nation where dialogue mass had so widely been forbidden would be required to accept a vernacular liturgy. Bewilderment was followed by incredulity and thence by widespread resentment. All this unpleasantness could have been avoided if the community had been prepared for it. Anyone who was reasonably in touch with Continental theology in the 1950s could have foreseen, if not the outcome of the Council, at least the possibilities in the realm of liturgy and ecumenism. When one considers the care with which the government prepared our nation for the adoption of decimal coinage, the lack of comparable preparation of the Catholic community for the decisions of the Council was little short of culpable negligence on the part of the authorities. When the Council had ended, the Church in this land lurched forward in a movement which illustrated perfectly the notorious dictum: "Everything is forbidden until it becomes obligatory".

The next few years were marked by a state of acute tension, but it was creative tension and the innovations were gradually accepted with conviction by the majority of Catholics. The most obvious change was that of English for the mass, and then the custom of the celebrant facing the congregation. Eventually, people found that it was not as bad as they might have thought; they actually came to like it, and in the 1970s it proved impracticable in most parishes to conserve the one Latin mass each Sunday which the bishops tried to maintain. People voted with their feet, and the parish priests were sensitive to half-empty churches at the Latin mass. By the 1980s it is only in really large city churches with about half-a-dozen masses each Sunday, that it has proved feasible to retain even one Latin mass.

Tension is not easy to live with, even when it is creative. In this immediate post-Conciliar period, up to 1968, not a few people left the Church. For those who stayed inside its ranks and came to terms with the Council, it was a time of great spiritual maturing. Everyone had to face up to deliberate decisions about religion, which they might have evaded had there been no Council. The result is hard to quantify, both on account of its complexity and because there has been so little research. Yet, bearing in mind these reservations, it would seem true to say that for those who are still committed members of the Catholic Church there has been a widespread maturing of the commitment to faith in Christ.

The conflicting interests of progressives and conservatives were retained in a state of creative tension up to 1968. In July of that year the encyclical letter on birth control, *Humanae Vitae*, was published and the harmony was shattered. The presentation of that encyclical has been likened to the assassination of President Kennedy. The announcement of both events was so traumatic to the hearers that they can remember to this day where they were and exactly what they were doing when the news broke. The delicate balance was destroyed, and tension was replaced by bitterness. Feelings of resentment were exacerbated because it soon became clear that the subject of birth control had been kept off the agenda, not only of the Vatican Council but also from that of the first international synod of bishops which met in Rome shortly after the Council.

Extremist pressure groups were formed among ultra-progressives and ultra-conservatives, accusing each other of betraying the Church or the Council. Polarisation of attitudes arrived at the point where neither side could communicate with the other. The bitterness and dissension were incomparably worse than anything which had occurred in the British Catholic community within living memory. In this sad situation of recrimination many priests and religious left the ministry and many lay people, abandoning Catholic religious practice, ceased thenceforth to consider themselves members of the Church. Morale deteriorated still further when the information gradually filtered through that, in reaching the decisions embodied in the encyclical, the Pope had disregarded the advice of the vast majority of his advisory commission, and that this fact had been kept secret.

The disputes surrounding the encyclical have done immense

damage to the post-Conciliar Church. It is a constant drain
on our morale and energy. It is one of those problems which
cannot be forgotten and will not go away, because all the
issues still remain unresolved. Sixteen years later, the
wounds have not been healed. Dissension has hardened
although bitterness may have worn off to some extent.
Viewed in the widest possible context, the encyclical had
some valuable and positive contributions to offer to contem-
porary society. In a culture where sex is so often debased as a
trivial pleasure, or a commercialised recreation, it was
important for the Pope to reaffirm that it concerns children
and the deepest commitment of human love. Unfortunately,
these positive aspects of the encyclical were overshadowed
by its total ban on contraception. Once again, we must view
this against the background of a world-wide context. All
serious-minded people are now concerned about the international population explosion. The most charitable construction which can be put upon the encyclical and its sequel is to
say that the Church has made no constructive contribution to
that problem. A less sympathetic opinion is that the Catholic
Church has exacerbated it, and shows less sense of moral
responsibility than certain governments in non-Christian
nations. Although the policies of these countries may include
methods of birth control which most Christians would
regard as immoral, they do at least accept the responsibility
for feeding their populations. The Catholic Church accepts
no such responsibility to provide food for the extra millions
who come to birth as a result of *Humanae Vitae* and its
consequences.

The theological arguments employed against birth control
up to the 1950s have all been discredited intellectually.
Vatican II gave rise to expectations that the Church would
approve it, because of the positive tone of the decree
"Gaudium et Spes", which was so different from any
previous encyclicals and Roman documents.

In the first place, the Conciliar decree spoke of the
purposes of marriage in a significant way:

> By their very nature, the institution of matrimony itself and
> conjugal love are ordained for the procreation and education of
> children, and find in them their ultimate crown. (Section 48.)

This is an ingenious formula, since it avoids the old dichotomy of subordinating the conjugal love to procreation, which used to be spoken of as the primary purpose of marriage. Neither here, nor elsewhere in the Council, is there any support for the old subordination of purposes. Clearly it is a deliberate and significant omission, and of great importance because that distinction and subordination of purpose was the principal argument against contraception in the pre-Conciliar period. The same document ("Gaudium et Spes") declared that sex was morally good. The wording is rather quaint, but its meaning is clear.

> This love is uniquely expressed and perfected through the marital act. The actions within marriage by which the couple are united intimately and chastely are noble and worthy ones. (Section 49.)

It means that it is morally good for a husband and wife to express love by sex even if there is no question of conceiving a child. To the average reader, this may seem too obvious to need comment, but in the context of Vatican II it was important because no previous official document of the Catholic Church had said so.

The size of a family was declared to be the responsibility of the parents, and nothing was said about methods of birth control, except that they must observe the divine law. (Section 50.)

The Council did not make any statement about which methods were in accord with the divine law or at variance with it. (It is agreed that abortion is immoral as a form of birth control: on this at least, Catholics are agreed!) It would have been better to have left the matter there, instead of pre-empting dialogue by an ill-timed encyclical.

In the decade which followed the publication of *Humanae Vitae*, no generally convincing theology was produced in support of the encyclical. The clergy were in a singularly difficult position but the laity were not. Having perceived that it was merely a dispute about methods, and not the principle, of family planning, and being aware that neither Bible nor Councils offered anything specific on the matter, they quietly made up their own minds. In 1979, Dr Hornsby-Smith published the first adequate sociological survey of English Catholics, and included a question on contraception. The proposition stated:

A married couple who feel they have as many children as they want are not doing anything wrong when they use artificial methods of birth control.

When asked for assent or not, 74 per cent agreed with the statement and 13 per cent opposed it.[7] It should not surprise us that people under 25 were more inclined to agree than those over 65. It is sad, but was probably predictable, that the wealthier and better educated people were more likely to agree than the less well provided. This discloses another and quite tragic aspect of the birth control dispute. Those who have been to university and whose minds are trained to think independently have quite easily made up their minds on a matter which they perceive to be peripheral to the business of Christianity. Poorer people who did not have such advantages are less able to adopt such an independent line. To put it bluntly, it is a sad example of the exploitation of the poor.

It is the opinion of many Catholics, with which I agree fully, that Pope Paul VI made a serious mistake in condemning contraception. It is also regrettable that his present successor appears to be making it a central element of his policy.

The public stance of the Church is ambiguous to say the least. The priests know perfectly well that the majority of their churchgoing parishioners have quietly disregarded the ban on contraception. Most of them say nothing in public, but a minority of the clergy are exceedingly severe about it. People soon find out which confessor gives which kind of advice. The bishops are well aware of the situation yet maintain a double standard. In public they support the encyclical but without obvious enthusiasm. In private they do virtually nothing to compel its strict observance by clergy and laity, either because they lack the theological conviction or because the shortage of priests deters them from removing any dissenters from office. Psychologically it is a demoralising situation.

In relation to the non-Catholic majority in the nation and the world, it means that our integrity is seriously compromised. It is disedifying to see a world-wide Church generating so much acrimony on a small detail after the general principle of family planning has been accepted. In relation to the arms race, the population explosion and other international problems, it is insignificant. The connection with the celibate clergy is disconcerting. It can hardly be an accident that no other large religious body or cultural institution takes the same view. The Catholic Church alone has made an issue of it, and this is the only religious body in the world where the official teaching and decision-making are exclusively in the hands of unmarried men. Only in such a specific group would this obsessive preoccupation with a detail of sex be likely to occur. The isolation of the Catholic voice on this matter is not reassuring.

In the normal course of events this debate should have petered out, leaving not too much animosity in its wake. The Catholic Church has mechanisms rather like the British legal system by which laws become dead letters and do not require deliberate repeal. This might well have occurred in the dispute about the methods of birth control. As I stated above, there is nothing specific in the Scriptures or General Councils, and clearly the Church's infallibility is not at stake. Unfortunately, we hear about it all too frequently. In the latter part of 1984 the Pope made speeches on the subject practically every week. The mood of the laity can be gauged by various indicators, one of which was a series of articles in *The Tablet* in October and November 1984, which culminated in a specific request that the encyclical be reformed.[8] In my opinion, this request is fully justified, and one hopes that it will be taken seriously by the hierarchy.

The disputes surrounding the encyclical have done immense damage to the post-Conciliar Church. It is a constant drain on our morale and energy. It is one of those problems which cannot be forgotten and will not go away, because all the issues still remain unsolved.

SECTION TWO: THE LIVERPOOL PASTORAL CONGRESS
As far as lay people are concerned, the most important event in the life of the British Catholic community since the end of the Council was the National Pastoral Congress which took place in Liverpool in May 1980, because the vast majority of the participants were lay people. It could have healed the rifts which date back to 1968, and produced harmony, but as this

section will show, the outcome fell far short of the expectations.

The initiative came from the National Conference of Priests who first approved the suggestion,[9] and it was accepted by the Bishops' Conference, who made themselves responsible for organising it. Every diocese in England and Wales undertook a programme of reflection and study, which was carried out in groups at parish level. As the exercise had been conceived of as a practical operation, the delegates to Liverpool took with them a large quantity of practical suggestions which had to be reduced to some sort of systematic order in the course of the four-day meeting. The deployment of hundreds of delegates in Liverpool was extremely well arranged. They stayed in private houses in the city, and were transported to seven main meeting places which had been assigned to the seven sections of the congress. This division, although inevitable in one way, marks the only serious flaw in the organisation. Because of their geographical dispersal and in view of the shortage of time, it meant that there were no plenary sessions which were real working meetings. This means that the resolutions which were voted on in the seven sections were not put to the meetings as a whole to see whether or not they commanded the assent of the whole congress. As a result, the opponents of the congress were able to make the rather petty and misleading criticism that none of the resolutions represented the mind of the whole congress.

A more serious criticism of its organisation is that it had no clear theological plan and no adequate sociological analysis of the society which it wished to help. The bishops' response (called "The Easter People") actually refers to the problems caused by the absence of reliable statistical information.[10]

However, the criticism about methodology pale into insignificance when one begins to analyse the two main documents which have been published in the wake of the congress. The conclusions and resolutions of the seven sectors of the congress were published in 1980 in a pamphlet entitled *Congress Report*,[11] and the Bishops' response was published later in the year in a booklet called *The Easter People*.[12] Basically CR is a series of suggestions, requests for action, and practical resolutions. One would have hoped that

EP would reply on the same plane. In the event, it presented itself as little more than a meditation on the state of Catholicism in England and Wales, and evaded the majority of the specific resolutions. EP Section 49 discloses the authors' understanding of its scope:

> We do not intend to provide comprehensive legislation or teaching for every area of our Church's life and mission. To attempt to do so would be seriously to misunderstand the enabling and co-ordinating role of a Bishops' Conference and the kind of spiritual leadership required of it: possibly to override the legitimate freedom and responsibility for mission which are the prerogatives of each individual diocese as a local Church under the pastoral guidance of its bishop or even to appear to encroach upon the allegiance and love which we owe to the Holy Father and the universal Church.

Elsewhere in the same paragraph it is made clear that the document is a reflection or meditation, and indeed the words "reflect" or "reflection" occur four times in a dozen lines. This attitude is regrettable since it shows a serious misunderstanding of the original intentions of those who initiated the whole process. The concluding paragraphs of *A Time for Building*, which summarised the National Conference of Priests' desire for a congress, said explicitly:

> At this Conference the priorities for the work of the Church and for the involvement of the whole Church in its missions should be agreed.[13]

It was consistent with this retreat into meditation that there was no follow-up to the congress, although it had been asked for specifically (CR p. 34, n. 17). The success of the National Conference of Priests (such as it has been) was due to its not being a once-only event, but an annual meeting. This means quite simply that the delegates have an opportunity to ask what has happened to their resolutions of the previous year. Although the NCP cannot force the hand of the bishops, the right to question is important. The absence of any sequel to the Liverpool Congress reveals just how unsatisfactory is the whole area of accountability in the Church.

A comparison of the resolutions of CR and the response of

EP will indicate that my criticisms are not ill-founded. CR recommended that a parish should become a communion of smaller communities within it (CR p. 12, n. 8). EP (120) assumes that this has already happened:

Whatever be its size, the parish is seen as a communion of Christian communities.

This is unrealistic. EP 122 pursued the matter:

Small groups and Catholic organisations and societies, properly established in a parish or deanery, can meet a variety of needs.

A careful reading of both documents indicates that the response was not quite in line with the request. CR also suggested that parishes should share a definite proportion of their income with the Third World (p. 13, n. 11), but this received no comment. There was a recommendation to review the promotion of priests to the position of parish priest by reason of seniority (CR p. 13, n. 12). The reply was:

A real brotherhood in the priesthood, founded on prayer and genuine sharing, can do much to overcome the obvious difficulties in a generation gap between the more senior priests of today and the younger men who respond to the call to priestly service. It is the development of this sense of brotherhood rather than administrative measures which will be the strength of the Church we desire to see. (EP 94)

The request that there should be a pastoral council in each diocese was passed over in silence. A strong plea to enter the British Council of Churches (CR p. 15, n. 24) gained the following response:

The recommendation expressed at the National Pastoral Congress of a need here and now to make a convincing gesture is itself a welcome and precious witness of concern for advancing the cause of unity . . . At this stage we commit ourselves to a re-examination of all these questions. (EP 74)

On the borderline between liturgy and ecumenism the Congress asked that permission be granted for giving Holy

Communion to non-Catholics in certain limited cases, like the partners in mixed marriages, bearing in mind that indiscriminate inter-communion was not desirable (CR p. 15, n. 25/26). The reply was:

> We keep this delicate matter under review, but while fully sensitive to the pain such exclusion can cause, we are unable to compromise these principles. (EP 77)

CR strongly urged the establishment of a National Liturgical Institute (p. 16, n. 28). But EP said:

> We are not at present convinced that this would be the best way to meet the needs of renewal which have to be tackled at diocesan and parochial level. (EP 69)

The congress asked that communion with the chalice should be regarded as the norm (CR p. 16, n. 30), but the reply was:

> We view this request sympathetically, but we have to make it clear that we are not in a position to give general permission indiscriminately. (EP 64)

They did not indicate why they were reluctant to seek special permission from the Vatican. By contrast, the request for wider use of general absolution in penance services (CR p. 17, n. 33) received a favourable reply, to the extent that this matter was indeed being pursued with the authorities in Rome. (EP 68).

The clerical side of Church life was dealt with in a variety of resolutions. The remoteness of the bishops was the motive for requesting that dioceses should be smaller, and consequently there must be more of them—many more, in fact (CR p. 18, n. 5). EP replied that since 1974 two more dioceses had been established, and plans for two more had been dropped (EP 116). CR affirmed its confidence in priestly celibacy but also suggested that the possibility of ordaining married men should be considered (p. 18, n. 8). EP gratefully seized upon the former (94), but was markedly less enthusiastic about the latter request:

> The decision rests ultimately with the Holy See where we may

be sure that careful consideration is regularly given to this question. There are of course many related issues, as was evident when the matter was discussed by the Synod of Bishops in 1971. We have ourselves considered the matter more recently and decided against making a petition to the Holy See at the present time. However, in bringing this request to the attention of the appropriate Roman Congregation we will emphasise the pastoral concern that underlies it. (95)

A mild suggestion that there be an exploration of the possibility of ordaining women (CR p. 18, n. 8) received even less encouragement (EP 96).

The section dealing with marriage and the family requested that there should be a working party to study marriage (CR p. 20, n. 3), but it evoked no response in EP. To improve the preparation for marriage the congress asked that there should be a nation-wide programme in which four months' notice would be required prior to a church wedding (CR p. 20, n. 5). EP replied:

> We propose to consider further the recommendation that engaged couples be asked to give the local parish priest a period of several months' notice of their intention to marry and of their willingness to undertake preparation for marriage. (107)

Needless to say, birth control was discussed and the congress called for a fundamental re-examination of the teaching on marriage, sexuality, and contraception (CR p. 21, n. 10). The reply was far from encouraging.

> The encyclical *Humanae Vitae* is the authentic teaching of the Church (EP 104) . . . We are convinced that the Church's mind on the full meaning of marriage and the human relationship within marriage needs continual examination and greater explanation to enable it to be better understood and lived. Any further development on the subject will of course be made in complete fidelity to the Church's *magisterium*. We remind our people that the Synod of Bishops later this autumn will be reflecting on the subject of the family and with the help of our prayers will contribute to a deeper understanding of the subject. (EP 106)

The situation of Catholics in a second marriage after divorce was considered carefully by both groups. The congress asked that the bishops should consider compassionately their desire for the sacraments, meaning of course Holy Communion (CR p. 22, n. 13). The reply was rather evasive:

> The question of the reception of the sacraments in such cases is one which the Bishops' Conference has been considering for some time . . . we take to heart the sympathy and compassion expressed by the Congress delegates as we continue our deliberations on this very sensitive doctrinal and pastoral issue. (EP 111)

Consideration of the family led on to discussion of those who do not enjoy the advantages of life in a stable family. The Church's duty to help them was expressed in a resolution to utilise our material resources for their benefit. In particular the congress envisaged

> The multi-purpose use of school buildings—the use of Church land for sheltered and other special housing—the building of hospices with the same effort that was applied to schools in the past. (CR p. 23, n. 16)

It was acknowledged that this would require a change of attitudes (CR p. 23, n. 15). The answer amounts to little more than generalised spiritual platitudes:

> We welcome therefore the call of the Congress for a more Christ-like attitude towards the poor, the powerless, the homeless, the handicapped, the deaf and the blind, the elderly and all who suffer in today's society. The parish community should place such people at the centre of its life and concern. As the Congress Declaration stated: "In them we see the image of Christ crucified, a focus for our love and care, whose needs we must recognise and meet, and from whom we receive a living witness of Christ's passion." (EP 124)

The section on evangelisation was the least satisfactory of the Congress's report. Possibly this area suffered more than all the others from the lack of statistical information, the absence of a sociological analysis of our society and its religious aspects, and from the neglect of serious theology. By the time that the conference met, one satisfactory survey was available, *Roman Catholic Opinion*,[14] but it had not been commissioned by the Congress organisers and received no official recommendation from them in the preparatory literature. One brief paragraph from the section on evangelisation will indicate the unresolved questions:

> We realise that England and Wales are now missionary countries, in need of renewal and of hearing the gospel again. Our Church must discover how to speak to the people of our time in their signs and language and according to their need. This is a task in which ecumenical co-operation is so essential it should be taken for granted. (CR p. 26)

The same page also speaks about bringing the Gospel to the pagans of the world who have never heard of Christ. In two brief pages the delegates encompassed some of the most intricate problems of pastoral theology without unravelling them. For example, what is the relationship between evangelisation and ecumenism? Is the neophyte to be encouraged to enter a sort of pan-Christian ecumenism, or does he become a member of one of the still separated Churches? This section of the congress report was disappointing. "The Easter People" did not supply the answers to its theological problems. It serves as an indication of the poor state of theology in this nation and its defective application to pastoral work.

The areas of Christian Education and Formation covered schools as well as catechesis in a broader sense. The Congress stated its conviction that adult catechisis is the most important branch of the exercise, and the bishops agreed positively:

> We willingly accept the practical implications of this decision, including the allocation of personnel and resources that may be proved necessary. (EP 145)

The working out of this intention in practical terms gives less ground for optimism. The congress advocated the establishment of a National Pastoral Institute, principally for catechical needs (CR p. 30, n. 9). Yet the reply was:

> At this juncture we are not in a position to do more than note the suggestion. (EP 153)

The congress recommended that there should be a full-time co-ordinator of catechists appointed in large parishes, or for groups of small parishes (CR p. 30, n. 10). To which EP replied:

> Dioceses and Deaneries may like to give thought to the appointment of full-time co-ordinators of catechesis in deanery areas and perhaps ultimately in parishes. (EP 129)

Another specific request was:

> That a common core of Religious Education be prepared at national level to ensure proper continuity and development in the formation of diocesan syllabuses. (CR p. 30, n. 12)

But all the sympathy which it received was:

> We shall consider the recommendation from the Congress about the provision of a common core Religious Education curriculum for national use. (EP 136)

Turning specifically to Catholic schools, the congress made a number of important and unambiguously clear recommendations. It was stated that the Catholic school is not the only agency for catechesis (CR p. 27, n. 6), and this was accepted, at least by implication in EP which speaks of the parish as the centre of all local catechetical activity (EP 128). The congress made the fairly obvious statement that Catholic schools should be communities of faith, for which they should have trained personnel committed to the formation of young people (CR p. 22, n. 16). EP agreed, but merely added a series of questions to the already recognised problems.

> The Catholic school must provide an experience of a living and worshipping community . . . It should be so inspired by the gospel that it is seen to be a genuine alternative to other forms of schooling. There are many questions which we need to ask about the Catholic school if it is to fulfil its role as a gospel-inspired community. How will its structure differ from those of other schools? What will be distinctive about its discipline? (EP 134)

Unfortunately, those questions remained unanswered. The explicit request for full-time chaplains to all secondary schools received an answer in two sections of EP:

> Regular visiting by local clergy, the appointment and training of chaplains, opportunities for in-service training . . . are all matters that call for our sympathetic, careful, and generous guidance. (EP 135)

And a little further on:

> We accept the need to appoint trained chaplains to Catholic secondary schools if these schools are adequately to fulfil their role in the Church. However, we have to acknowledge that not every priest is suited to this work and that local shortages may make it difficult to find the right man. (EP 138)

There was no attempt to suggest how the local shortages might be remedied.

The request that young people proceeding to tertiary education should be prepared for it more adequately (CR p. 28, n. 15) received an affirmative response from EP:

> We willingly endorse recommendations for religious education courses specifically designed to prepare 5th and 6th formers for entry into tertiary education. (EP 140)

The suggestion for a commission to study the whole area of tertiary education (CR p. 31, n. 23) gained only a lukewarm reception:

> We hope to develop a national policy also for those in higher education. (EP 40)

And, further on:

> We must consider carefully the possibility of the expansion of the Department for Catholics in Higher Education. (EP 144)

Two further requests were passed over in silence, firstly that seminarians should spend part of their course in an ordinary tertiary education environment (CR p. 31, n. 26), and that a bishop be appointed with sole responsibility for tertiary education (CR p. 31, n. 25). It is worth remarking that the university chaplains were opposed to this because it would weaken the link between the university community and the local bishop.

The final section on justice raised many issues which could hardly expect a swift practical remedy, but even so, the lack of positive response in EP was disappointing. The suggestion that dioceses and parishes should seek ways of providing alternatives to prison (CR p. 39, n. 13) was passed over in silence. The sub-section on peace, defence and disarmament, had some quite specific observations and suggestions. It criticised the arms trade, stated that it was impossible to justify nuclear war, and advocated a search for non-violent alternatives to war (CR p. 39, nos. 17, 18, 19). These received nothing more practical than a quotation of the relevant paragraphs of *Gaudium et Spes* from Vatican II and the restatement of the English Bishops' declaration about peace in October 1978 (EP 169). To answer a practical request with a restatement of already-known general principles does not bring a practical solution any closer to realisation. The plea that more resoures should be devoted to the work of Justice and Peace (CR p. 39, n. 15) received more than cautious treatment in the words that:

> We will study the recommendation that each diocese should appoint a full-time worker for justice and peace, and should create its own diocesan commission to promote active interest in this vital subject. (EP 167)

It is not surprising that Northern Ireland featured in the discussions, and the congress made a strong appeal to the bishops to convene, jointly with other Church leaders, a major conference on the matter (CR p. 40, n. 23). However, the bishops did not "feel able to make an unqualified commitment to accept" such a course (EP 170). Four years later, the prospect seems to have been forgotten completely.

Finally, the congress urged that we must strive for better relationships in society (CR p. 41, n. 27), which is admirable, but they also indicated that such relationships would improve the institutions and structure within society (CR p. 41, n. 27). Personally, I would suggest that just the reverse is the case. Peoples' lives and their relationships are usually shaped by the institutions in which they live, and not the other way round. If relationships are to be improved, it is normally necessary to reform the structures.

After analysing the Congress Report and the Bishops' reply, what assessment can be made of that vast exercise? On the whole it seems not unfair to describe the response as an evasion of the practical demands made by the congress. A few pages above I noted that the strong statements about warfare, and the armaments trade, were met with a quotation from Vatican II and from an earlier statement of the bishops. This I think typifies the tone of the dialogue. To reply to urgent pleas merely by quoting documents which were known and accepted before the congress, was effectively an evasion. That would have been the kind of place at which a practical undertaking should have been made. (And it was not the only point at which a practical commitment was called for.) The number of options open is almost past numbering, but something simple like a firm undertaking to introduce courses in peace studies in all the seminaries would at least have been a gesture of good will to the congress.

Basically what was missing from "The Easter People" was any sign of a willingness to make institutional changes. After that great congress, and all the sensible suggestions which were made, not one element of structural change was undertaken by the bishops. Resolutions were answered with platitudes and the whole apparatus of Church organisations and institutions went on as before without any modification being introduced. Four years after the event nothing of major significance has emerged from its deliberations and the exercise must be considered frankly as a failure.

In case the reader thinks that I am too harsh in my assessment of the congress, let me summarise its results. The report contained approximately 40 specific resolutions, recommendations or practical requests. Of these, only one received a positive encouragement, namely General Absolution (EP 68), and that matter had been under discussion between the bishops and the Vatican before the congress started. The only specific decisions in EP were refusals to act, such as declining to set up a National Pastoral Institute (EP 153). One asks oneself, was there any positive detail which emerged from the congress? I have combed the report with care, and the only sign of hopeful initiative which I detect is the unwillingness to pursue the conferring of minor orders of Acolyte and Reader on laymen, lest it should be prejudicial to the activities of altar boys and women readers (EP 98). I do not wish to sound cynical, but all I can say is: "Let us be grateful for small mercies."

The last few pages of the report rounded off the whole operation on the safest possible territory of an appeal to holiness (EP 183–200).

Where is the memory of the congress now? For most people it has been forgotten as completely as if it had never taken place. Elsewhere it has been washed up on the inhospitable shores of parish discussion groups. In September 1984, one diocesan newspaper gave the following glimpse of the uninspiring scene:

> The working party of the Response has met, and we have tried to respond to the message, to answer the question: How can we do something of practical value about prayer and the Bible in our parish? The suggestions that follow attempt to tackle this priority, but are not meant to be blueprints for all to follow rigidly. Certainly not that! Some groups have already worked out a programme tailored to suit local needs. Far better to follow such hard work through than to drop it merely for conformity's sake. But if you are looking for material to help you discuss, consult, and plan—here are the outlines of what we shall offer from October onwards in each month's *Catholic Voice*.[15]

Having started with parish discussion groups, the wheel has turned full circle and the congress is once again, at parish level, being buried quite effectively.

SECTION THREE: THEOLOGICAL COMPETENCE

One of the most serious weaknesses of the Catholic Church in this nation has been the failure to study theology seriously. The causes of this malaise are several, among which is the imprecise, yet powerful, disincentive generated by the attitude of most bishops, many religious superiors and vast numbers of clergy that it is basically unimportant and must always yield place to the practical tasks like building churches and conducting schools. It has also been hindered by the comparative absence of institutions, money, and manpower devoted to its development. Seminaries educate only the future priests, which limits their effectiveness in disseminating theology. There is no Catholic university in this country, and for this let us be grateful. But it does force us to ask how and where theology is to be studied?

The Catholic colleges of education have departments of theology and religious studies, but their programmes are orientated to the production of school teachers who will impart religious education to children. They do not offer honours degrees in theology, nor do they plan for post-graduate studies. Admittedly, a Catholic is at liberty to study non-denominational theology at any of the thirty or so British universities which offer it, but this does not constitute an opportunity for the Catholic community as a whole to make a corporate creative contribution to the development of theology in this nation.

In spite of the overall depressing picture, there is one area, that of adult education outside the universities, where the Catholic community has a network of extremely successful institutions, namely the pastoral centres. The pioneers in this field were communities like the Grail in West London and the Dominicans at Spode House in Staffordshire. As far back as the 1950s they were organising short courses for adults in every sphere related to theology. They also served as centres for retreats and spiritual exercises. After the Council many other religious orders and dioceses imitated the pattern, with the result that practically every diocese now has a residential centre for adult religious education. It would be difficult to count up how many people have passed through them in the last twenty years, but it amounts to many thousands. Their effectiveness has been phenomenal. All the programmes are what we would call short courses (like study week-ends) or part-time evening courses. This means that their participants have sacrificed precious time out of busy lives. It implies that the students have a high degree of commitment, especially if they are giving up holidays in order to attend a summer school, for example. The result of all this effort has been a record of undeniable success. Earlier in the chapter I stated that most people still in the Church as practising Catholics had re-thought their commitment in faith; it is now time to point out that they have also re-educated themselves theologically. It is largely due to pastoral centres like Spode House that this vast re-education of the adult population has taken place. The process has been assisted by the quality of the book trade. This too has been an indirect by-product of the Council.

There are about half-a-dozen publishing houses who have devoted their efforts for at least thirty years to the dissemination of serious theology at both the academic and popular levels. There is a similar number of newspapers and periodicals circulating in Great Britain which present theology and an analysis of the daily life of our community in a manner which is helpful to our mission. Comparisons are odious, and one does not wish to cause offence, but there is only one journal produced by the English Catholics which is of a sufficient standard to find a place in the theology section of an average university library.

One further factor which has favoured the development of theology has been the amelioration of the official censorship procedures and the virtual disappearance of the unofficial censorship. It may not be superfluous to look back to the 1950s to recall how the latter mechanism operated. A certain large church in London had been destroyed by bombing during the war and was being rebuilt in the mid-1950s. The *Catholic Herald* published a letter in which the writer regretted the reconstruction of an unimaginative Victorian gothic edifice, since architects were then capable of creating really imaginative buildings like the French church in Leicester Square. The following week another letter was published saying how wonderful it was that the old style was being repeated without any concessions to modernity. Unfortunately, it came too late because the parish priest had already forbidden the sale of the *Catholic Herald* at the entrance of the said church!

The neglect of academic theology by the English Catholic community has been so serious that it can be stated confidently that, since the death of Cardinal Newman in the last century, we have not made any significant contribution to the theological life of our nation or the universal church. The indicators of this situation are numerous and unambiguous for those who face up to them. Until the last few years there was nothing even vaguely like a department of Catholic theology in any university. Twenty years ago, not

one Catholic was a full-time lecturer in divinity in any
university. I know of only two theological books by Catholic
theologians which have been translated from English into
another language.[16] In the mid-1960s I was studying theology
in Switzerland at the universityof Fribourg, and I cannot
recall that any lecturer referred to any English Catholic
scholar since Cardinal Newman, although famous non-
Catholic authors from this nation were quoted with respect
and studied attentively. As far as serious theology is
concerned, it would have made no difference if the Catholics
of Great Britain had simply not existed for the last eighty
years: there has been a theological vacuum.

Fortunately, things are improving now, thanks to the
initiative of a few enlightened individuals. These forces are
now showing signs of progress, and indeed the development
of theology in the last few years is one of the most
encouraging signs of the post-conciliar period.[17]

In April 1984 a group of Catholic theologians meeting at
Upholland decided to set up a national theological association. Fr Mahoney of Heythrop was elected as president,
and a further election produced a committee whose equitable
balance of interests could scarcely have been improved even
by deliberate planning. It comprises two lay women, two
laymen, two Jesuits, two Dominicans, and two secular
priests. On another basis of division, the committee members belong in almost equal numbers to the universities of
Cambridge, London and Oxford, with one from Leeds.

For more than a decade ecumenical considerations have
inhibited the creation of a specifically Catholic association,
and before that we had lived for too long in psychological
ghettos of our own making. However a substantial period of
Catholic commitment to the ecumenical movement has
exorcised those anxieties, and every participant who spoke
stressed that we did not intend to establish a new ghetto, nor
would we withdraw from the inter-Church dialogue. Moreover it was agreed that a reasonably defined denominational
base is an advantage in ecumenism. We are not aiming to
achieve the lowest common denominator of non-disputed
theological greyness. Each Church must reflect upon its roots
to enrich the dialogue with distinctive contributions. From
the practical point of view it saves an immense amount of

time if the ground rules can be pre-supposed instead of being debated at length at every meeting prior to discussing the business in hand.

That April meeting reflected the shift to universities which has taken place almost unperceived over the last two decades. Twenty years ago there was not one Catholic full-time teacher in the divinity department of any university in Great Britain. Now there are about twenty thus employed, and two of them hold professorial chairs. All but one of them are lay people, and this too is significant. A few months ago I was in conversation with a recently retired professor of divinity of a provincial university. He remarked that it had been a matter of regret to him that during the whole of his career no Catholic had ever taught in his department; every other mainstream Church had been represented among the lecturers. That observation is symptomatic. The universities and the other Churches are not keeping us out; we have excluded ourselves. A few lines above I noted that the twenty Catholic lecturers are mostly lay people. They have complete freedom to plan their own careers, but the clergy do not.

It is no secret that most bishops and religious superiors are reluctant to allow their priests to devote to the further study of theology, that amount of time which would be necessary to qualify them for university teaching. Their justification is that there is a grave shortage of clergy, and this is perfectly correct. The fact that most of the parochial clergy celebrate three masses each Sunday has masked the underlying shortage of priests. There is no denying that the parishes are neglected spiritually. Yet the scale of this shortage is so great, that the diverting of half a dozen priests to advanced studies in theology would make no appreciable difference to the nationwide problem. In France, for example, they have never shown a similar disregard for the intellectual life although their shortage of clergy has been more acute and has been with them for a far longer time.

Basically it is related to one's view of the priest's mission. Is the teaching of theology part of the Church's mission? And if so, is it suitable for a priest? The Church's established practice since patristic times would seem to have given unambiguously affirmative answers to both questions. It is therefore sad to see that in England the clergy are dropping behind the laity in the theological field. By that I do not mean that I would wish to see the laity withdraw from theology; what I regret is the relative absence of the clergy. The practical consequences of this imbalance should be weighed very seriously. It is said that the pen is mightier than the sword, and that is true in Church affairs too. Our present practices in ecumenism and participated vernacular liturgy are the direct consequences of the consensus which theologians reached in the late 1950s. The same thing will happen in the future. Is it desirable that the clergy should be absent from the genesis of ideas which will shape the Church's future policies? Let us make no mistake about the force of apparently theoretical ideas. Policies which are based on sound theology will prevail because they will command confidence, and if serious theology is absent no amount of disciplinary activity or penalties will make up for it.

How does the aspiring theologian embark upon his pilgrimage? For a layman it is straightforward (if he or she has the intellectual ability). Let me describe the career of a friend of mine whose name I will withhold. He studied theology at a provincial university, took a first and came to Cambridge to research for the Ph.D. in ecclesiastical history. He was successful and by the age of twenty-four was looking round for a university teaching post. After a post-doctoral fellowship in a northern university, he obtained an assistant lectureship in another university, and now has a full lectureship somewhere in England.

The training of the clergy is somewhat more complicated. It is orientated towards specific goals and after their entry into a particular diocese or religious order the individuals have little choice in the planning of their studies. For the most part they are destined for work in parishes, monasteries, teaching in schools, and a limited number will be designated for work in seminaries (or providing the theology in colleges of education). For parish work they are given six years in a seminary, and much the same applies to monks. For school-mastering they will be sent to university for a first degree in a secular subject if they did not have one at the time of their entry. Those destined for the staffing of seminaries will usually have studied a slightly longer course, at Rome for instance, and a minority of them might take a doctorate there too. Ushaw and Allen Hall have special arrangements with the universities of London and Durham whereby some of their students (all too few, I regret) combine their six seminary years with study for an undergraduate degree in divinity. What has been conspicuously absent from this programme is the intention to equip any of the priests to teach theological subjects in the secular universities of this country. This is at variance with the age-long practice of the Church and the cause is nothing other than the mediocrity of our aspirations concerning the nature of our mission to the nation.

In spite of the poor record of the last century, recent years have seen some signs of hope. An increasing number of laity and clergy have been seriously concerned about the absence of high achievement in theology. Furthermore it has become clear that these aspirations must be translated into institutions if progress is to be made. If individuals are left in virtual isolation they can achieve very little, even if they possess great personal talent. Cardinal Newman has influenced the Church's theology after his death by his writings. During his lifetime he had little appreciable effect upon the life of the English or world-wide Catholic community. Most of the structures which he planned were frustrated. How often could we count upon the emergence of a genius of his stature? And if he was so curtailed by the lack of suitable organisations, how much more devastating will it be for those of less talent.

Wherever Catholic theology has developed successfully in the last hundred years, it has been on account of the existence of organisations which have been established to promote its serious study, and which have integrated satisfactorily into the intellectual life of the nation. There is no uniformity of pattern, and in places as different as the United States, Canada, France, Belgium and Germany a variety of "schools" have been established, varying in response to the Church's position as a national Church or a minority group, and to the organisation of universities in those nations.

At long last England too now possesses an interesting variety of experiments and newly established teaching organisations. Ushaw's arrangement with Durham has resulted also in the seminary lecturers teaching in the university. In Bristol there is a carefully structured Catholic participation in an ecumenical department of theology. The University of Kent has admitted the Franciscans who moved their seminary to the campus, so that their students can combine their domestic theology with a university degree.

The most ambitious of all these schemes was undoubtedly the transfer of the Jesuit theology house from the remote Oxfordshire village of Heythrop to the centre of London, whence it has been incorporated by Royal Charter as a college of the university. Among its students the laity outnumber the clergy and nuns. It has supplied a long felt need, namely the enabling of laity to study Catholic theology for an honours degree financed by a personal grant like any other student. This means that ultimately they can earn their living on theology. It may not be the most elevated way of evaluating the academic life, but one must be realistic. In a society like our own the possession of a university degree is the negotiable coinage of intellectual achievement. Unless these diplomas can be obtained, and unless they are recognised by the nation as a whole, lay people will not be able to afford the luxury of studying theology.

A final contribution to the different Catholic enterprises of recent years is the series of changes which have been made in St Edmund's House in Cambridge. At the end of the last century it was established as a sort of lodging house where priests lived while studying for first degrees in the university, being matriculated at other colleges. The recent history of St Edmund's is too complicated to retail in detail here, but the end result is admirable. We now exist in our own right within the university, admit our own students and present them for examinations. Most of them are post-graduates because the first stage of our new existence was when we availed ourselves of the university's plan, in the mid-1960s, to establish about half a dozen small colleges designed for postgraduate students who were engaged upon research. Students at St Edmund's can now research into any subject which the university offers including divinity in all its related parts.

One unanswered question must now be faced: is there such a thing as Catholic theology? The establishment of the Catholic Theological Association in 1984 has, by implication, brought this to the fore. Catholics do study theology, but is the subject matter of their enquiries different from that which is taught to other Christians, or indeed to agnostics who study it as a cultural phenomenon? The question is so far-ranging that I must limit myself here to merely two observations. Firstly, the unity of the Catholic Church and our self-identity are to some extent connected with the awareness of shared norms, values, and beliefs. We have nothing remotely like the political establishment of the Church of England here or the Lutheran state Churches on mainland Europe. Secondly, the consiousness of agreed values and norms is related to our attitude to traditions which comprises scripture, patristic consensus, General Councils, the *sensus fidelium*, and more. A sympathetic agnostic is entitled to regard all of it as the expression of a community's consensus which he will accept or reject with as much detachment as he gives to the American Constitution (assuming that he is not an American citizen). For the believing Catholic it is different. Conciliar decisions and the rest connect with the Church's life as a community, in which the believer is incorporated, and through which he expresses his faith in the person of Christ.

Whatever view one might take of Catholic theology, it cannot exist in a vacuum, and the individuals who study it might integrate it with their overall pattern of life. Since theology is a science, one of the places for its development is quite naturally a university. Since the English scene is one of cultural pluralism, the natural habitat will be the secular university. (It is agreed on all sides that there is no place for a Catholic University in Great Britain.) Should we aim for faculties of Catholic theology like the German universities? Or Catholic communities like St Edmund's which are more open to the theology presented by the secular universities? Having stated the choices let us be grateful that it has not been answered exclusively one way or the other. It is much to our advantage that we have about half a dozen different models operating at the moment. Only the passage of time and their own achievements will indicate what is desirable for the future. Let us not prejudge the outcome from the standpoint of theoretical principles.

There is, however, a minor consideration, that of geography. If a Catholic wishes to make a contribution to the academic life of this nation, by teaching theology in one of the universities, then it will be a considerable advantage to have done his postgraduate studies in a British university.

Quite simply it will mean that he knows his way round the system. History is reasonably clear about this. The many priests who have gained a doctorate in Rome over the last hundred years or more have never integrated satisfactorily into the English academic life, although some of them have been scholars of outstanding ability like the late Canon D. J. B. Hawkins. They have tended to look back to Rome as their natural academic habitat.

Finally, lest I seem to stress unduly the importance of institutions let me recall to the memory of my readers one example of importance, namely the past history of Trinity College, Dublin. Thanks to that college the Church of Ireland was able to make a contribution to the nation's culture out of all proportion to their small numbers. It serves as an almost classical paradigm of what a minority group must do to preserve its self-identity and make a creative contribution to the wider society in which it lives. The recently established theological association, and the various institutions which we have fostered at university level should be able to perform the same service for the Catholic minority in this nation.

The case of the twenty teachers of theology, referred to above, raises disturbing questions about the nature and exercise of authority in the Catholic community here. Prescinding from Heythrop which is a special case, of those other twenty in universities only one is a priest, and this is surprising. Since all priests have to study theological subjects for six years before ordination, they should have an incomparable advantage over the laity in this field. What we see is just the reverse, which can only mean that some other factor is at work to counterbalance inherent advantages which are enjoyed by the priests. It is my considered opinion that the other factor is the manner in which ecclesiastical authority prevents the clergy from developing their theological potential. As I indicated above, lay people can plan their own careers, but the clergy must obtain permission from their superiors if they are to pursue further studies or teach theology at a university (granted that they have the native ability). Not only can the religious superiors forbid a priest to pursue theological studies, but they can also effectively prevent it. Without going into details, which would involve persons who are still alive, I can think of all too many incidents where priests have been denied educational opportunities, have been dismissed from teaching posts, or denied permission to publish, simply because their opinions have been considered too "advanced" by their superiors.

In analysing the relationships between laity, clergy, and bishops in the areas of theology and Church discipline, we see a discouraging scenario. Lay people advance in theology because the bishops cannot stop them, clergy are held back in this field, but the laity too suffered frustration at the Liverpool Congress, because in that situation they came effectively under the control of the bishops. In these important areas it seems that ecclesiastical authority is operating in an exceedingly negative fashion.

This gives rise to many questions about the nature of authority and its exercise in the Church. Much has been written on it in the last thirty years, which has not been assimilated, so I will recall some of the principal points of agreement, but briefly.[18] Authority does not exist as an end in itself, but it is a means to serve the work of the Church. This means that it must be understood in the context of the Church's mission, and for the exposition of this notion I can do no better than quote the words of the Vatican Council:

> To fulfil this mission Christ the Lord promised the Holy Spirit to the apostles . . . By his power they were to be witnesses to Christ before the nations and peoples . . . Now, that duty which the Lord Committed to the shepherds of His people, is a true service, and in sacred literature is significantly called "diakonia" or "ministry".[19]

Corresponding to the superior's right to command, is the subject's duty to obey. In the theology of St Thomas Aquinas the virtue of obedience is classified as one of the related parts of justice and its exercise is governed by the same considerations as justice. This means that its moral excellence consists in achieving the virtuous mean, which is not giving too little or too much obedience. The wisdom of this insight must surely have been appreciated by every reflective person when the Nazi war criminals were tried at Nüremburg (and subsequently in Germany and elsewhere). Frequently the erstwhile SS officers justified their conduct on the plea that they acted under obedience. In fact their conduct demonstrated perfectly that it is morally reprehensible to give too much obedience to a legitimate superior.

Political life in the free world illustrates a mature appreciation of how authority should act. And in spite of some abuses, and many criticisms, one can see in a nation like Great Britain, a number of authentic institutional arrangements to ensure that the exercise of power in the nation is morally satisfactory. It is achieved by a sophisticated system of checks and balances in which free speech and criticism are presupposed, and universal suffrage is the background. There is the important division of power between the legislature and the judiciary, and in Parliament itself the Leader of the Opposition is paid a salary which is second only to that of the Prime Minister. This last detail is most significant because it indicates that opposition is valued. Institutions of this kind indicate that one is dealing with a genuinely mature society.

How does this apply to the Church? I make no apology for using civil society as the instrument of comparison. The nature of authority and its corresponding attitude, obedience, are not essentially different whether exercised in Church or State. The main practical difference between the two is the manner of enforcement of the decisions of the superiors. A quaint example may help to illustrate this point. Up to the time of the French Revolution the Church would either use the civil power, or imitate its methods, in order to secure obedience. In the case of ecclesiastical dress, the clergy could be punished by a fine in the civil courts if they were not wearing it. This occurred in the Papal States and in Catholic nations of Europe.[20] This gives rise to the question, how does the Church enforce its commands when it is not possible to fine the offenders? This is crucial in relation to the laity, because they cannot be coerced by the clergy. It means quite simply that authority in the Church must repose upon consent between superiors and subordinates or else it is virtually non-existent. This conclusion should have been evident from a study of the Church's mission, but it has been obscured in history by a variety of accidents, thanks to which the clergy have been able to use the civil power for their own purposes, and also to imitate it as far as they could.

Because the Church, for so long, could count upon the civil governments to act as their executive arm in coercing miscreants, it is not surprising that ecclesiastical authority now shows some anomalies in its exercise. After the French Revolution, and the other insurrections associated with it, the Church has no longer been able to exert power in that fashion. What has been created as a substitute? It should have been the building of a system of trust and confidence, but unfortunately that has not yet been achieved. In many respects we are still living through the classical problems which have been immortalised in King Lear. As is well known, the two elder daughters of the ageing King are flatterers while the youngest criticises and opposes him openly. The older women do not give him obedience but subservience while they are under his domination. As the play approaches its tragic conclusion, it is clear that the younger daughter is truly loyal to her father in spite of her outspokenness. Lear only appreciates this when it is too late, and therein lies the tragedy.

Unfortunately there is all too much of the Lear syndrome in the Catholic Church's exercise of authority, certainly in this country. Flattery is still rewarded, and authority is frequently seen to be powerless where punishment cannot be enforced. We have yet to achieve a system reposing upon trust and the ability to inspire confidence. There is, however, one ray of hope. The laity cannot be coerced, and free speech has come to stay. History has yet to see the consequences of free speech operating in an autocracy.

CHAPTER FIVE

Handing It On To The Next Generation

Many young people aged about twenty, who were brought up in Catholic families, hold views on religion and morals, which are so much at variance with the implied presuppositions of Bishops' Pastoral Letters, for example, that we must acknowledge the existence of a credibility gap of staggering proportions. The lack of adequate sociological investigation in this field is distressing since it shows a lack of pastoral concern, but the phenomenon is so widespread and so unmistakable that we are justified in studying it despite the paucity of scientific evidence. The parochial clergy, and enlightened lay people have all recognised instances of widespread abandonment of Christianity. The kind of thing which I have in mind is the situation of Catholic families, where both parents are committed members of the Church, but whose children have all, or nearly all, abandoned the practice of religion. The most obvious sign of their attitudes is the complete abandonment of mass and the sacraments; they may also deliberately refuse to marry the person with whom they are living, even after the birth of children. But what is significant is that these rejections of institutional religion may well be accompanied by a high sense of moral responsibility in other areas, total fidelity to their partners, and sincere concern for all that concerns the well-being of persons.

The background to their attitudes is exceedingly complex. In contrast to their parents who probably grew up in the 1930s and 1940s, they have enjoyed a high material standard of living, education and television have presented them with virtually an unlimited range of choices in life, and yet in more recent years sombre influences have been perceived. The presence of nuclear weapons, and the scale of unemployment make them feel helpless.

The most powerful of these negative attitudes to life would seem to be the nuclear armaments. It is difficult to generalise, but it appears that for a significant number of them, there comes a time in adolescence when they are mature enough to appreciate the destructive power of the nuclear arsenals which the larger nations now possess. The girls generally arrive at this realisation sooner than the boys because they mature earlier. The sensitive and perceptive ones will sometimes experience a lengthy and almost pathological depression at this point. It is justifiable, I think, to assume that the articulate and sensitive young people probably experience more poignantly, what the less articulate know but cannot state. This attitude shows itself in a feeling of present helplessness, looking towards a pointless future. In practical terms they become discouraged about undertaking the hard work required for "A" level exams and university studies, saying: "What's the point of it: the world probably won't last until I am middle-aged." A variety of public opinion surveys indicate that a significant number of young people (perhaps 50 per cent) consider that there will be a nuclear war during their lifetime. One young man of my acquaintance, aged 28, says that he has no intention of marrying and raising children because the world has no future. I feel sure that he is not the only one who holds that view.

If it is difficult to generalise about the attitudes of young people towards religion, it is still harder to identify the precise causes which have estranged them from its institutional manifestations. However the problem is so serious that one must attempt some assessment of the reasons behind their rejection of conventional religious practice. Moreover the phenomenon is so widespread, and the people in question are so frank in discussion, that it is not difficult to discern recurring patterns in their behaviour and attitudes. My own impressions on the matter have been built up over about thirty years of varied pastoral work in parishes and universities. It is the result of countless discussions with resentful young people, sad parents, worried teachers, and a large number of genuinely humble people who are painstakingly searching for the right methods, and asking honestly: "Where have we failed?"

Whether or not they are completely accurate, the reasons which young people often allege when talking about their antipathy to institutional religion, include such allegations as that parish priests, bishops, nuns, and teachers of Religious Education have been experienced by them as unpleasant authority-figures. If religious allegiance becomes entangled with school discipline, loyalty to the Church will undoubtedly suffer. They state frequently that official pronouncements display a negative attitude to life, that they are obsessed about sex, display little that could be categorised as "life-affirming", and contribute nothing to such values as joy, creativity, freedom, and justice. One perceptive young lady told me that in school they had not been taught to pray. (But is this possible in a classroom?) In addition to all these, there is the often repeated complaint, which I regard as the most dangerous, that institutional religion is quite simply irrelevant to their lives.

The present situation is extremely disquieting. To some people it appears that we might lose the majority of the next generation who seem set to abandon the religious convictions of their parents. How did we arrive at this state of affairs? What were the policies, the presuppositions, or the accidents, which produced it?

To judge by unspoken assumptions it would seem that in the nineteenth century it was presumed that children more or less inherited Catholicism from their parents, in the same way that they acquired nationality and surnames. The commitment of faith was taken for granted, or else overlooked. From the age of five the school took over from the home and imparted the intellectual content which was judged to be the appropriate expression of their faith. Together with the parish, the school processed them through confession, communion, and confirmation; and inculcated a code of conduct, by which the children grew up keeping the Church's rules. The homogeneity of the operation was helped by the fact that the all-age schools had catchment areas which were co-terminous with the parishes, and the sense of community was further strengthened by the fact that many of the parishes were for the most part ghettos of Irish immigrants. Up to 1914 the coherence of these parish communities was strong and they seemed to produce generations of practising Catholics, although one may question the validity of the methods. After the Second World War most of these sociological presuppositions had vanished. The parishes were no longer Irish ghettos, the Catholics no longer felt like strangers in the nation, the senior schools were not co-terminous with just one parish, and thus effectively destroyed that element of community building. In the years following the Council, theological criticisms of the old catechism, the syllabusses, and the methods of teaching, have been severe. As a result the system which looked so effective up to the First World War is now seen to be in disarray.

To some readers it may seem that the assessment of Catholic schooling which I have presented in the preceeding paragraphs is inaccurate and unduly pessimistic. There are some who defend the system against all criticisms, and reinforce their position by claiming that spiritual values cannot be verified by empirical research. This is a misleading allegation. It is perfectly true that the inner reality of religious conviction is incapable of quantifiable measurement, but its effects in life, conduct, and rationalised attitudes can be observed. One suspects that a large scale operation to evaluate the Catholic educational process might be so devastating to the supporters of the policy, that they could not face up to the possible disillusion, and prefer to pre-empt the danger, by discountenancing the project. It is a fact that no wide-ranging investigation of the school system has been undertaken.

Although research in this field is lamentably incomplete, a number of relevant surveys have been made, and I will examine five of them which have a bearing on the transmission of religious values to children. The first comes from the University of Bristol and was undertaken on behalf of the Medical Research Council National Survey of Health and Development.[1] The sample totals 5,362 individuals who were born in March 1946, and who were selected so as to constitute a fully representative section of the nation. These people were studied or interviewed at intervals of two years up to the age of 26. The religious affiliation in infancy was noted in the survey, and at the age of 26 the participants in the survey were asked whether they still held the religious belief and denomination of their childhood. A significant number had abandoned it, either in favour of another Church, or by admitting no religious affiliation, or simply declaring themselves non-believers. Of those baptised into the Church of England 24.7 per cent admitted to non belief at the age of 26. For the Church of Scotland's adherents 24 per cent had taken this step. For the Methodists it was 30.5 per cent. Other Non-conformists recorded it as 39.8 per cent. And for the Catholics 26 per cent had moved into non-belief.[2] The figures are not identical across the board, but in the words of the authors who analysed the survey: "Total loss rates (i.e. losses from belief to non-belief) were surprisingly evenly spread across religions or denominations."[3]

A straightforward deduction from these figures is disquieting. The loss of religion by the age of 26 is not significantly different between Catholics and other Churches, in spite of the massive efforts devoted to our schools. One is justified in deducing that the elaborate school programme makes no appreciable difference to the children in safeguarding the transmission to them of their parents' religion. As far as specific investigation of the Catholic schools is concerned, the first satisfactory survey was that of Dr Hornsby-Smith in 1978.[4] Before analysing his results in detail, I will quote a general statement about religious practice, since it is a reasonable indicator of personal conviction.

> Since only about one-third of Catholics attend mass on Sunday and two-thirds attend Catholic schools, it follows that at the very least, one half of the children attending Catholic schools subsequently cease to practice.[5]

This calculation is dependent upon the overall number of Catholics in the nation, which is not known with any accuracy. However the author safeguards himself against this uncertainty, by indicating that the 50 per cent practice rate is the highest that one can infer.

More specific information came from a survey of 47 secondary and middle schools in the diocese of Southwark in 1975. It involved 11,032 girls and 10,921 boys. Concerning mass attendance they were given four questions:

How often do you attend mass outside school?:

1) More than once a week?
2) On Sundays and holidays of obligation?
3) Occasionally and only when I feel in the mood?
4) Never really.[6]

Those who identified with the latter two can be judged effectively to have abandoned the normal practice which is expected of Catholics. By the age of 15, the number who identified themselves with that non-practising group was 44 per cent of the boys and 36 per cent of the girls.

Clearly mass attendance is just the crudest and clearest of indicators. Carefully framed questions about belief were also addressed to children of a similar age group. The fifth form pupils of three Catholic comprehensive schools in the south of England, were questioned in 1973. Altogether 419 Catholics completed the questionnaires, and one London Education Authority school served as a basis of comparison. They were given half a dozen statements about God, and asked to express assent or dissent. Proposition 1 stated: "I know God really exists and I have no doubts about it." Proposition 6 was: "I don't believe in God." Between these extremes were graduated positions of which Proposition 2 stated: "While I have some doubts, I feel that I do believe in God.." Proposition 3 expressed it thus: "I find myself believing in God some of the time but not at other times." After that, the statements express disbelief in one way or another. Adding together the pupils who agreed with the first three, and who can be called the believers, we find the following results. The three Catholic schools scored 76, 78, and 78 per cent of the pupils in that category, and the non-Catholic LEA school recorded only 43 per cent believers among its pupils.[7] The near uniformity between the Catholic schools is striking, but the fact that nearly a quarter of their pupils could not rise to assent on so simple a statement as belief is disquieting.

The same schools were questioned about Jesus, with the following propositions:

1) Jesus is the divine son of God and I have no doubt about it.
2) While I have some doubts I feel basically that Jesus is Divine.
3) I feel that Jesus was a great man and very holy but I don't feel him to be the son of God any more than all of us children are.

Subsequent propositions were even less affirmative of the

divinity of Jesus, and in fact it is only the first two which really satisfy Catholic belief. The three Catholic schools mustered barely half of their pupils into that bracket, namely those who agreed with propositions one and two. The percentages were 59, 49, and 51, and the LEA school showed only 25 per cent.[8] While the pupils of the Catholic schools show just about twice as many believers in Jesus's divinity as a non-Catholic sample, it is still far from re-assuring in terms of religious conviction.

In assessing the findings of these surveys Dr Hornsby-Smith makes the following observations (concerning the mass attendance): "There is clear evidence that the process of lapsation from this institutional requirement is well under way in the early years of secondary schooling."[9] As an interpretation of the motives behind their behaviour he states:

> Four themes emerged as important in the interpretation of the religious socialisation of the young Catholic:
> 1) The struggle of the adolescent for the personal autonomy of the adult;
> 2) Antagonism or indifference to the "official" religion of the institutional Church and the existence of a more privatised form of religion;
> 3) The impoverished conceptualisation of God and religion leading to its rejection as "childish" in adolescence; and
> 4) In the absence of structural support from family or peer groups much lapsation appears to be due to laziness and "drift" rather than conscious choice and decision.

Among the really strong factors influencing the convictions of children, the author identifies the family:

> There was clear evidence of the strong influence of the home background of senior pupils on their reported religious beliefs and practices. Particularly important were parental and familial religious identification and behaviour.

This leads immediately to the consideration of one factor which is an imponderable at the moment. If it be granted that parental attitudes are strongly influential on their children's beliefs, then it may be that the school is simply superfluous. In other words it may be just one more consequence of the parents' convictions that they have sent their children to a Catholic school. So far we are not in possession of any research which has examined the question in sufficient detail to arrive at firm conclusions on this hypothesis. However, the experience of many university chaplains would support it, because we meet so many committed Catholics who have not been to Catholic schools, and for whom the parents have been virtually the only source of spiritual inspiration.

Prescinding from that latter conjecture, the results of Dr Hornsby-Smith's investigations do not give a reassuring picture of the performance of Catholic schools. The next relevant survey was a combined operation of Gallup Poll and the University of Surrey, for which 1,023 adult Catholics were interviewed in the spring of 1978.[10] Catholic education occupied only a small part of the overall enquiry, but its findings are valuable. Before studying their assessment of the causative influence of the schools on the religious convictions of the adult, it is instructive to note some general trends. Two generations ago the vast majority of Catholics received all their education in Catholic schools. For the age range 50 to 64 years, 77.7 per cent were in this position. But for those aged between 15 and 24, only about half (53.3 per cent to be precise) received the whole of their schooling in a Catholic establishment.[11]

This situation is reflected in their attitudes. When asked if they agreed or disagreed with the proposition: "Catholics should be educated in separate Catholic schools", 29.7 per cent agreed, but 36.4 per cent disagreed. The remainder were made up of various shades of agreement, dissent, or uncertainty.[12]

There were some surprising replies to the question: "If there was one change you could make to the Catholic School system, what would it be?" No change, was the reply of 26.9 per cent; 24.7 per cent didn't know. After that the most numerous category (13.1 per cent) said: "Less religious instruction/education/emphasis." The next closest to this was: "Less dogmatism", scoring 4.8 per cent.

These facts, figures and attitudes do not convey the impression of a system which works well and commands confidence. As far as the operational success of the schools is concerned, the authors are very cautious. The most that they would venture is that Catholic schools are marginally effective, but other variables are powerful.[13] The nature and influence of these variables can be seen in assessing the simple indicator of mass attendance. High scorers here were the products of Catholic schools, but occupational status and sex were as influential in the process as the schools, and the influences of spouse or parents were even stronger.[14] Frequently the authors refer to other influences, especially the home, whose causal power cannot easily be discerned in an enquiry which is based upon straightforward answers to a standardised questionnaire.[15] In their conclusions they say:

> Catholic schools appear to be effective in producing adult religious outcomes although the actual effect is small, especially in relation to the effects of variables, like parental religiosity, and spousal religiosity which measure the impact of the home . . . where the adults familial environment is not religious at all, however, the impact of Catholic schooling is lost.[16]

In view of which I feel inclined to draw the inference that if the family environment is strongly religious the school is superfluous.

The next investigation of the effectiveness of Catholic schools generated more heat than light. "Public Schools– Shock Report" said *The Universe* of 11 November 1983. It was quoting the Catholic chaplain to the University of Cambridge who made some startling revelations about the mass attendance of known Catholics in that university.[17] Exactly 900 Catholic students were known to the chaplains, of whom 337 were at the chaplaincy on 10 October which was the Sunday designated for counting the mass attendance. In particular he noted that students from the best known and most expensive Catholic public schools were poorly repre-sented, only 27 out of 37 freshmen from these schools being at mass on that Sunday. This led him to comment:

> The figures make nonsense of the claim of Catholic public schools that they are forming Christian gentlemen who will be the future leaders of lay Catholic opinion and action. . . . Very good company, immensely likeable, and totally impervious to the Gospel—such are the most intelligent products of our "best" public schools.

The exercise was widely criticised because of the unrepresentative nature of the sample. In addition to the chaplaincy, there are in Cambridge half a dozen parish churches and religious houses offering nearly twenty masses at which the uncounted students might have assisted at mass if they were not at the chaplaincy. Undoubtedly this fact must have a bearing upon the figures which were quoted. Nevertheless the chaplain's conclusions were borne out by my own experience during seven years as Chaplain to the University of London.

The last survey which I will analyse was undertaken in the summer of 1982. It is the product of an unlikely partnership between the University of London (Bedford College) and the Catholic Women's League.[18] The sample was somewhat restricted, but has its own special interest as a result. Questionnaires were received from 165 young people aged between 16 and 30, whose mothers were members of the Catholic Women's League (Plymouth Branch). It is important to bear in mind that the latter organisation represents a self-selecting group of convinced Catholics, whose children are likely to have benefited from very positive religious influences. The Plymouth diocese is a region in which Catholics are a very small minority of the population, and where few parishes have a sufficient concentration of Catholic people to warrant a school system such as exists in Manchester or London.

The simplest indicator of religious practice is that of mass attendance, and in this group 59 per cent went regularly, as against 41 per cent who did not. Let it be remembered that these are the children whose families are convinced practising Catholics. Their attitudes showed an even greater divergence from the official norms: 57 per cent were in favour of divorce if the marriage had broken down; 64 per cent approved of premarital sex; and 83 per cent accepted the moral correctness of contraception.[19]

In seeking for the causes of these attitudes the researchers faced the question as to the influence of a Catholic school, and faced the specific problem: Was it a cause or merely an effect of religious conviction? To quote the words of the authors:

> In certain limited areas there are hints that a more careful measurement and investigation may reveal a causal association. However it may still result in showing that causality is following

in the direction of people choosing Catholic schools as a part of their lifestyle rather than the school affecting their Catholicity.

The same conclusion is expressed in slightly different words by the other researcher:

> Careful study was made of the type of schooling to see whether young people attending Catholic Primary and Secondary schools were more likely to continue practising their faith, than those sent to non-Catholic schools. The survey found no evidence to this effect: there was no appreciable difference between the two as far as continuity of practice was concerned.[20]

If the Catholic schooling was ineffectual, there were two causes which actively undermined the religious convictions of the young people, namely disillusionment with the parish or parish priest (about which more will be said in the next chapter), and most frequently the all embracing, but devastating factor or irrelevance.[21]

While the surveys of the last decade give no cause for optimism about the performance of the Catholic school system, there is a similar disarray in the theoretical expositions of the same period. More than a century ago the hierarchy seems not to have been troubled by doubts as to the need or effectiveness of denominational schools. The first Westminster Synod in 1852 expressed its mind unambiguously:

> The first necessity therefore is a sufficient provision of education adequate to the wants of our poor. It must become universal. No congregation should be allowed to remain without its schools, one for each sex. . . . Indeed whenever there may seem to be an opening for a new mission, we should prefer the erection of a school, so arranged as to serve temporarily for a chapel, to that of a church without one . . . And it is the good school which secures the virtuous and edifying congregation.[22]

In the period after the Second World War, and more particularly since the Council, there has been considerable discussion about the value, and specific purpose of denominational schools. The volume of literature is considerable, so I will limit myself to the examination of a few representative studies. A symposium held in 1974 was edited under the title *Theology and Education*,[23] and contains papers dealing with all the basic problems. At the very start the editor admits that the enterprise is fraught with uncertainty:

> The whole book is tentative in that it is looking for a framework within which further work can be undertaken. At present, our Church is faced with considerable uncertainties and confusion in its educational policy and practice.[24]

Without wishing to appear cynical, I cannot refrain from remarking how extraordinary it is to have pursued a policy for more than a century, involving so much expenditure of money and manpower, and yet to be so deficient in theoretical conviction.

By contrast, one of the contributors, a Catholic, who was the headmistress of a state school, gave a clear, if imprecise definition of the objectives for which her school strove: "I can think of no better way of describing the values of the secular school than the ancient trilogy of truth, beauty, and goodness."[25] Further on a Catholic priest, working inside the Church system tried, but without much conviction to derive a definition of the objectives from the Vatican Council's document on christian education.

> Thus the Second Vatican Council suggests among the distinctive purposes of the Catholic school, in the first place, that "it aims to create for the school community an atmosphere enlivened by the gospel spirit of freedom and charity", but one might wonder whether the Catholic school can do this, while continuing to be such a close institutional counterpart of the secular school as it is at present . . . Do the theological dimensions of either community or freedom have specifiable consequences for education?[26]

Towards the end of the book the editor supplies what looks like a description of the assumed role of Catholic schools; and he offers it in the context of not surrendering to complete secularism.

> Indiscriminate involvement in secular education runs the risk of dissolving the Church in a general wave of educational change

and progress, and thus destroying the distinctive contribution which the Church has to give. To preserve her identity, to transmit the gospel, to educate her children to maturity in faith, this inward-looking purpose is a *sine-qua-non* of her educational work. We might call it Church Education.[27]

Unfortunately it is almost a direct contradiction of what was said by one of the other contributors to the symposium:

It is my belief that we have something vitally important to contribute through our Catholic schools which derives directly from the Christian insight, but only if we abandon our confessional approach to education.[28]

This kind of divergence on basics scarcely generates confidence in the rationale of the system.

Shortly after the Liverpool Congress, the Catholic Teachers Federation published a pamphlet entitled *Aims and Objectives in Catholic Education*.[29] The title gives rise to reasonable hope that here one will find an explicit statement of what is distinctive about a Catholic school, and why a separate system of Church schools should continue to exist. Certainly the author was qualified to speak on the matter since he is a former president of the Federation. However, misgivings begin with the first paragraph where the author starts with a general disclaimer that the pamphlet "lays no claim whatsoever to originality and still less to being an epitomised formulation of a philosophy of Catholic Education, even assuming that such a formulation is feasible." After this disappointing start, the reader is offered half a dozen attempts to formulate the aim of Catholic education, none of which amounts to the clear definition of an operational objective:

The main aim of Catholic education is to form the true and perfect christian, and to use whatever means are possible in the life and organisation of the school to achieve it . . . Within this aim must be included the development in the children of responsible freedom. . . . If we seek a reason for Catholic education and for the Catholic school as a separate entity, it is to be found in the christian faith. . . . To take this point further, the educational programme should be directed to the development

> of the whole person, so that we have Catholics who are
> responsible people . . . Catholic education is an expression of the
> mission of Christianity. . . . The school should be a praying
> community.[30]

This list of admirable aspirations still leaves us without a clear
definition of Catholic education, since they could apply to
schools which are not Catholic, or to communities which are
not schools. The organisation and the writer of the pamphlet
are not outside the mainstream of the enterprise. It is
significant, and indeed serious if a clear sense of purpose
cannot be found in such an association.

The last document in which I will try and discover a
definition of the aims of Catholic education is an official
report. At the meeting of the Bishops' Conference in
November 1977, a study group was set up, with wide-
ranging terms of reference, namely: "To review the principles of Catholic education and to make recommendations."
The pages of the report indicate the laudable desire to
assimilate the insights of the Vatican Council, ecumenical
perspectives, and modern developments in education.[31] Less
explicit, but strongly pervasive was the quest for a convincing reason why Catholics should maintain a separate
system of schooling. In spite of pages of laudable ideals, it is
my opinion that no convincing principle was elaborated
which could justify separate Catholic schools. The following
sentence is representative of the tone of the whole document:

> The Catholic school is committed to the development of the
> whole man, since in Christ the perfect man, all human values
> find their fulfilment and unity . . . If, like every other school, the
> Catholic school has as its aim the critical communication of
> human culture and the total formation of the individual, it
> works towards this goal guided by its Christian vision of reality
> . . . Its task is fundamentally a synthesis of culture and faith, and
> a synthesis of faith and life.[32]

All the sentiments are praiseworthy, but lack the precision of
a definition of practical working objective.

The section which is entitled "The Distinctive Nature of
Catholic Education" is refreshingly frank about the difficulty
inherent in the quest. Having spoken of faith in Christ, the

report states: "Catholic Education proceeds from this explicit belief, which is made more concrete in the proclamation (kerygma) and in the doctrine (didache) of the Catholic Church". In the next sentence we read the honest avowal; "As a statement of principle this has an enviable clarity, but the situation becomes less clear when the attempt is made to discover how in practice this principle ensures a distinctive character to Catholic education."[33] The authors try to achieve it, by identifying four key elements, which are eventually woven into something like a definition, which is expressed thus:

> Catholic education should be characterised essentially by its communication of a perspective of human life centred in Jesus Christ; by its respect for the individuality and integrity of all; by its consequent concern with education for freedom, proceeding by way of illumination rather than indoctrination; and by its promotion of a sense of justice and of mission. A first concern of the Church's educational mission must be for the poor and disadvantaged. In a word its task is redemptive.[34]

This is the nearest we get to a definition of what is distinctive about the practical goals of Catholic education.

None of these attempts in the three documents which I have analysed have given a satisfactory definition of purpose, which is sufficiently specific to justify the retention of our school system. All of them presuppose that the pupil has made a definitive act of faith, they are theoretical and insufficiently practical, they could apply to christian schools of any Church, or to organisations which are not formally educational, and they neglect the importance of adult education. In 1972 the Vatican published the *General Catechetical Directory*, and in 1979 came the document *Catechesi Tradendi*, both of which stress the major role of adult catechesis.

In spite of its official character, *Signposts and Homecomings* has not settled the uncertainty about the goals of education, and this was recognised quite explicitly at the Conference on Catholic Schools at Nottingham in the summer of 1984.[35]

Having exposed at some length the ineffectuality of the Catholic schools, and the uncertainty about their working objectives, I now wish to pick up the pieces, and with the help of the decisions of Vatican II, sketch out at least a framework of a viable policy. For this we must start with the parents.

Assuming that the parents wish to hand on their religious convictions to their children, their first task is, in technical language, to announce the gospel to them. There is no exact blueprint for this operation, as it will vary considerably in each family. Birth into a christian family is the first grace for the child, and the explicit announcing of the gospel will begin with such simple operations as the first steps in prayer, answering the child's questions, and explaining the significance of festivals like Christmas.

As the child approaches the age of reason the element of personal freedom will begin to make itself felt. At this point it is profitable to turn to the Decree on Religious Freedom in Vatican II. It was drawn up for the political situation where governments suppressed christianity in the name of Marxism for instance, or where Protestants were harassed in the name of Catholicism. Nevertheless, the principles which were invoked derive from the necessary freedom of the act of faith, and can apply validly to the education of children as to the police surveillance of churches and synagogues.

The basic principle is enunciated near the middle of the Decree: "The act of faith is of its very nature a free act."[36] It gives rise to the right to religious freedom, which the Council declared should be enshrined in civil law (*Dignitas Humanae*, section 2). The Council also extended the scope of religious freedom to the family and the education of children, in these words:

> Since the family is a society in its own original right, it has the right freely to live its own domestic religious life under the guidance of parents. Parents, moreover, have the right, to determine in accordance with their own religious beliefs, the kind of religious education that their children are to receive. (*Dignitas Humanae*, section 5)

This implies that if a government agrees to provide specifically religious schools, as in Great Britain, it is on account of the parents' rights that they are organised, and not because the Church authorities have asked for them. The distinction is a fine one, but extremely important. The Council also indicated that the method of education must also be in accord with the basic freedom of the act of faith:

> Truth however is to be sought after in a manner proper to the dignity of the human person and his social nature. The enquiry is to be free, carried on with the aid of teaching, or instruction, communication, and dialogue. In the course of these, men explain to one another the truth they have discovered, or think they have discovered, in order thus to assist one another in the quest for truth. Moreover, as the truth is discovered, it is by a personal assent that men are to adhere to it. (*Dignitas Humanae*, section 3)

Bearing in mind the inherent differences between infant school and adult education, these principles have a direct bearing on the Catholic education programme.

Granted that the schools are already in existence, and cannot be wished away, there are three theoretical patterns upon which they could be organised: Presumption, Conscious Detachment, and Elected Silence. The first pattern presupposes that the child has made the definitive act of faith, and imparts theological information to give it satisfactory content. It is caricatured by the teacher's well meaning heartiness as he threatens the class with: "We do believe this, boys, don't we?" I am convinced that it was the unquestioned basis of most Catholic schools up to the Second World War, and perhaps up until the Council. It can easily lead to resentment in the pupils, and cannot easily be reconciled with the Council's teaching on the freedom of the act of faith.

The pattern of Conscious Detachment reacts against the former model and presents Catholic doctrine like any other subject, or like other faiths in a study of world religions. "This is what Muslims believe"; "This is what Hindus believe"; "This is what Catholics believe". The process is perfectly detached, and no element of personal commitment intrudes upon the presentation of the facts. The process is akin to literary criticism in that the acknowledgement of goodness or beauty is not arbitrary, but nor is it empirically determinable. The disadvantage is that it raises theological problems which are as serious as the Presumption model. Is a christian entitled to retail the message of the bible as a purely cultural exercise, without presenting it as an invitation to belief? It is arguable that silence, at least through the years of childhood, would be preferable to displaying christianity on a "take it or leave it" basis.

This leads naturally to the option of Elected Silence. It presupposes that teachers cannot totally conceal their inner convictions from the pupils, even if they wanted to! If they hold strongly to a philosophy of life, or a religion it will become apparent in countless ways. Every subject, including mathematics, can serve as its vehicle, but more particularly it will be disclosed in the process of discipline, and the overall way in which the teacher deals with his pupils as people. One could conceive of a school in which all the teachers were committed Catholics, where the objectives of the school were inspired by the gospel, as was the discipline, but in which there was neither religious instruction nor worship. It could have a powerful effect upon the pupils by a sort of osmosis, and would serve as an admirable support to the values of the home. Can one reasonably ask more of a Catholic school? Yet to many people it might appear costly, or even extravagant if so much religious commitment had to work in silent witness instead of articulate evangelisation.

Having cleared the ground sufficiently, I would now like to offer a definition of Catholic education, which avoids the criticisms expressed in the preceding pages. It is the definition which has been elaborated by the Conference of Catholic chaplains to Universities and Polytechnics. After years of reflection and discussion, it was refined to a precise form of words, which was approved by a massive majority at the conference in July 1983. The formula is:

> The aim of Catholic education is the establishment of a relationship of trust with the institutional Church, in the context of which the individual will re-affirm, or make for the first time, a personal commitment to Christ.

This formula has many advantages. It implies that the act of faith is a personal commitment to Christ, and not primarily a grasp of doctrinal propositions. It does not pre-suppose that this commitment was made in infancy, or during school years, yet it holds the individual in a realistic relationship with the community while that decision is in the making. It does not state, or imply, that the theological information should take place in childhood rather than in adult years. It is concerned with personal relationships, to the believing community, and to Christ. In regard to the community it is distinctively Catholic. Its flexibility is such that it could apply to a school, a parish catechetical programme, or a students' chaplaincy. It could also be verified perfectly in a school which offered neither worship nor instruction, but which aimed at the transmission of Catholic ideals by the silent witness of the teachers' deeply held convictions impinging upon the pupils' personalities.

In addition to the general criticisms of Catholic education which I have outlined in the preceding pages, there are some special problems which arise out of the deliberate planning of one section of the schools, others that arise out of the lack of planning, and others which are the consequence of our society. I will begin with the unplanned phenomenon. Up to the time of the Second World War the establishment of fee-paying convent schools seems to have been undertaken without any systematic planning at all. Their distribution appears to have been motivated by the impression that no parish was complete without one. There seems to have been no rational investigation of population trends, and the matching of school places to the needs of the locality. The result of all this is that many convent schools have as many as 50 per cent of non-Catholics among their pupils. The motive for sending the girls there is not usually stated explicitly, but it can be discerned as the middle class status which is apparent in behaviour and speech patterns. Clearly there is no theology behind it, but it may be harmful in a nation which is so badly split on social planes as is ours.

There is another category of schools which cannot be viewed so leniently from the standpoint of social divisiveness. In the 1920s and 1930s a number of the older Catholic boarding schools made the deliberate decision to model themselves on the non-Catholic public schools, in order to secure for their pupils the educational advantages which the public school system offered. Stated thus it sounded relatively innocuous, and they have been extremely successful in achieving their objectives. However, after fifty years it has become clear that several of the built-in goals and aspirations are seriously at variance with the ideals of the gospel. I have in mind the latent snobbery which is completely different from academic achievement, and also the practice of purchasing privilege. The matter is so delicate that it is rarely spoken of in public, yet everyone knows what is at stake. The privileges to be bought are so valuable that the parents will pay astronomical sums to gain them for their children. If the school comprises Catholicism as well, it seems like yet another benefit in the package, yielding the perfect marriage of worldly ambition and spiritual profit. The points of divergence from the New Testament's ideals are not immediately apparent, because these schools are well provided with chapels, priests, and good works. They give rise to a whole set of values and assumptions which are scarcely ever set out in writing. They go behind the acquisition of privilege, and the likelihood of advantageous social contacts and career prospects. They engender in their pupils, in an insidious manner, the belief that they are superior human beings, and with that goes a corresponding form of self satisfaction. Apart from its being so far from the brotherly simplicity of the gospel, it does great harm to our nation. Social classification is damaging in any case, and in England many conflicts like industrial strikes are aggravated by the unspoken assumptions of superiority and resentment in the contending parties. It should be one of the clearest missionary tasks of the Catholic Church in Britain to work for reconciliation within the body politic. Instead of that, our most expensive schools are propagating the kind of social divisions which fortify these harmful class structures.

There are even wider questions which must be faced by the organisers of the Catholic school system. Great Britain today is a thoroughly pluralistic society, in which all Churches and faiths are to be found, and all of them as minorities. Most of the nation has no committed religious position. Political diversity is wide-ranging and free speech ensures that all ideologies are canvassed vociferously. If such is our society for the adult, one may well ask if a denominationally exclusive school is the best preparation for life? There are good reasons for thinking that an infant will benefit from a school which reflects the values and beliefs of the home. But at university level no denominational institution exists, and the chaplaincies cater very well for students immersed in this irreligious environment. This means that at some point the animal has changed its colour, if I may express it thus. What provision is to be made for the pupils at the transitional stage of that metaphor, the children in senior schools? Before one envisages a detailed solution, it is valuable to reflect upon a consideration put forward some years ago by the Grail organisation. They declared that a child should meet atheism, religious indifference, or immorality, for the first time when he is young enough to turn to his parents for guidance. This is a realistic assessment which does justice to parental responsibilities, and to the cultural pluralism of our society, but it also throws doubts upon the value of Catholic schools which take their pupils up to the age of 18.

Having spoken at length of the shortcomings of the Catholic schools' system, there is one other area of activity which might redeem it, because so much effort has been devoted to it in the last dozen years or so. Is it possible that the massive injection of good post-conciliar theology into the text books and syllabuses could save the situation?

Apart from the Decree on The Church, it is the document about Revelation (*Dei Verbum*) which has been of particular value in catechetical programmes. After a complicated history, a long dispute was resolved, and the Council enunciated in general terms that the Bible is the record of revelation. Revelation for its part is the process by which God discloses to mankind his nature, his attitude, and his plans for us. He does this through events like the deliverance of the Israelites from Egypt, and sometimes through the messages of the prophets. The supreme event in this process is of course the Incarnation, and all that goes with it, namely the death and resurrection of Jesus, not forgetting too his teaching as recorded in the gospels. To many people this may all seem so obvious as not to require any explicit statement. Yet in view of pre-Conciliar teaching methods and text-books, it was most important that the Council made clear that faith is not primarily the intellectual assent to a set of statements about God. It is firstly a response to the person of Christ:

Through this revelation therefore the invisible God out of the abundance of his love speaks to men as friends and lives among them, so that he may invite and take them into fellowship with Himself. (*Dei Verbum*, section 2)

One of the first milestones in theological writing after that Decree was Gabriel Moran's *Theology of Revelation*, published in 1965. He develops the basic notion that revelation came in events and in the person of Christ, eliciting a personal commitment to that same Christ. Since then there has been a praiseworthy effort in all nations to write a whole range of books by which religion, and specifically Catholicism, can be presented to children. I do not wish to belittle their efforts, but one must ask the searching question: can the problem be solved by good books?

My answer is simply, No. Back in the 1940s when the old notorious penny catechism was much in evidence, many of us were well taught by teachers of integrity who succeeded in spite of the books. In more recent years teachers of equal integrity have failed with pupils who are basically no worse than the previous generation, and in spite of much better books and visual aids. It is the system itself which is at fault, and cannot be remedied more than marginally by improving the text books. In the changed climate of the modern, post-Conciliar world, the classroom with its captive audience is the inescapable problem.

For the sake of completeness, I would like to end this chapter by describing one area which is unquestionably successful, and whose methods and presuppositions could possibly be used in other spheres of education. I refer to the chaplaincies which now exist in all the universities and many of the polytechnics in Great Britain. Each one has developed in response to the nature of the university which it serves. Some are based on a small house, others on student hostels. All have some kind of chapel, and the dwelling of the chaplains is normally an open house to all. The chaplain is the animator, not the dictator, and he can encourage the development of a whole range of small communities based on colleges, departments, or halls of residence. In these units the students themselves assume the lead, and take on the real responsibility for running the groups. In the most general terms one can say that the object of the exercise is to create communities in which the students can integrate their religious convictions with their secular education and emotional development.[37]

I am writing about students, but I am well aware that they are a minority in the age group of 18 to 21. The way in which they are gathered together enables an observer to comment on their attitudes with greater clarity than he could achieve in talking about their contemporaries who are dispersed throughout the fully adult world, working, yet continuing to live at home. Compared with them, the students' time at university is almost like a passage through a controlled sociological experiment. Youth has been siphoned off from the mainstream of life, and the pattern of this youth culture can be examined without too much interference from such disturbing elements as unemployment or the exigencies of child-rearing. What I say about students and their religion applies also to their contemporaries who have started work, but the processes are not so self-conscious, nor so pressurised.

There is no doubt that theirs is to some extent an artificial world, and it is a transient phase in their lives. But so was childhood transient (and not less important for that). This section of their life's journey is the first in which all the decisions are made on their own responsibility. They are free from financial worry because the grants are adequate. They have to work harder than at any other time in their lives, and their intellectual and emotional development is literally precocious. They do not yet have the responsibilities for other people such as will come to them when they start work or get married. But for all that, the quest for lodgings, doing the shopping, cooking, keeping up with their studies, and socialising, constitute the elements of an extremely healthy process of maturing. (I only wish that the seminarians could experience something equally positive, instead of living every day in large institutions where their meals are cooked by someone else, and their laundry is taken care of too.)

It is an atmosphere of an environment in which they can suspend judgement on many issues, and experiment until they find ways of life, thought and culture which they find satisfying. Religion comes in for the same sort of treatment at their hands.

The university itself is impartial. The lecturers take care

not to influence their students by their own attitudes to philosophy, religion, politics or morals, though in the long run these inner convictions cannot be totally concealed. One lecturer in economics was at great pains to conceal his political persuasions from the students, and there was a big row at one of the medical schools because a lecturer had made a disparaging remark about religion in front of the student audience. Whatever may have been true in the past, science does not breed atheism. I cannot speak for other Churches, but Catholics are present at all levels of the teaching side in numbers which are at least up to our national average, if not higher.

The student body into which they move is tolerant towards religion, as it is tolerant towards much else. Nonconformity in dress is the symptom of acceptance of everything. If people wish to spend their free time playing rugger or bridge, the Students' Union will facilitate it, and even pay vast sums for gliders and other apparatus. Ballroom dancing, wine-tasting, pot-holing and yoga receive the benign blessing of the student body, which tolerates practically anything within its ranks. Occasionally the gay parties are smashed up by the hearties when they are drunk, but this is rare and it is frowned upon. Should I say that religion benefits from this attitude of tolerance? No obstacle is placed in its way, but I fear that apathy is the source of it, and nothing more positive. At the ideological level the student world is remarkably bored. They do not look to the political parties to effect social changes which they judge to be the effects of international economic forces over which Parliament (and still less the Student Union) has little control.

What precise effect does all this have on the religious attitudes of the students, and on the Catholics in particular? No satisfactory research has been published on this subject, and although the chaplains' conference initiated a move to evaluate the whole process of Catholic religious formation, nothing has yet come of it. I must make it quite clear to the reader that my observations are the result of personal impressions formed in the universities of London, Cambridge and Fribourg at which I studied myself (spread out over various periods of my life up to my late 30s), and seven years as university chaplain in London. These impressions will have all the limitations of one individual's experiences, but, as London is by far the largest university in the nation, it provides a fair sample to the study. I will attempt to describe the representative tendencies, and if they appear to be universally held among the student body, I will say so.

Let us start with Sunday mass. Students will attend it if the liturgy is the expression of the life of a Christian community. And what more could we ask for? This is the classical expression of what church-going should be, and the students will go for no other reason. To attend mass out of a sense of obedience to the Church's rule is almost meaningless in their attitude to life. In this they differ notably from previous generations of English Catholics in whom such patterns of regular observance were once reasonably characteristic.

During the course of their student years, which for most of them is a three-year period, the majority will have rethought their religious position to a greater or lesser degree of explicit articulation. A few will even go through the whole corpus of belief with a chaplain, not unlike the process of instruction for a convert. Some students are remarkably (almost surprisingly) conservative in their attitudes. I have known individuals who disassociate themselves from university chaplaincies, finding them too trendy and seek out mass in conservative parishes, perhaps even with a Latin liturgy. It is impossible to generalise, but this may be motivated by the subconscious desire to evade the demands made by a more challenging liturgy and community which call for involvement.

By contrast there are those who have accepted fully the pattern of Church life which Vatican II has established. In fact many of them can scarcely remember the Latin mass, and they have grown up in a Church which has been enriched by creative tensions. This means that none of them can escape the fact of free speech in the Church, and criticism. At first they may feel that they are being disloyal to the Church (and to God) if they criticise any part of the Catholic package deal. Later on, if things develop normally, they will acquire the poise to be able to disregard what is unhelpful, and remain firm in their attachment to the essentials.

This I regard as truly mature faith, and it is very encouraging to see them moving steadily towards it. It would be a symptom of gross immaturity if they were to abandon Catholicism on account of something accidental like antipathy towards the religious order which conducted their secondary education. At the other end of the scale it is edifying to perceive the personal commitment to Christ which they develop in the context of the Catholic community, while deliberately excluding from their lives items which they find simply irrelevant, like mass stipends, for example.

Their attitude towards the institutional Church is problematical. Personal relationships are immensely important in their lives, and as a result they can appreciate the value of an authentic community. The bureaucracy of the Church makes virtually no impression upon them. Their attitude here is consistent, and it is reflected in other Christian Churches too. Nationwide bodies like the Student Christian Movement are shadows of their former selves, and, in our own camp, organisations like the Young Christian Students make very little impression on the lives and outlook of the majority of students, compared with the local eucharistic community of their own chaplaincy. It is not easy for them to have a vivid experience of the institutional Church, but does it matter? Fortunately the world of the university enables them to experience something a little different, but vastly more important, namely the universality of the Church.

It is not unusual to have more than a dozen nationalities present at a normal Sunday mass, and what is more to the point, the foreigners fit in easily. Once again the direct simplicity of the students seems to have grasped the core with surety. The universality of the Church is important; institutionalism is not. Unfortunately most of them do not look to the Church at large as an instrument for social change in the world, for the betterment of the human race, but whose fault is that?

I think it is their lack of interest in institutions which confuses their outlook towards ecumenism. They are for the most part Christians first, and members of a denomination secondarily. The customary reasons advanced against intercommunion cut little ice with some of them; it looks like bureaucratic tidiness, and to them it seems more authentic to receive the eucharist if you share the worship of a community. Their understanding of the eucharist is such that

receiving communion is the normal expression of participat-
ing in the mass. To attend the liturgy without communion is
very rare. On the other hand confession occupies only a small
place in their piety. They understand the meaning of
reconciliation, and realise that it is comparatively rare in the
life of the average believer whose vices are not dramatic.
When they do seek this sacrament it is almost invariably in
the face to face pattern. Their dislike of the wire grille is
consistent with their impatience with anything which suggests artificiality. Authenticity is the watchword, and the
direct simplicity of the way in which they make their
confessions is altogether edifying.

Authenticity is also the character of their prayer. I can only
speak for minority groups, because the prayer pattern of the
total student body is too vast for simple categorisation.
Charismatic prayer groups have given help to a number of
students, but there are others who say frankly that it does not
appeal to them, and they prefer to pray, in groups, in a form
of silent yet relatively unstructured prayer. Older patterns of
devotions like the stations of the cross, or the rosary, have
almost vanished as far as I can see. I make no value
judgement about it, I merely note the fact.

However, I cannot help thinking that their popularity in
the past had some connection with the fact that the mass was
in Latin and active participation was absent in practice. The
enormous development of liturgical piety in the last decade
has brought about the atrophy of some erstwhile practices of
corporate prayer. Piety which had nothing but the mass
would be one-sided, and the most satisfactory line of future
development would seem to be the divine office. A small
number of students do make use of this kind of prayer. One
young man who planned to enter a seminary after his finals
used to have a breviary which he left around more
prominently than the rest of the students thought fitting, so
they placed between its pages a press photo of a lady cut out
from page three of a well known daily.

Whence come these attitudes? And what are the influences
which have shaped the students' religious stance? If we can
identify them will they help us to understand the young
person's convictions or lack of them? Undoubtedly they will:
we cannot hope to respond sensitively to their religious needs

unless we attempt to evaluate the causes of their present position.

In my experience the parental influence is so important that any other contributory factors to their religious formation are secondary at the best, if not peripheral. The value of a school is problematical. All I can say is that some of the people who have been most fully committed to the Catholic cause at university were never at Catholic schools. Although it seems that a totally Catholic home is desirable, one truly committed parent can usually engender full commitment in the child.

Although the schools vary greatly in their good or bad influence, one fact in my experience is so clear that I must draw attention to it, although it is not edifying. I will not name them, but it is not difficult to draw up a list of the ten best known public schools and other Catholic boarding schools for boys in England. In the last four years, at the University of London, only two young men from that group of schools have come forward to play an active part in the work of the Church. Since there are several religious orders involved, and since the characters of the schools are different, it seems clear that it is the fact of being a boarding school which is the harmful common factor. I have come to the conclusion that by the age of 18 a Catholic boarding school has had the effect of switching them off religiously.

I have heard it argued that later on they return to the faith of their childhood. I hope this is true, but since no one has done any research on the matter I remain sceptical, but open-minded. Even if the supposition of the return were true, we would have to admit that there was something strangely amiss with a system whose finished products so frequently contracted out of religion as soon as they had left the schools which had been established precisely to promote it. At other universities it may be different, but I would feel uneasy if the boys from public schools felt at home only in the Oxbridge manifestations of Catholicism, for example.

The ex-pupils of day schools fare considerably better, but all of them have suffered from the loss of nerve which overtook the teaching of Religious Education in Catholic schools immediately after the Council. It has left them unsure of the content of their belief. The pedagogical collapse was

bound to have occurred sooner or later because so little had
been done to improve the teaching methods of RI and the
syllabus for about a century. By contrast, in every other
department of school work serious attention was given to
presenting the humanities in such a way which could be
assimilated efficiently, and so as to retain the pupils' interest.
By comparison religion has been at a disadvantage, being
transmitted sometimes by mechanical answers to catechism
questions, or retailed from the pulpit in a dogmatising
authoritarian manner. These two extreme forms of the
"authority" approach contrast sharply with the climate of
education in which children are now trained from primary
school upwards, namely the encouragement to examine the
world enquiringly. At university they are urged to be actively
critical, and their religion must be able to stand up to the same
standard of scrutiny.

The principal casualty in this dichotomy of attitudes is the
vexed question of sexual morality. If one desires to discourage
premarital sex, it is quite useless to say that the Pope says it is
wrong. Recent documents from the Roman Curia have not
helped here, because they do not speak in a way which the
students find convincing. I do not for one moment wish to
imply that the students are immoral. There are certain
authentic principles to which most of them adhere with
conviction. They consider that sex is the expression of serious
emotional commitment, and regard promiscuous "sleeping
around" as clearly wrong. They also have high standards of
self discipline, and when on holiday it is not uncommon for a
boy and girl to share the same room or tent and not have sex,
which some people might find hard to understand.

To return once more to the influences which have fashioned
the students' outlook, it seems that the parish is almost
nowhere to be seen. I find it difficult to recall any instance
where the home parish has been a strong influence on the
student's religion. The impression which I derive from my
students is that the parishes from which they come are simply
not communities; administrative units, yes, but institutions
which are too large and wrongly structured to serve as
communities in the authentic sense, and which could give to
the young people an adequate sense of belonging and
involvement.

How then do the chaplaincies react to this kind of religious outlook in their students? The first priority is to try to create real communities. Within their context we generate an attitude of acceptance. The student soon learns that he will not be subjected to a theological means-test. His individual doubts, uncertainties, or convictions will be respected, and in a non-judgemental atmosphere he or she can work out the hoped-for synthesis of religion, life and study, to the point of integrity. The liturgical reforms of Vatican II have been of the utmost value to us. In general (and I speak as an erstwhile parish priest) the university chaplaincies enjoy more flexibility in their apostolate than any other institution in the Church's mission. We can adapt our method of work to whatever the situation requires.

Within my experience, one example of religion which really works is the students' annual pilgrimage to Walsingham at Easter. This entails walking with a heavy pack and carrying the large cross 20 miles a day for a week. It is physically exhausting, but purposeful, emotionally involving, and spiritually deep. All the ingredients are authentic and the effect is quite striking. At the midnight liturgy of Holy Saturday I have seen the students spontaneously start dancing in church as an expression of sheer joy. There was nothing contrived about it, nor irreverent, but it made me realise that religious practice and exuberant happiness ought not to be strangers to one another.

Since authentic experience is one of the key notes of student awareness, we make sure that theological education, in whatever form it may come, will be geared up to illustrate the relevance of religion to everyday life.

There is one thing which the chaplaincies cannot give them, and that is experience of life. One of the most zealous of our collaborators was a post-graduate student who came back to university significantly after two years of Voluntary Service Overseas work in the West Indies. Similarly a newly-qualified teacher said to me: "The problem with RI is not just the giving of information to the believers about what they believe, but to try to engender faith in the non-believers in the classroom." Yes, precisely, but he could not have realised it until he was faced with the responsibility of being in charge of a class. In my study I have a photo of the arrest of the Jews in the Warsaw ghetto. It never fails to move me profoundly, but the students regard it with the same sense of sympathy which they extend to the victims of the Black Death. It is already history for them. Memory is short, and the future cannot be anticipated. The most that we can do is to dispose them so that they will react positively to the increasing responsibilities which they will meet in the adult world.

Vatican II created the climate for a thoroughgoing re-appraisal of the value of the Catholic schools system. So far the operation has been mostly destructive, particularly with regard to cathechisms, text books, and syllabuses for which theological and pedagogical examination had long been overdue. The schools as institutions have also been subjected to searching scrutiny, and here too the results have not been reassuring.

Unless a new policy which is convincing and decisive can be elaborated quickly, the whole system will be under threat. Already there are signs that the parents are no longer as convinced about their value as were previous generations. Added urgency accrues to this quest for effectiveness because, like the cuckoo in the nest, the school system has taken precedence over all other areas of education and apostolate in the allocation of resources. If the system cannot be made effective it will have inflicted a double deprivation on the Church.

CHAPTER SIX

The Nerve Centre

When we recite the Our Father we do not pray for the well-being of the Church, but that the Kingdom should come. As I showed in Chapter One, the proper mission of the Church is not simply its own numerical increase, but the establishment of the Kingdom, which in the simplest terms means that the will of God shall be operative among men, even if they are not inside any christian Church. In the last chapter I showed that the vertical transmission of christianity from one generation to the next is hampered by the schools; in this chapter I will examine how the horizontal dissemination of the Church's mission is inhibited by the structures which we have inherited. Here we have the most tragic example of old wineskins trying to contain new wine, particularly in regard to the deeper concept of mission which has been given to us by the Vatican Council.

Lest it should seem that I am being too hard on the familiar structures by accusing them of inhibiting the Church's mission, let me cite specific examples concerning the establishment of the Kingdom of God. When we consider the progress of humanity in the last couple of centuries there have been a number of positive advances which cannot be regarded as other than God's will for the betterment of mankind. The clearest example was the abolition of the slave trade, and I have no hesitation in categorising it as the will of God, and an instance of the Kingdom of God being realised. In a similar way we should welcome other advances such as the existence and legal recognition of effective Trades Unions, free education for all children, the emancipation of women, giving them university education and parliamentary rights, the right of conscientious objection against military service, and the National Health Service. This list is not exhaustive, but it does indicate, in our nation and elsewhere, achievements in which the dignity of the person is recognised and where his or her basic rights are safeguarded.

It is significant that all these advances were achieved without noticeable help from Catholicism, although in some cases other christian Churches were very active.

The same picture emerges from a brief glance at the notable evils of recent history which have not been ameliorated or curtailed by the Catholic Church. The list of humanity's problems is vast, and I will limit my observations simply to those which could reasonably have been remedied, at least to some extent, by the Catholic Church. In this short list, I would include the cruelty of warfare, notably in the two World Wars which have been fought out on European soil, the exploitative tendencies of colonialism, particularly apartheid, and anti-Semitism culminating in the persecution of the Jews by the Nazis. None of these evils was notably opposed or limited by the activities of the Catholic Church, although many of them were perpetrated in regions where Catholicism was represented at least by substantial minorities.

This ineffectuality of Catholicism is shown ironically in one area where doctrine and social pressure should have combined to strengthen it, namely matrimony. The survey on English Catholics by Dr Hornsby-Smith has showed that the rate of matrimonial breakdown among Catholics is the same as that of the rest of the nation.[1] This is perhaps the most telling of our failures. It is a purely domestic issue in which the Church should be completely in control. It does not require the co-operation of any outside agency, we are not trying to influence the conduct of an unwilling nation, but even so we have failed. It seems to suggest that the preaching in church as well as the teaching in our schools and the idealism in many families have resulted in a pattern of behaviour which for all practical purposes is indistinguishable from that of the rest of the nation.

In the face of this record of ineffectuality and failure it might perhaps be claimed that the Catholic Church cannot be blamed for failing to advance the Kingdom of God, because in England at least it is a small minority. There are several answers to this allegation, and the first is that minority groups, if they are well organised, are extremely influential. Moreover a minority which comprises at least 10 per cent of the nation cannot be dismissed as negligible. Furthermore it can be seen that in countries where the Catholic Church accounts for a quarter or half the population the ineffectuality is just as bad. In Germany in the 1930s the Catholics made no effective opposition to Hitler's anti-semitism. The heroism of a handful of protesters merely highlights the acquiescence of the majority. In the United States where Catholics make up a quarter of the population, and where they are by far the largest and best organised single Church, they have not been in the forefront of opposition to apartheid. Nor have they made any significant contribution in the field of other social evils like the absence of an adequate health service, or the deplorable gun trade and the violence which it generates. Even if a Church includes the majority of a nation in its ranks, it may well be ineffectual as a missionary instrument for the Kingdom, if its institutions are wrong. This was the sad record of the Anglican Church during the time of the early industrial revolution, when they did so little to ameliorate the hardship of the industrial workers, in contrast to the Methodists and other Non-conformists. Later in this chapter I will examine in detail the causes of this ineffectuality of Catholicism, but for the moment I will note one detail, namely the damage done when the clergy become a privileged class. For centuries the Established Church had preached to the poor the duties of obedience, but something new came in with the early years of the industrial revolution. When confronted with the massive abuses of child labour, Lord Shaftesbury declared that, with the exception of one parson whom he admired: "The Anglican clergy as a body will do nothing."[2] Cobbett made a similar accusation of the Methodist clergy, when he perceived that they were deserting the pattern of the primitive days and aspiring to social status similar to that of the Anglican clergy. The professional ministry, as opposed to the local preachers were described by him as being "the bitterest foes of freedom in England".[3] Lest I seem biased against the clergy of other Churches I feel bound to add that the same psychology can be seen undermining the social conscience of the Catholic clergy too. The gigantic presbyteries which were built in the poorest parts of Liverpool in the middle of the nineteenth century can only be explained by the desire to live as a privileged class by clergy who had lost touch with the sufferings of the poor.

In addition to the Church's failure to promote mankind's well-being and ameliorate its sufferings, there is some evidence to suggest that the picture is even worse. There seem to have been forces at work in the Catholicism of England and Ireland which has actually fostered badness. For many years the prison chaplains in Great Britain have remarked that the proportion of Catholics in prison is far above our percentage in the population as a whole. The disproportion is so great that it presents a recognisable problem regardless of the uncertainty about the exact number of Catholics in the population. This, and allied problems formed the subject of a conference in London in 1981, whose findings I summarise here.[4] The impression current among field workers is that Catholics, forming about 10 to 12 per cent of the United Kingdom population, account for about a quarter of prison inmates, and an even higher proportion of drug addicts and alcoholics, though for the latter categories accurate statistics are hard to come by. The simple explanation of this is that crime is often an index of social marginality, and the detainees in prison are those who are too poor to pay fines. It is then alleged that the Catholics in prison are drawn from the poorest immigrants, mostly Irish, who have here no roots, nor homes, nor employment. There is undoubtedly an element of truth in this, but it is not the whole explanation. Whatever may be the failings of the individuals who find themselves in prison, it must also be admitted that the Church has failed them. Irish immigration is not a new phenomenon. They have been arriving in large numbers since the first part of the nineteenth century. Our failure to devise a system of absorbing them into caring communities is a reproach against the Church as a whole. It should also be remembered that the Poles are not found in large numbers in prison, and they arrived here at the end of the Second World War not only poor, but with language difficulties as well. Two further observations about the Irish in Britain should be noted, research about battered wives has shown Irish women to be more at risk than many others, and many young Irish people here tend to be not just lapsed but positively anti-Catholic.[5] The conference, which studied this problem, suggested a number of causes in addition to the poverty of immigrants. It seems that in Catholic education in England and Ireland the concept of "saving my soul" has taken precedence over "loving my neighbour". Moreover the negative attitude to sex has led to an inability in the men to form enduring relationships with women. So the man is thrown back on casual contacts with fellow males, often in pubs, where the habit of hard drinking is easily formed. Similarly Catholic education has contributed to this state of affairs by its pre-occupation with avoiding sin as distinct from attaining love and the motivations which it offers.[6] Clearly it would be unwise to place too much reliance on the findings of one conference, but the danger signals are sufficiently clear to warrant serious research into this terrible possibility that the presentation of Catholicism has actually damaged people as human beings.

The record of the immediate past is extremely depressing. Quite simply the Catholic Church has not benefited the human race as one wuld have expected. Into this gloomy picture the Vatican Council presented its vision of renewal and reform, in such a way as to give rise to reasonable expectations that the Church could adapt its mission in such a way as to tackle mankind's major problems. This optimism is reflected in so many passages of the Conciliar documents that it would be impossible to cite all of them. It is unnecessary because anyone who has read them in their entirety will have glimpsed this vision of hope. By way of examples I will quote a couple of sections from the Decree on the Laity since they express succinctly the Church's awareness of its missionary task and its confidence in being able to achieve it.

> Christ's redemptive work, while of itself directed towards the salvation of men, involves also the renewal of the whole temporal order. Hence the mission of the Church is not only to bring men the message and grace of Christ, but also to penetrate and perfect the temporal sphere with the spirit of the gospel.

Further on the same document states in somewhat more practical terms:

> The laity should accustom themselves to working in the parish

in close union with their priests, bringing to the Church community their own and the world's problems, as well as questions concerning human salvation, all of which should be examined and resolved by common deliberation.[7]

The ideals of the Church's mission could not have been expressed more clearly. These and other passages in the Conciliar documents gave rise to the well founded hope that the Church was determined to live out this vision of its vocation.

Clearly ideas of this kind cannot be immediately translated into practice. The appropriate structures must be devised, if they do not exist already. From the vision of the Church as presented in the Conciliar documents it is simple to see what kind of instrument is needed for the accomplishment of this mission. It is clear that the Church must be embodied everywhere as a real community (not just an administrative unit), and the characteristics of this community must be worship, charity, apostolate and witness. The first of these four needs little comment, it is the living expression of the personal relationship with God, and together with prayer it forms the highest activity of which mankind is capable. I have used the word "worship" in this context as distinct from "prayer", because the latter activity can be performed by an individual alone, whereas liturgical worship requires a group. Charity needs no justification. Every page of the New Testament proclaims it, and the plight of the Irish immigrants described above would never have occurred if we as a community were living as the precept of charity would require. The quality of apostolate applies to both aspects of the Church's mission, namely the recruitment of believing christians from among erstwhile non-believers, and the promoting of the Kingdom of God among men. Witness can be considered from many points of view starting with martyrdom. It represents the determination to live by, and proclaim the ideals of the gospel even when we cannot share them with others, and when hostile organisations prevent our attempts to penetrate them with the spirit of the gospel.

We must now ask ourselves how things stand twenty years after the Council. Have we animated the world with the ideals set out in the Conciliar documents? Are we living our

christian life in missionary communities such as I have
described in the preceding paragraph? In short have we begun
to bring about the Kingdom of God as a way which is notably
more effective than in the period leading up to the Council?

In the period after the Council the Church was in an
unusually advantageous position. Three powerful sets of
influences converged to provide the impetus for radical
renewal. The history of the immediate past showed how the
Church had failed in alleviating mankind's sufferings. It was
appreciated most clearly with respect to the holocaust.
Europe as a whole suffered from a guilt complex about the
treatment of the Jews, to such an extent that many nations
and other societies experienced something like a collective
purpose of amendment, in the desire to ensure that nothing
like it should happen again. Secondly the documents of the
Council enshrined a dynamic vision of the Church, which if
taken seriously could certainly transform it, and eventually
human society as a whole. It remained to be seen whether
they would be enshrined for too long, simply to become
entombed. The third set of influences comprised the collective
realisation that the period described as "You've never had it
so good" had come to an end, and that the problems revealed
by its demise were basically moral dilemmas. At the very
start of the 1980s the *Observer* devoted a perceptive article to
this realisation as a way of marking the commencement of
the new decade. It is sufficiently important to quote some
extracts from it, which are all the more valuable since they
were not written from an overtly religious viewpoint.

> The late 1950s and the 1960s with their tidal wave of change and
> euphoria—the coming of affluence and television, the Kennedy
> era, the youth and pop "revolutions", permissiveness in social
> mores and the arts, the rebuilding of our cities—were the last
> moments in time when it was possible for most people in our
> culture to look forward in hope to an as-yet unrealised future.
>
> If we examine the nature of that optimism, that wave of
> expectation which so markedly died away in the 1970s we may
> see that it was rooted in precisely those same sources of hope
> that have sustained the human race throughout the twentieth
> century.
>
> The twentieth century dream has had three central interwoven
> strands:

1) The belief that through science and technology, we should be able to unlock all the "secrets of the universe", we should be able to "master" nature, and thus create a materially secure and comfortable life for the majority of mankind.

2) The Utopian belief that, through drastic political and social re-organisation, aided by the greater use of State planning, we should be able to create an entirely new kind of just, fair, and equal society.

3) The belief that, through the dismantling of all the old repressive taboos, and conventions of the past—whether in social attitudes or the arts—individuals would be able to enjoy a much greater degree of freedom and self-realisation.

The importance of the Seventies was that, in each of these great avenues of human exploration, they had marked a "moment of truth" a point at which, more obviously and inescapably than ever before, the dream ran out.[8]

In spite of this auspicious convergence of influences, whereby everything was poised for the Church to make a major breakthrough in human affairs, the twenty year period since the Council had given us virtually nothing. The major moral and social problems of the nation have taken their natural course unchecked by any perceptible alleviation from the Catholic Church. The North of Ireland is perhaps the most striking instance. Violence there did not begin in the 1960s, but in 1968 a significant change came about. In that year the civil rights movement, which had tried to shift public opinion by non-violent means, was overtaken and pushed aside by a new escalation of violence, which has continued undiminished up to the present time. No christian Church has made any appreciable contribution to its diminution, nor have they presented even the beginnings of a peaceful solution. This conflict is all the more serious for christians, because the religious loyalties (or so it is claimed) are at the heart of the dispute. Another social problem with serious moral implications is that of unemployment. By 1985 the number of those out of work was well over the three million mark. The field of industrial strife was marked by the coal miners' strike which lasted from 1984 in to 1985. And finally the Cruise missiles arrived, thereby introducing a qualitative change in the arms race.

In the face of these problems Church leaders of all denominations expressed regret and sympathy, but in practical terms no christian body put forward any realistic plan to improve the situation. I hesitate to criticize Churches of which I am not a member, but for the Catholic Church I have no hesitation in saying that our record is no better than that of the forefathers facing the problems of the 1930s or earlier. It seems clear that our responsibility is all the more acute, because no other Church has had the benefit of a major reforming Council in the immediate past.

In the simplest terms I think it is fair to attribute our impotence to our failure to take the Council seriously. In practical terms this means our inability or unwillingness to devise satisfactory institutions through which to channel the reforming insights of the Council into the avenues of real life.

Throughout this chapter I have indicated that our mission will be ineffectual if we do not devise the appropriate structures. I have shown also that the inherited structures have proved to be inadequate. The time has now come to indicate precisely which structures are at fault. The realisation of where the trouble lies is best achieved by analysing a typical situation. Some years ago I knew a German Jewish family who had come to England in 1936. The incident which gave them the final impetus to leave was when their children, in the State schools, were obliged to sit in a special part of the classroom. This segregation was decreed in order that the Aryan children, who had not so far perceived the difference, should learn that the Jews were an inferior race. This situation prompted the emigration of my friends, but it should also have prompted some serious soul searching in the teaching profession. This is the kind of situation where a committed christian must refuse obedience to his superiors. It is an act of witness to the gospel, which must be made even if the teacher risks dismissal. Granted that it is a difficult decision, where would he turn to for guidance and moral support? Clearly it must be the parish, not the diocese or any other unit, because it is in the parish that the average Catholic meets his co-religionists on a normal regular basis. It is the group in which he could reasonably expect to find other people in the same dilemma, if it were working properly as a community.

The fact that the parish is the eucharistic group is another reason why we should search here for any failure in the mission to establish the Kingdom of God. I am not saying that the parish was instituted by Christ or the Apostles. It is the eucharistic gathering which can be traced back to our Saviour, and since this activity is absolutely central to christian life, the group which enacts the eucharist will inevitably be the basic unit of the Church's mission. Since the Middle Ages the parish as we know it has been the eucharistic community for the vast majority of the laity, and it is therefore the parish which bears the principal responsibility for the success or failure of the Church's mission.

What of the diocese? Could this be the level at which the apostolate could be most effectively pursued or frustrated? Clearly it bears some responsibility for the success or failure of the Church's mission (and I will discuss it at more length in Chapter Eight). For the moment I will merely note that it is just the wrong size. It is too large for any individual Catholic to feel a member of it in the sense of knowing the other members personally. A teacher in Hitler's Germany would not normally look to it as his basic support group. As far as national policy is concerned it is too small to negotiate with the government. This has been made clear in recent years with the publication of the American bishops' joint letter on the moral issues of warfare, and the provisional publication of their document on economic policy. Of all the ecclesiastical structures, it is the national episcopal conference which is most suited to deal directly with the government in an attempt to influence the nation's policy. The diocese has other responsibilities, one of which is the proper co-ordination of parishes, the clergy, and their training. I will deal with these matters in Chapter Eight. For the present it is clear that the basic unit of missionary zeal or neglect is the eucharistic community, which in the modern world means the parish.

In the two decades since the Vatican Council there have been a number of real achievements in the workings of some parishes for which we must be grateful. The establishment of parish councils has resulted in a real sharing of responsibility between priests and lay people. Ecumenism has seen many successful initiatives at parish level especially the sharing of churches in rural areas where the concentration of population does not warrant a separate Catholic church. But the most obvious benefit of the Council has been in the liturgy, and especially the lay participation which has been made possible by the introduction of English in place of Latin. Some English liturgies are uninspiring, but if the priest has a measure of imagination it can be reasonably satisfactory. A considerable amount of really good liturgical music has been composed and deserves to be better known. In this we are somewhat behind nations like France where liturgical experimentation was well advanced before the Council was opened. We still have not produced anything comparable to the Psalm settings of Père Gelineau. Communication has been facilitated by the English language and by moving the altars so that the celebrant at mass faces the people. However, an authentic community celebration involving real communication requires more than this. The architecture of most churches and the large numbers involved mean that it is extremely difficult to achieve an authentic community experience in the average parish church. That is why baptisms, marriages, and the liturgies of smaller gatherings more easily achieve this effect.

In fact the success or mediocrity of the liturgy depends to a large extent upon the personal qualities of the priest. This applies to other areas of parish life too. It is my conviction that in this post-Conciliar period, really outstanding priests can turn their parishes into reasonable communities if they bring to the exercise personal charisma and do not rely too much on the structure. Their success is achieved in spite of, and not because of, the parish structure. Every diocese has a number of such parishes, which the bishop can look on with pride, but they are vulnerable, because it is not the intrinsic dynamism of the parish which sustains the enterprise.

To illustrate this point I would like to quote verbatim a letter from a dissillusioned Glaswegian which I received after I had published these ideas in a magazine.[9] I will allow the letter to speak for itself, making no changes except where it is necessary to conceal the identity of the writer and the parish.

Let me tell you our experiences. Several years ago we had a priest in our parish who had the same ideas as in your article. We had eight high rise blocks of flats and many other types of houses. With an estimated Catholic population of 2000 about 800 were practising. We had a parish council with lay responsibility for many of the tasks which were to be accomplished. One leader was selected from each block of flats and he was responsible for communicating, encouraging, motivating them. We had house masses once a month in each of our homes and organised the liturgy to fit into such themes as Justice and Peace, Amnesty International, Abortion, Nuclear War. We tried to create a eucharistic community encouraging each other to open our homes and hearts to the gift of hospitality. We had sponsored walks, helping the outcast of our society, liturgy meetings once a month, prayer meetings once a week, social evenings once a month. The parish council met every two months, the deanery meeting was every three months. There were formation programmes for the young people, disco etc., and week-end trips; bible study groups once a month, passover meals, adult education weekends, retreats, etc. Not only our homes were open but the parish priest's own private house was open and every person was welcome and encouraged to come in and feel at home in an atmosphere of joy, love, and peace. There were many more activities which I have not mentioned, so theory with a lot of hard work were put into practice.

But then things started to go wrong.

Our parish priest moved to another parish. I can still see that fear which we had just before he left when we were discussing the coming of the new priest, and how we were committed to carrying on as usual, so that nothing would change. Alas change did come. Our new parish priest was promoted and his first assignment was to take over the community of ——. He came from a small country parish where he was a hospital chaplain for many years. He was totally bewildered so that even the sign of peace was completely new to him. He used to call us the pressure group. He used to carry Vatican II under his arm and try to educate himself in the ways of Renewal. But slowly and gradually this dear and holy man did change things conforming them to his ways of thinking in the way in which he had been taught.

Now five years on about 90 per cent of all the activities which I have mentioned have disappeared. There is very little going on, if any at all for the young teenagers. Apathy is rooted well into the community now.

The situation depicted in that letter could happen anywhere, because the benefits of Vatican II are achieved in spite of the parish system, and not because of its inner dynamism. As a result they are always vulnerable as long as the present pattern of organisation remains with us.

In one way I admire the efforts of these heroic priests who contrive to achieve so much, yet in another way I am inclined to look upon them as G. K. Chesterton described the slave owners of the past. He said that it was the benevolent slave owners who constituted the most serious obstacle to progress, precisely because they disguised the intrinsic faults of the system.

The Glasgow parish described above was ultimately unable to cope with Vatican II. Parishes of that kind are not able to cope with the pre-Conciliar holding operation either. To clarify that contention let me describe simply just what are the expectations put upon a parish, both as a missionary unit, and as performing a holding operation in the old-fashioned sense. A tragic instance from a parish in which I worked some years ago will illustrate what is at stake. An Englishman who had worked abroad married an Indonesian woman who was a Catholic and eventually returned home with her and five children. After a year he left her and lived with another woman. I leave it to the reader's imagination to envisage the plight of his wife caring for five children, thousands of miles from her own family, socially cut-off because she was not quite white, and still bewildered by the complexity of English life. The effect upon the children was so serious that a twelve-year-old girl attempted suicide by lying in the road in the path of oncoming traffic. The parish failed her completely. Her situation was so serious, that she would have needed at least one hour a day of supportive contact by someone who would listen sympathetically, advise her, and generally compensate for her isolation. The priest could not devote adequate time to her difficulties because he had far too many people to care for, and there were many other problems in his district which were just as serious as hers. Furthermore, one may well ask whether the priest was really the best person to help her. Other married women would have been her most obvious allies, but somehow the parish did not automatically link her to potential helpers.

Fundamentally it is the structure which is at fault. We should not blame the Glaswegian priest who walked round with Vatican II under his arm. He is more victim than villain. It is the parish itself which is institutionally incapable of responding to the challenge of Vatican II or caring for the casualties which society has been producing long before the Council emerged as a source of hope. The parish as we know it is an obsolete structure inherited from the Middle Ages. Neither the old Code of Canon Law, nor its modern counterpart, nor the Synods of Westminster have re-cast it to make of it a suitable community capable of carrying out all that is required of it. It originated in northern Europe in the early Middle Ages, and was a superficial christianising of the Teutonic pagan arrangement by which the landlord was obliged to supply a priest and shrine for his tenants. The priest became a christian and the shrine was renamed a church, but basically nothing else changed. The Third Lateran Council of 1179 secured for the bishop the right of nominating the priest.[10] The organisation took place after Europe had been converted to christianity, so that neither the parish nor its clergy ever acted as missionaries.[11] The bonds of community were assured by the social cohesion of the small villages and towns of medieval Europe. The parish did not create community theologically.

With the passage of time, nearly all the presuppositions of the medieval parish broke down, revealing the ecclesiastical unit as basically inadequate for its functions. In many nations the Reformation destroyed the confessional unity. Industrialisation and the mobility of population destroyed the natural cohesion of village life. Secularisation meant that church was no longer a normal focus of everyday life, and modern social services removed the caring activities from the sphere of church influence. Believing christians should not lament any of these evolutions. They are either the inevitable consequences of the modern world, or else laudable achievements like the National Health Service whose ethos is in perfect harmony with the gospel.

A few instances from modern parish life will indicate that the preceding paragraphs are not exaggerating the realities. For more than a century the Society of St Vincent de Paul has existed in many parishes, for the care of the poor. It is in all respects laudable, but its very existence indicates that works of charity were not regarded as normal for practising Catholics. Church law requires attendance at mass each Sunday, and this has come to be regarded as the mark of normal Catholicism. It would be more in keeping with the spirit of the New Testament to consider works of charity as the norm. The mere existence of the SVP betrays the fact that the parish's intrinsic dynamism does not group people in such a way that they will support one another naturally. The same is true of the Catholic Missionary Society. It is a group of priests which was created in the last century for the conversion of England to Catholicism. The presuppositions behind that organisation are extraordinary. It is absurd to think that it could be done by a dozen priests. And even so, what were the other five thousand priests doing? The decision to create the CMS was mistaken if the originators thought that a dozen priests could do the task, but they were perfectly correct in their appreciation that the parish clergy were not converting England. This was not through lack of zeal on their part, but that the structure of the parish prevented it.

The limitations of the parish are not confined to the previous century. On 31 December 1984 one church in Cambridge arranged a vigil service to mark the advent of the new year, and to pray for peace in 1985. About 40 people were present from a large town with several Catholic, Anglican, and Free-Church parishes. There was no rival activity (apart from New Year parties) which might have taken people elsewhere. The fewness of the congregation for that service indicates how little the average parish lends itself to serious issues like ecumenism and work for peace.

Another grave disadvantage of the parish system, to which the clergy fall victim, is the way in which the priests have been established as a privileged class. Basically it is because they do not earn their living like other men. They are not paid by results, nor does promotion depend upon efficiency. The system of remuneration from Church funds is so secure that they need never fear dismissal. The isolation from everyday life is reinforced by the nature and lifestyle of the presbytery, by clerical dress, and most of all by the law of celibacy (which will be discussed in Chapter Eight). The cushioning from the pressures of ordinary life has the effect of cutting off the priests from the laity because they do not really share the hardships and dangers of their parishioners. A priest in Belfast told me that in 1968 the start of the troubles meant that many Catholic families had to leave their homes in "mixed" areas and seek refuge in the Catholic districts of the city. Ordinary people opened their houses to the refugees, but this did not happen in the presbyteries.

All the shortcomings of the parish stem from the fact that it is too large and unwieldy to be a community. Whether or not a group becomes a community depends upon simple factors like size and structure. When I was chaplain to the University of London, I lived in a student house which accommodated about 80 students. Each year it had a completely new intake, and each year a community formed. The size enabled this to happen, whereas the larger inter-collegiate halls with two or three hundred residents remained anonymous non-communities. Most parishes manifest some measure of community around the priest, and this is due to his personal out-reach. A certain amount of research has been done in this matter by the Anglicans, but their parishes are sufficiently different from ours to make it somewhat artificial to extrapolate directly from their experience. Anyway, it is an area in which the personality of the parish priest is the most important variable. On average he may be able to maintain a working relationship of some kind with perhaps 40 or 60 people. This linkage will constitute the working group in most parishes, and the people in it will in practice undertake the activities like church flowers or parish bazaars. It is a mechanism which attracts to itself those who are naturally gregarious. It does not help those who are naturally shy or reticent on account of religious difficulties or personal tragedies. Once again my mind travels back to parishes in which I worked. I recall a family who first became known to me when their eldest child died of leukaemia at the age 12. Ten years later the husband and wife parted company, but the wife and her surviving children received no support from the parish. She was made to feel like an exile. This did not happen because of culpable neglect on anyone's part. It was simply that the structure did not automatically bring the sufferer into contact with other Catholics. What was lacking was horizontal contact. As I stated above, a priest may have personal links with perhaps 60 people. It can be called vertical contact, rather like the relationship between a doctor and his patients. It might perhaps be likened to the spokes of a wheel emanating from the hub. But what is required is horizontal contact between the laity themselves, or like the rim of a wheel, if one may mix the metaphors for the sake of emphasis. For a number of years the parish structure has been criticized severely, and there is a growing consensus that the Church needs smaller groups if its apostolate is to be effective. Arising out of this realisation, there has been a proliferation of small units within the existing parishes. Some of them date back to the pre-Conciliar period, like the Young Christian Workers or the Legion of Mary. In more recent years they have expressed themselves in a less specialised fashion, in prayer groups, family groups and study groups of various kinds. They differ from the older patterns in that they have both sexes in the same groups, and usually meet in private houses rather than presbyteries or church halls. They have achieved undeniable but limited success. Thanks to the Council they can celebrate mass in their meetings, and indeed in private houses. This has been an immense benefit. Nevertheless they have their limitations, mainly because the parish by a sad irony, inhibits them, without being able to offer a positive alternative.

It is not only in the religious sphere that one organisation can inhibit the development of another. Ordinary life provides striking examples. Private hospitals act as parasites on the National Health Service. By confining themselves to wealthy patients and simple operations, they evade the most difficult problems in the medical field and in the task of sustaining the health of the nation. Since doctors and most nurses are trained in National Health Service hospitals, the cost of this programme is borne by the NHS until they are qualified, and the private sector can then seduce them with higher wages. In various ways they hinder the progress of the NHS. Similarly the public schools damage the nation's educational system. Although it is not spelt out on any prospectus, the parents know that they are purchasing privilege. These schools can expel troublesome pupils and teachers without difficulty. They can restrict their entry to the cleverest children. Thus they can attract to themselves the more talented teachers, as well as the more exacting and wealthy parents. In such a position they could hardly fail to get good educational results; and they cannot fail to undermine the state schools whom they leave with the task of coping with all the real challenges of education and society.

In my experience the normal parish inhibits the small groups in ways similar to the counter-productive activities of private schools and hospitals.

This is how the matter stood nearly two decades after the Council and on the eve of the publication of the new Code of Canon Law.

Having seen the limitations of the parish in practice the time has now come to examine the New Code of Canon Law[12] to see if it holds out any promise for improvement in the future. As I mentioned in the Introduction, the arrival of the New Code in 1983 was one of the occasions when we might reasonably have hoped for a definite "lift-off" for the Conciliar insights to have borne fruit. In this particular instance it is profitable to compare the vision of the parish as presented in both the old and new codes of Church law.

The Code of 1918 embodies the canon law which dated back to the Middle Ages, the reforms of the Council of Trent, and for the parishes, the customary practice of the Catholic nations of Europe after the Reformation. It did not recast the legal system, and as far as parishes were concerned it was a work of systematisation, not of creative thinking. It reflects the outlook of Italy at the beginning of this century, which is not surprising since Cardinal Gasparri was its principal architect. The implied presupposition of its treatment of parishes is that the parish was a benefice in the medieval sense, whereby a source of income was attached to certain responsibilities. The appointment of the parish priest was entrusted to the bishop, who had a grave obligation to nominate the most suitable priest available (canon 4359). In England that was set aside, and promotion by seniority was the rule. The duties of the parish priest are set out in canon 467 where he is enjoined to celebrate the divine offices, administer the sacraments to the faithful, to correct the wayward, care for the poor, and similar tasks, not forgetting the instruction of children. Canon 462 lists those functions which are reserved to him. It is a strong concept, but emphasises the legal overtones of the whole system. They include such functions as taking the last sacraments to the dying and giving the solemn blessing of houses on Easter Saturday. In another part of the Code altogether there is an oblique reference to non-Catholics, stating that non-Catholics dwelling in the diocese or parish are commended to the care of the bishop or parish priest (canon 1350). Every item in this programme bears the mark of the unwritten assumption that the Code envisages a nation whose population is solidly Catholic. There is no harm in this except for the fact that this same legislation was the rule which has governed parishes in England, whose situation has been totally different. One canon is devoted to the curate. The bishop shall appoint one if there are too many people, or if the parish priest is too old and infirm to care for them alone (canon 476). It implies that the one priest benefice is the norm. In this whole section the laity are not mentioned except as the passive recipients of the priests' ministrations.

Since this programme is so far removed from the exigencies of the English scene, one had hoped that the new Code would be an improvement. As I will show below, this expectation has been sadly disappointed. This part of the legal system has not been recast in the light of the theology of Vatican II, it has simply been subjected to a superficial modernisation. Canons 1740 to 1752 of the New Code deal with the legal procedures for the dismissal or transfer of a parish priest who is unwilling to move. The details need not detain us here, but the procedure implies that the old concept of a benefice is still the underlying paradigm. This impression is confirmed by the fact that the bishop is enjoined to assign a priest to a parish for an indefinite time, so that he shall enjoy stability (canon 522). The actual selection of the candidate is envisaged more imaginatively than in the old Code. The bishop shall appoint the priest who is, all things considered, suitable, and he may even consult lay people if the situation would warrant it (canon 524). His duties are described somewhat more imaginatively than in the old Code. Basically he is carrying out the care of souls (*cura pastorali* – – – – *fungens*) (canon 519) expressed in the threefold formula of teaching, sanctifying and ruling. It is definitely paternalistic, and a holding operation. Nowhere do we read a phrase which might suggest that he is the animator of a missionary community. He is required to announce the word of God to the inhabitants of the parish (*in paroecia degentibus*), which is a strange way of describing a community. He must also care for the instruction of children and youths, and encourage Catholic organisations. He is required to make the eucharist the centre of the life of his parochial congregation, and must promote the liturgy (canon 528). The next canon urges him to care for the poor and needy, expressed in a slightly more modern tone than the old Code, since it mentions refugees and the lonely. The second part of that canon (529), mentions the laity, in cautious terms: "The parish priest shall recognise and promote the laity's own part in the mission of the Church, by encouraging the organisations for these religious purposes." It sounds just a little bit half-hearted. However the parish council receives special mention, albeit cautiously expressed. Canon 536 announces it in these words:

> If it should be opportune in the judgement of the diocesan bishop, having taken the advice of the council of priests, a pastoral council shall be established in each parish, which will be presided over by the parish priest, and in which the faithful, shall give their assistance to further the pastoral work, together with those who participate officially in the pastoral care.

(The latter phrase applies to curates, for instance.) Without wishing to be cynical, it sounds like a grudging concession forced out of an unwilling administrator, who would have been happier to have omitted the matter from his otherwise tidy scheme of law. But the restraints are spelt out in the second section of the same canon: such a council has only consultative authority. It cannot force the hand of the parish priest, and he is entitled to veto anything which they might agree upon.

In the new Code the curate receives more lengthy treatment, but acquires no greater status or responsibility than in the old law. Canon 545 envisages the circumstances of the appointment in these revealing words: "As often as the proper fulfilment of the pastoral care of the parish renders it necessary or opportune, one or more parochial vicars (i.e.

curates) may be assigned to the parish priest . . .". It is extraordinary that they are linked firstly with the parish priest and not with the community. The curate's duties are spelt out in the next three canons. Canon 548 speaks of his "obligations and *rights*", in fact though he has none, unless local law should provide what the Code does not. In this respect there is no advance on the old Code.

Any hopes that one might have entertained that the new Code of Canon Law would re-vitalise the life of the parishes in the spirit of the Council, have been totally deflated. The canons dealing with parishes and their clergy are merely a cosmetic operation on the old Code and not a re-casting of the law. The ecclesiology of Vatican II is so little in evidence that the Council might as well not have taken place. All the minor adjustments in the modernising of this part of the Code could have been effected without the Council. The legislation still implies the assumption that a parish is a benefice, and the laws concern primarily the benefice holder (i.e. the parish priest). It is not simply a question of clericalism. The curates have no rights. For instance a curate can be moved by a letter from the bishop, but the transfer of an unwilling parish priest requires a complicated legal process. A comparison with secular professions, and the working relationships between any chief executive and his colleagues indicates just how unbalanced is the situation of the Catholic clergy. The head of a school does not completely dominate the other teachers. The senior partner in a group of doctors or solicitors has more responsibility than his colleagues, but it is only a difference of degree. It is difficult to think of any other group of professionally qualified men in which the junior partner has so little responsibility, so little stability, and so few safeguards for his work or his person, as in the Catholic clergy. It is extremely bad for the morale of the junior priests, and unquestionably harmful for the Church's mission.

Since the Code assigns such an insignificant place to the assistant priests, it is not surprising that the laity too receive scant recognition. Basically they are not given proper responsibility in any area of the Church's mission. One could list any number of particular criticisms of their status, but the root of the trouble lies in the basic orientation of this part of the Code. The legislation does not indicate anywhere that the laity constitute what one might term the centre of gravity of the Church. Clearly the legislators have not realised that the clergy exist for the sake of the laity, and not *vice versa*. Granted that these presuppositions are absent, one is forced to admit that the parish, and the laity in particular, can hope for very little from the new Code of Canon Law.

Thus far we seem to have arrived at a total impasse. The traditional parish is too large and unwieldy to be a community, yet having acquired a life of its own it acts as a parasite effectively working against what the small groups might achieve. Not only does it inhibit their proper development, it has proved dangerously impervious to the spirit of the Vatican Council, and has sufficient life of its own to take up the energy of many good people especially in matters like fund raising to maintain the fabric of the buildings. Is there any way out of this deadlock? Fortunately yes, there is a relatively easy solution.

Quite simply we must move the Catholics' centre of gravity from the parish to a smaller group by shifting the eucharist to the said small group. As long as the parish church remains the meeting place for the weekly mass, it will always inhibit any other community, precisely because the eucharist is absolutely central to Catholicism. What I propose therefore is that people should be divided according to natural groupings, assembling about forty people in one street or apartment block. Within normal expectations one could anticipate that about twenty of them might come to mass regularly, and their Sunday eucharist should be in the home of one of the members. This simple mechanism would ensure that the small group is no longer marginal, but is the main focus of the religious life of the average Catholic. It is worth recalling that this system would be closer to the New Testament scheme than the present parish. At its origin the eucharist was instituted in the context of the Jewish passover which was a domestic religious meal celebrated at home, and not in the synagogue. The present parish church has taken its size and function not from New Testament inspiration, but by a complicated history from the temples of ancient Rome and pre-christian paganism in Europe.

Let us work out the consequences of people meeting

regularly in one another's houses for Sunday mass. Without any contrivance or artificiality they would get to know one another personally. The casualties could not be concealed. Invalids would simply be present, matrimonial failures could not remain hidden, and in that way they would become aware of the group's problems. It would be a small step from that realisation to offer help, without anything as artificial as creating the SVP to deal with it. In short, charity would result.

We must be frank and realise that there would be friction, and the members of these groups would get on each other's nerves. Far from being a disadvantage this would be a step towards spiritual maturity. In the present parishes people can float along at a polite distance from each other, and the social classes can keep apart effectively. The infant Church faced the same problem and brought about the dramatic reconciliation between Jews and Greeks. If the Catholic Church cannot effect reconciliation between different temperaments in a small group, then there is no hope of our achieving anything in the more serious areas of conflict like industrial disputes or the north of Ireland.

Such a group could also form the basis for introducing potential converts to the Church. It would be sufficiently informal for them to be present without embarrassment. For the non-churchgoer, the artificiality of church is quite devastating, and difficult for the regular worshipper to appreciate. If it were apparent that the small house groups were really concerned about issues of charity and justice then it is not unrealistic to hope that people would seek to join them. This would seem to be the most natural way for the Church to expand, rather than by propaganda operations or anything resembling an advertising campaign. In other walks of life people are attracted to organisations which obviously achieve their avowed objectives. Students try to enter good universities and colleges. Good regiments in the army attract recruits in a similar way. The spiritual pilgrimages of Ronald Knox and Cardinal Newman are not typical. Both those men, and others like them, were in search of what might be called a more satisfactory ecclesiastical pedigree. It is an ideal which will appeal to professional theologians more than to the average man in the street. It is not unreasonable to hope that a small eucharistic group whose members bore one another's burdens, and who showed themselves to be concerned for social justice, would develop a spiritual dynamism which would attract other people to join them.

If the group is small enough to prevent anonymity, and if the eucharist becomes the centre of its community, then a whole series of forces will be released which will enable it to achieve the functions described at the beginning of this chapter, namely worship, apostolate and charity. What is crucial is that it should be the normal place for Sunday mass, otherwise the believers will not take it seriously enough.

The danger of isolation must be faced. These small groups could fragment the Catholic population into cliques, in which the atmosphere could become precious or suffocating. This could be avoided by ensuring that they all attend larger eucharistic gatherings on a regular basis. They could assemble in the parish church once a month, or even once a fortnight. This would do them no harm, and much good, provided that it was clear that the small group was the basic unit for them and the centre of gravity of their religious life.

In case it might appear that I exaggerate the possibilities of these groups let us examine their remarkable success in other nations, particularly in Latin America where they have acquired the technical name, *communidades de base*, basic communities.

CHAPTER SEVEN

Basic Communities

Christians in many different countries have felt the need that their primary community should be a group of manageable size. I will give a couple of examples drawn from widely different societies to illustrate how well these communities work. The first concerns a group of four or five families meeting in a suburb of Cologne in 1982. The families formed the nucleus of the group, and they were joined by half a dozen students from the university. Most of the families were Vietnamese boat people, and they lived in run-down apartments in a poor area inhabited mostly by immigrant workers from Turkey. They met every Saturday evening in one of the flats, in the sitting room. The meeting was unhurried. They spent the first hour or so just chatting, then a priest said mass. There was nothing special about the mass except its simplicity. The priest used an upturned beer crate as a table, because there was very little furniture. Children wandered in and out. After mass the children moved into the kitchens in several nearby flats where the students helped them with their homework. The adults remained behind chatting, mostly about how to find work. Two questions arose during the time in which my correspondent was involved in the group. Firstly, should the children be given religious instruction rather than help with their homework? It was decided that they should not, because this was better done by their parents and could be arranged by them during the week. Secondly should other children be allowed to join the group whose parents did not come to mass. It was decided that they could, and as a result many Turkish children came, and as a consequence of this the Vietnamese became better integrated into the Turkish community who occupied most of the apartments. Much of the discussion between the adults was about how to get work. They also arranged baby-sitting for the following week, usually for the times when people were going out job-hunting.

The second example which was brought to my attention comes from the north east region of Zimbabwe. It is a large village consisting of several family kraals comprising about 80 people altogether. The community is animated by a totally uneducated man who is a full time (paid) catechist. He was never at school, but taught himself to read and write. He has a very strong personality and is a committed Catholic. He started his activity by reading the bible to the people, since most of them are illiterate, and too poor to purchase their own. He then encouraged them to apply its message to their own situation. A thriving community developed which started its own pre-school group, a farming co-operative and a co-operative for making school uniforms. They meet several times during the week in smaller groups where they discuss these various projects, pray, and read the bible together. A German missionary priest goes there once a month to say mass. The catechist recently organised a week-end retreat and about 250 people came for it. The priest was invited, but not asked to say mass, which was significant. In practically every sense he is an outsider, although he speaks their language tolerably well. The people now want to build a church, and have already collected several hundred, not dollars, but bricks.

The examples from Germany and Zimbabwe show how adaptable is the structure, but as is well known, it is in Latin America that the development of these groups has been most in evidence. It was there, in the 1950s that they acquired the semi-official name *communidad ecclesial de base*,[1] which in English speaking countries is translated as basic communities. It was the conjunction of unusual circumstances in Latin America which has favoured their rapid development. The population explosion has resulted in the mushrooming of enormous shanty towns outside every city. They are well beyond the boundaries of the old parishes, and in any case the shortage of priests is so acute that they could not cope with these new districts in the traditional manner. In short, the system of old-style parishes has broken down sufficiently so as not to inhibit the development of the small groups. This is in marked contrast with England where the old structures persist, with the appearance of coping, and with enough life to inhibit small authentic groups within them.

In addition to the numerical breakdown of the old parish arrangements, the poverty, violence, and other social injustices in Latin America are so acute that they have galvanised clergy and laity into action. The method which is seen to be useful in that situation is the basic community. Fortunately the Church is in the forefront of the struggle for social justice, and it is to the credit of the christians of Latin America that so many of them have suffered for this cause. Since 1968 over 900 religious, clergy, and bishops have been arrested, tortured, expelled, or murdered. It is not surprising that the Church experienced the need for a dynamic structure which would correspond to the realities of their mission. The basic communities have fulfilled this need, and the contrast between their life style and the flower festivals in the parishes of the English home counties is literally heart-breaking.

By 1980 approximately 50,000 such communities had been established in Brazil. In Honduras there are an estimated 4,000, and in Guatemala in the diocese of Huehletenango alone there are more than 700. They are also numerous in Chile and Peru.[2]

In the two large conferences of the Latin American bishops these basic communities received official sanction. At Medellin in 1968 the bishops' declaration stated:

> Thus the christian basic community is the first and fundamental ecclesiastical nucleus, which on its own level must make itself responsible for the richness and expansion of the faith, as well as of the cult which is its expression.[3]

A similar confirmation of this statement was made at the Puebla congress in 1979:

> In 1968 base level ecclesial communities were just coming into being. Over the past ten years they have multiplied and matured, particularly in some countries, so that now they are one of the causes for joy and hope to the Church. In communion with their bishops, and in line with Medellin's request, they have become centres of evangelisation and forces of liberation and development.[4]

Clearly the movement has come of age and the communities are beginning to bear fruit. In order to show how valuable the basic communities have become, and how great is the promise which they hold out for the future, I will describe briefly their development in other continents, and record also the decisions of a variety of bishops' conferences which have pronounced in favour of them.

In Africa the movement started a few years after it had become established in Latin America, and it was to some extent provoked by the success of the pentecostalist churches and independent sects. In 1975 at the meeting of the Symposium of Episcopal conferences of Africa and Madagascar, the bishops resolutely opted for implanting the Church not by adaptation, but by incarnation or localisation. They declared: "The Church becomes incarnated or authentically localised in the measure in which the living and running of Church life is actively and consciously assumed by local christians."[5] They indicated that small communities were ideal for this purpose.

It is in East Africa particularly that the movement is strongest, possibly because christianity has been established there for a comparatively long time in relation to other parts of the continent. In 1973, the Episcopal Conference of Eastern Africa held a study conference to deal with planning for the Church in East Africa in the 1980s. It became clear that the Church had to put serious effort into getting people into small communities:

> Church life must be based on the communities in which everyday life and work takes place: those basic and manageable social groupings whose members can experience real interpersonal relationships and feel a sense of communal belonging both in living and working. We believe that Christian communities at this level will be best suited to develop real intense vitality and to become effective witnesses in their natural environment.[6]

Again, when preparing for the 1974 Synod of Bishops several episcopal conferences stressed the significance of grass-roots communities: "We strongly recommend that present Church structures and attitudes be modified, for example, by establishing basic communities." The topic of grass-roots communities was selected for the study conference of the bishops of East Africa in 1976, which brought together at Nairobi the 80 bishops of Kenya, Malawi, Tanzania, Uganda and Zambia. This decision was taken after a survey in which 42 dioceses participated, from which it appeared that the creation of christian communities should be given absolute priority.

The theological presuppositions of this policy were developed in the opening address of Bishop Kalilombe of Lilongwe (in Malawi):

> Until now the force that keeps the Church going at these levels (dioceses, parishes and even outstations) does not come from inside the local communities themselves, but from outside. The Church is too dependent on priests (all too few) who come from outside the communities. As long as this state of affairs persists the Church in East Africa will remain an infant Church incapable of really standing on its own feet, unstable and at the mercy of changing historical circumstances. To remedy this state of affairs ecclesial life has to be based on small Christian communities. That is why the text quoted above from 1973 is so important. It marks a decisive landmark in our pastoral policy in East Africa. For bishops, the resolve to base Christian life and witness on small Christian communities is not just one way among many possible ones; it is not just following a passing fad in the Church today it is a basic commitment: a serious shift in pastoral emphasis.
>
> It is deliberately intended to modify deeply our pastoral systems, policy, and practice. Until now the avowed common system was to base the life of the Church on the parish level, rather than on the sub-parish level. The parish was taken for granted as the basic or nuclear expression of the local Church. Any sub-parish division was not really considered as an adequate realization of the Church, capable of being the centre or basis of a full ecclesial existence.

It will not have escaped the notice of readers in Great Britain that the Bishop of Lilongwe had identified the precise cause which has inhibited the development of small communities in our own country. Any grouping smaller than the parish has been treated as a subordinate in such a way as to inhibit its potential effectiveness.

The Bishop of Lilongwe continued his observations:

> In fact parishes are too big and not adjusted to the natural communities. In them, "the Church" is identified primarily with

the hierarchy and the clergy, the laity being generally considered the clients of such a Church. Moreover the main objective of this Church was to be a sort of service organization: to minister to the people as to individuals. It was too little involved in the tissue of the total life of a truly concrete community; it met only its sacral needs. But it is only in an actual community that the Church can fully become a bearer of salvation. The parish then becomes a network of veritable grass-roots communities, in which their vitality (thanks to flexible application of the principle of subsidiarity) and their links with one another receive their proper due.

It is not possible to determine the size of these communities in terms of precise numbers . . . but the community should be such as to group together a sufficient number of adherents and variety of ecclesial charisms to be able to provide the ordinary non-ordained ministries or services that can keep the local Church community alive and active in its normal day-to-day life.[7]

In different African countries the basic communities have demonstrated their flexibility by accommodating their dimensions to those of the towns or villages in which they live. In Tanzania for example the basic communities are formed from two to fifteen families which means in practice from 50 to 150 people. This enables them to coincide with the size of the community villages in the rural areas. In Zambia on the other hand, the problem was the lack of community spirit in the urban parishes. In 1973 the parish of Chilenje in the archdiocese of Lusaka divided its territory into 117 sectors, each one comprising 50 or 60 families. This gives some idea of the unwieldy size of the original parish. From Burundi there is an interesting report of the creation of a network of small communities in the parish of Mbogora in the archdiocese of Gitega.

From the beginning of the month of February 1974 we wanted to place our parish in "mission state", and this was certainly on account of the shortage of priests but above all because of the new vision of the Church of Burundi which has become ever more adult. With this aim in view we proposed new structures . . . Every large outstation will be considered as a parish, a viable basic community, and will be directed by a central 10-member committee: six men and four women. Why these ten members? Because this committee, assisted by the chief catechist will be asked to meet every Sunday morning and thus the presence of a sufficient number of members will be assured.[8]

In Zaire the factor of distance seems to have been their major problem. The parish of Birmbizo has 40,000 Catholics served by 45 chapels half of which are more than 40 kilometres from the main church. The experience of missionaries was that a visit to a chapel every four months and the short instruction given on that occasion produced meagre results. The missionaries, chapel leaders and catechists decided to regroup the parish into communities of 10 to 15 families. Each community had to meet and select a working committee consisting of one man, one woman, a young man and a young woman. By 1974 more than 400 such leaders had been inscribed for training sessions.

In the Congo the Bishops' conference in 1973 explicitly encouraged the establishment of small communities. They were organised at village level, or in the different neighbourhoods in the towns. Meetings were conducted by the lay leaders, the priest's role being that of ensuring contact with other communities and with the bishop.

In Cameroun Archbishop Zoa of Yaounde put forward a plan for a conference in 1974 in order to give priority to small local communities. One obstacle was the clerical mentality of many people concerning the ministry. Possibly with this in mind, they decided that the animators of these communities should not be called catechists. They foresaw that in the future they might celebrate the eucharist.

In Mozambique the need for smaller groups has been made more urgent on account of the disruption caused by the war of liberation and the subsequent guerilla fighting which still disturbs the whole country. A few years ago Bishop Pinto of Nampula declared:

> The era of missionaries from outside is over. The time has come for the inhabitants of Mozambique themselves to be the missionaries of Mozambique. Traditional seminaries are going through a crisis, and it would certainly seem that not enough priests can come from them to satisfy the needs of the communities. Is it not high time to think seriously of ordaining married christians, proposed by the communities and acceptable to them.[9]

The development of basic communities in Asia varies considerably according to the proportion of Catholics in the overall population. For instance in India there are comparatively few groups, since the Catholics are a very small proportion of the population, and their missions and parishes have the cohesion and community sense which comes from being numerically small, and moreover being a minority group. However in the Philippines the situation is different, since the majority of the population are (nominally at least) members of the Catholic Church. In 1974 the synod of the bishops of the Philippines made this statement:

> For the effective evangelisation and participation of our people, the formation of small basic communities (in our barrios) and other natural groupings, in co-ordination with the wider communities of the parish and diocese, is indispensible.[10]

In Malaysia in the month of August 1976 the bishops withdrew priests from parish work for time to reflect. Parishes were left to the care of lay readers. At the end of the time of reflection they published a joint letter stating:

> All 126 of us have agreed on the following conclusion: the most important and most central need of Catholics in the peninsula of Malaysia is the formation of basic christian communities, drawing their inspiration from the first christian communities of the Acts of the Apostles.[11]

In Europe and North America there are a variety of movements which group their members into small communities. They do not have quite the same role in the Church as do the basic communities of Africa, Asia, and Latin America. The reasons are complex. First of all the shortage of clergy is not so acute as in the Third World. On the whole there are enough priests to keep the old structures functioning with the appearance of normality. Most people live within reasonable travelling distance of a church. Many people have cars. Furthermore the movements of Catholic action have a relationship with the political scene which is different from that of the basic communities in the Third World. So for a variety of reasons the movement has not developed as swiftly in the "old" world (including North

America, which has reproduced perfectly the institutions of European Catholicism). Nevertheless as I indicated in the previous chapter, small groups like the basic communities are just what we need in Great Britain, and in other parts of Europe.

Having sketched out the widespread development of these communities, the time has come to look closer at the sociological and theological factors entailed in their pattern of life. By the mid-1970s it had become apparent that the prophetic aspirations of the French pioneers such as H. Godin[12] and G. Michonneau[13] have not been realised. Even with the advent of Vatican II it has so far proved impossible to re-vitalise the traditional parishes and make them into authentic communities. The traditional structure of the parish, and the growing anonymity of urban life defeated those endeavours. But it means that in Europe as well as in the Third World, people were in search of authentic community experience. To this extent the quest for grass-root communities is not exclusively an event confined to the Church. It is a phenomenon belonging to the realm of general anthropology and is an expression of the quest for new relationships between persons. There appear to be three determining factors in the sudden flowering of a variety of grass-roots groups, small communities, non-official groupings etc.:[14]

1) There is first of all the increasing pressure from social structures which limits the liberty of the individual as well as his interpersonal relationships. The isolation and anonymity which is the lot of urbanised man and the vicious circles caused by the incessant round of production and consumption are making people more aware that they are prisoners of all kinds of social alienation. They long for a return to something smaller, more tangible, where responsibilities can be more easily taken on again.

2) An important factor in the process of alienation is the weakening of intermediate groups within society. The family finds itself forced to abandon a great number of its functions to society, the mass media, and organized leisure. It seems that big organizations have become too vast and too impersonal to satisfy men's aspirations and that the family is too small and too intimate to face up to its own responsibilities.

3) Man's deepest needs on both the effective and the ideological

plane require social structures on a smaller scale and of greater variety. Psychology and pedagogy have laid bare these often repressed needs and encouraged man to become more free and creative, but by the same token have rendered him more vulnerable in face of conflict and frustration. The tension between his conscience and his personal convictions on the one hand and the need for social recognition on the other have led him to look for new ways of being integrated into society, which will guarantee him a minimum of personal harmony and allow him to be recognized and recognizable in his "otherness" at the social level.

The experience of all these forces in the context of religion has given rise to the rapid development of the basic communities. The theological characteristics of these basic communities can be summarised as follows:[15]

1) Basic communities start at ground level, more or less spontaneously, as the result of a number of men and women feeling a need to share their faith, their commitment and their spiritual searching, sometimes to the point where they are willing to live in community. They are different from parishes and Catholic Action groups of former times in so far as they are built up from below.

2) Many people join a group because they need to meet other people to establish human relationships, and such persons give importance to the more effective aspects (togetherness); traditional roles are blurred; there are few formal leaders and more group responsibility. The essential thing is the experience of being brothers and sisters and partners.

3) All are anxious to arrive once more, by some new road, at an authentic community of faith after the model of Jesus and his disciples. Even if the eucharist is not celebrated regularly it is always of central significance. When this significance is lost an ecclesial grass-roots group easily develops into a basic community that is purely secular and political in aim. Most communities try to take up a new position vis-a-vis man's classic idols: possessions, power, and sexuality. But the actual way in which they express their liberating criticism concerning these idols varies greatly from group to group.

4) For the majority of these communities a life according to the

gospel has no meaning if it is not related to the needs and problems of man today, in a context that is real. The importance attributed to an exemplary personal life along the lines emphasised in days gone by is increasingly being transferred to the giving of witness through the committed life in a group; or else the important thing is the community's own witness; sharing in man's adventure as he creates and suffers, working for the liberation of a new humanity and here what counts is the liberating of the other person, not one's own personal perfection. The ascetical practice and mystique of these groups are profoundly different from those held in honour twenty five years ago.

5) There is great variety among the groups and it is very difficult to reduce them to any one type.

I have dealt at some length with the phenomenon of basic communities as they have developed in several continents, because they have supplied the answer to the problems raised in the previous chapter. As was apparent in that chapter, the parish system in Great Britain is not only useless, but in many cases presents a barrier to our mission to establish the Kingdom of God. Theoretical considerations seemed to point to the need for small groups of believers, and the experience of the basic communities had vindicated the correctness of that theoretical projection. Moreover they have flourished especially in those regions where great distances, or the population explosion have caused the old parish system to break down. This has meant that the parish has not inhibited them as has been the case with more marginal groups in England.

Earlier in this book I indicated that an authentic christian community must have four characteristics, worship, charity, apostolate and witness. In the basic communities they occur almost automatically. The case of the German priest celebrating the eucharist on an upturned beer crate in Cologne shows how easily it fits into their life-style. Charity needs no planning, because the casualties cannot be hidden in so small a group. But it is probably christian witness which has proved to be their forte. The development of the basic communities has gone hand in hand with the struggle for justice in Latin America. Their very existence has been a

witness to their determination that they will transform their
societies so that men and women can live as the gospel
indicates, and not under exploitation. It seems too that they
hold out the best hope for apostolate. Not only do they work
explicitly to advance the Kingdom of Heaven but they have
the dynamism which can bring outsiders within their ranks.
In a large measure they have succeeded in revitalising the
faith of thousands in Latin America, which even thirty years
ago was regarded as a continent of merely nominal Catholicism. Clearly they have generated enough dynamism to
attract people to them. It is difficult to prove it but, that
would seem to be the authentic way for the Church to make
its numerical increase. In the days of the apostles, the outdoor
public speeches of St Paul were the exceptions. As soon as he
had established a viable community he moved on. From then
onwards these small cells were self diffusive, and that was
how christianity achieved its rapid expansion in the Roman
Empire in the first three centuries. The growth of small
communities, like the division of cells is closer to the infant
Church's life than publicity campaigns in which the product
is orchestrated like a sales' promotion drive.

One thing will not have escaped the reader. If the eucharist
is to become central to the life of these groups, they will need
more priests than we dispose of now, and also they will need
priests whose life style is very different from the conventional pattern inherited from the Middle Ages. This is a
complex problem and I will devote the next chapter to it.

CHAPTER EIGHT

Basic Priests

Drawing together the threads of the last two chapters, one can say that in Latin America the basic communities have flourished because the parish structure has not inhibited them. By contrast in England the parish, though stretched to the limit and failing in many of its responsibilities is yet able to suffocate the development of smaller groups within its boundaries. In this, and other ways the parish actually inhibits the Church's mission. In spite of the difficulties which would be encountered in establishing them, our first priority is to establish basic communities in this country. They would have to be co-terminous with a small village, a block of flats, or one street in a city. In such a setting, a stranger, for example coming from Liverpool to London, in search of work could be accepted automatically in a way which would be impossible with parishes of the present dimension. If these groups are to maintain their corporate existence against the inhibiting influence of the parish, they must be the communities in which mass is celebrated. This would be a major recasting of the ecclesiastical geography, but it is a re-organisation which must be undertaken. Thus far the post-Conciliar parish has undergone merely cosmetic treatment, in a limited endeavour which has aimed at nothing more than optimising the performance of the existing structure.

It is obvious that these communities, being the eucharistic focus of their members, will require many more priests than the Church can dispose of at the moment. Even if each group did not have its own priest, and if three or four groups were cared for by one priest, it would still be necessary to ordain about five times as many priests as we have now. Clearly they could not be recruited or trained in the conventional pattern. It is obvious that they would have to be chosen from among married men as well as celibates, and about that I will speak later in the chapter. Before discussing the relative advantages of married priests, there are other considerations which are even more important in deciding what kind of ministers these communities would need.

The starting point must be a perception of the communities themselves, and the first consideration is a paradox. Although these relatively small groups require a priest, his ministry must be of such a kind that the lay people are not excluded, inhibited, or rendered superfluous. As I showed in Chapters One and Three the laity are integral to the Church's mission, simply in virtue of their baptism. There is a danger at the moment that the shortage of priests in England might be remedied by ordaining more deacons, and employing full-time lay workers in parishes. Both of these would deprive the laity of their rightful participation in the apostolate. The latter expedient of employing, for example, graduates in theology as parish workers is a deceptive solution. Although they do not receive holy orders (some of them are women), they are functionally clerics. Being employed full time in the work of the Church, and having no secular occupation, they ought to be regarded as clergy, from the sociological point of view.

One final consideration, about the type of priests which the basic communities would need, is financial. Their numbers and life-style must not be an undue burden on the laity whom they serve. Fortunately this problem will solve itself. Other christian Churches in England are finding it exceedingly difficult to pay their married clergy adequate salaries. For the Catholic community it would be quite impossible.

Having sketched out the requirements of the priests both positively and negatively, the correct solution virtually identifies itself. The priests in question would have to be ordinary wage earners like the laity, and this would solve all the problems automatically. They would impose no financial burden on their communities, and there would be no agonising decisions about how much they deserved to be paid. This is purely a practical consideration. What is really important theologically is that they would share the conditions of life of the rest of the community, with its worries,

joys, and sufferings. It would be impossible for them to live
in any sense as a privileged class. It is artificial to try to
speculate how much time they might be able to give to
pastoral work, but for the sake of clarity it is useful to make
some kind of assessment. As an arbitrary figure I would
suggest two hours a day on average as the upper limit. Once
again a problem would be solved automatically. This would
mean that the laity would have to shoulder the responsibilities of making the group work as a real community. My
own experience as a parish priest has convinced me that most
of the tasks which enable a community to thrive do not
require holy orders. Assisting people with difficult teenagers,
or elderly relatives are best done by other lay people, as are
the support needed in times of bereavement, or matrimonial
difficulty. From every point of view the working priest is the
ideal minister for a basic community; he would have to be the
animator and not the factotum.

I would like to stress the value of a priest being a wage-
earning worker like other people. Little has been written
about the day to day life of the clergy before the fourth
century, but what has survived is very revealing. From the
fourth century onwards the emperors conferred benefits on
the christian clergy so that gradually they became a privileged class with salaries in various forms. Before the fourth
century this was not the case. One recent writer who has
investigated the matter extensively has arrived at these
conclusions: "In the earliest decades of christianity the
functions of christian ministry seem to have been for the
most part less than a full time occupation."[1] It is possible that
the bishops may have lived on "alms" or family estates, and
the deacons too (since they were far less numerous than the
priests), but the priests were most probably workers,
devoting to the ministry what we would call, part time
work. There are indications in Cyprian's letters that priests
who lived on alms were forbidden to indulge in secular
business.[2] In other words the infant Church was displaying
that admirable characteristic of pluralism, which was to be
seen in other areas of Church life also. For example the
children of christian parents were sometimes baptised in
infancy, whereas in other christian families the younger
generation accepted it only in adult years. Pluralism of this

sort was one of the strengths of the infant Church, which we would do well to initiate, as I will show later in this chapter when dealing with the question of celibacy.

An unusual pointer to the state of things has been revealed by the excavation of the world's oldest church at Dura-Europos, in modern Iraq. It is a house church dating from the middle of the third century, and it could not have held more than 60 people. Clearly a community for which this building was adequate, would not have needed full time clergy. Most probably they were part-timers, who earned their own living for most of the week.[3]

At Elvira in Spain there was a council in the year 300 (or possibly 303) whose canons give the most valuable glimpses of clerical life, mainly by implication. Canon 18 states:

> Bishops, priests, and deacons shall not depart from their districts for the sake of business; nor shall they follow up profitable business deals going round the provinces. For earning their living, let them send a son, a freed man, a servant, or friend, or anyone: and if they wish to negotiate business, let them do so within the province.[4]

The precise enactment is clear, lest they neglect the care of souls their business journeys must be relatively short, inside the province and not beyond its borders. But the implications are most illuminating. Quite clearly it is regarded as normal that all the clergy, including the bishops are business men. This in turn implies that they were not devoting all their waking hours to specifically ecclesiastical tasks. Canon 20 of the same council speaks about usury (that is to say, lending money on interest):

> If any cleric shall be detected accepting interest on a loan, it is our decision that he shall be degraded and excommunicated. Also, if a lay person shall be proved to have accepted interest on a loan, it is our decision that he must promise after correction to cease from the practice and not to revert to it, and then be given pardon; if however he persists in this iniquity he shall be expelled from the Church.[5]

Once again the implications are more revealing than the immediate prohibitions. It is clear that the clergy were sufficiently involved in commerce, for them to lapse into a practice about which the infant Church was exceedingly strict. There is evidence from the south of France for the same attitude. The Council of Arles in 314 made a similar prohibition, indicating that the same situation obtained in the background there also.[6]

After Constantine became emperor he soon began to bestow financial privileges on the clergy. After his victory at the Milvian Bridge he gave a large donation to the clergy of Africa. Later in his reign he exempted the clergy from the five yearly tax on business transactions known as the Lustralis Collation.[7] The frequency with which the latter privilege was renewed indicated that large numbers of clergy must have been involved. Donations of the kind made to the clergy of Africa led eventually to regular payments which formed the normal incomes of the clergy. By implication this sort of payment by the then Christian empire and its agencies, indicates that in the period before such subsidies were forthcoming, the clergy must have been self supporting for the most part.

It is easy to understand how the clergy would become dependent upon financial support of this kind. In the latter part of the fourth century it seems to have been taken for granted, since the ecclesiastical historians remarked on the fact that Julian the Apostate withheld the clergy's payments from the imperial revenues. They were restored by the next emperor Jovian, to the evident satisfaction of the same historians.[8]

The rest of the evidence from the fourth and fifth centuries shows the variety which existed in the payment or work life of the clergy. St Jerome criticises the cleric who has risen from poverty to riches by means of commerce.[9] It was not the fact of his working which annoyed St Jerome, but the evident love of money which had crept in, and we may infer that working for his living was normal. One cannot help recalling that St Jerome's journeys to Palestine and the biblical work which he undertook, were financed by gifts from an immensely wealthy christian widow and her daughter. So he cannot be accused of inconsistency when he urged on the laity the duty of generosity to the clergy in his commentary on the Epistle to Titus![10]

A glimpse into the fifth century is given by a document traditionally known as the *Statuta Ecclesiae Antiquae*. It was once thought to have been the record of a council in Carthage in 389 AD, but is more probably to be assigned to Southern Gaul in the second half of the fifth century. Plurality of practice is evident. Canon 49 presupposes a salary when it says: "A cleric who is absent from the (liturgical) vigils, apart from the excuse of bodily indisposition, shall be deprived of payment." A little further on in the same document canon 52 presupposes work: "A cleric shall provide for his food and clothing, by manual work or agriculture, without detriment to his official duties."[11] Generally agriculture was held in high esteem and was stressed by hagiographers as showing the humility of the saints.[12] Work which would be incompatible with the ideal of poverty was considered reprehensible, such as the management of large estates.[13] Towards the end of the fifth century Pope Gelasius placed limits upon the kind of work which would be permitted to the clergy, expressing his wishes in terms which indicate that involvement in commerce was normal for them:

> Many clerics are involved in business which is dishonest and reprehensible . . . Thence they must learn to desist from this kind of unworthy commerce, and must refrain from all astuteness and cupidity in business, otherwise they will be forbidden to take part in the liturgical offices, no matter what rank they may occupy.[14]

This longish digression, about the payment and wage-earning occupations of the clergy in antiquity, should reassure any doubters who might feel that worker priests are at variance with christian tradition. As I will show in the next section, it is the privileged status of the clergy which is harder to reconcile with the ideals of the gospel. In the 1940s the worker priest movement was initiated in France, and spread to other European countries after the war. In 1953 the movement was suppressed by order of the Vatican, in dramatic circumstances which have remained in the memory of most people. As a form of ministry it was approved by the Vatican Council[15] though this has not been remembered as vividly as their suppression. The experiment was taken up widely, and communities were to be found in the most unlikely places. I remember vividly visiting friends in a conservative Catholic canton in Switzerland, when I was taken to a certain meeting. We assembled in a small apartment in the ancient quarter of the city, and a number of men came in at about six in the evening with grease and oil on their clothing, clearly having finished a day's work in a factory. After some informal talking, one of them put on a chasuble and started to say mass on the kitchen table. I learned afterwards that all of them were priests. They lived in an unpretentious apartment and worked all day in local factories. Unfortunately the bishops in Great Britain have shown no enthusiasm for the movement. A dozen years ago there were four or five scattered over the length and breadth of the country. They were too few, and too marginalised to make any significant contribution to pastoral experimentation.

However, it is my conviction that something like the worker priest pattern is required to provide the eucharistic ministers for the basic communities which I have described earlier in this book. If they are married and earning their living like other men, the basic pattern of their life will be established. How they would relate to the groups which they are to animate must be worked out by experiment. Trial and error is the only way to establish a pattern of pastoral work, it would be impossible at this stage, and dangerous, to offer a theoretical blueprint. However, before they are deployed in their basic communities, there is one element which must be planned, that is their theological instruction. Since they would administer sacraments, say mass, and preach, they must be competent in biblical studies and theology. If they had not studied it at university or at a college of education, some scheme will have to be devised. Once again, I do not intend to go into detail at this stage, but it is relevant to remark that the training of the married deacons has indicated basically how it can be done. Since the deacons preach they have been given theological and scriptural formation. Various schemes have been tried, and all of them are basically part time education, by correspondence, in the evenings. The trainee deacons are guided by a director of studies whom they visit occasionally. It entails much hard work for the aspirant, but assuming that the motivation is strong, a satisfactory theological formation can be acquired over a number of years. Apart from the pastoral work which they now undertake, the married deacons have given the Church this added bonus that they have demonstrated the feasibility of part time theological study, which could work just as well for worker priests. (The other indirect benefit which has arisen out of the permanent diaconate is that it has brought to an end the strong psychological taboo about sex and holy order.)

It seems clear from many considerations that the future development of the church's mission in this country, requires basic communities served by priests whose life style is very different from that to which we are accustomed in today's clergy. I have indicated that they will have to be wage-earning workers, but that is not all; other changes are needed. Clearly the law of compulsory celibacy must be altered, but I will speak of that last, because it is not the only remaining obstacle to effectiveness. It is equally important, but less obvious, that we must bring to an end the clergy's status as a privileged class, living differently from the laity in so many ways, all of which are at best irrelevant to the gospel message, and mostly harmful to its diffusion.

Ironically the beginnings of clerical privilege can be traced to the christians themselves, in the period of persecution. Tertullian, the ex-lawyer turned theologian employed the term "ordo" for the christian clergy. He did not invent the term. He was adopting the well known name of the social classes in the empire, namely the Ordo (order) of the senators and the order of the populace. When the empire gave official approval to christianity it was quite simple to insert the clergy into the legal system as the third "ordo", indeed the nomenclature was employed officially as early as the year 395.[16]

In addition to the title, the clergy began receiving legal privileges in the reigns of Constantine and his successors, especially Gratian.[17] The first of these privileges was the exemption of the clergy from civic duties known as the *munera civilia* by various laws of October 313. In 321 the Church was allowed to receive inheritances, and in 333 came the first of the laws which gave to bishops some initial legal competence in civil cases. When Gratian became emperor in

the West he confirmed the clergy's exemption from some of
the taxes, and in 379 he exempted from the industrial tax
(chrysargurion) those clerics who were engaged in commerce. The year 398 saw further extensions of the bishops'
powers to act as judges. Finally they were empowered to
settle any civil matters in which the parties were in
agreement. When St Augustine was bishop of Hippo, he
spent every morning in this occupation. In 392 the churches
acquired the right of sanctuary, and the clergy were given the
privilege of being tried in their own courts. This was to
prove one of the most powerful factors marking-off the
clergy as a privileged class in the Middle Ages.

In addition to the strictly juridical privileges, the clergy
began to acquire status symbols, which in the Roman Empire
were conferred by imperial decree and not just by the whim
of an ambitious individual. Since the time of Constantine the
higher clergy were given titles of rank such as *Clarissime*,
illustre, and *gloriosissime*, which scarcely need translation!
They were also entitled to wear articles of clothing which
denoted civilian rank such as the pallium, the stole, the
sandals, and possibly too the maniple.

All these marks of privilege seem strangely out of accord
with the primitive observance of Gallilee. Had they not
resumed the broad phylacteries about which Christ spoke so
scornfully? Were they not delighting in being called Rabbi,
just like the ancient pharisees? It is encouraging to learn that
protests were made against this scramble for privileges. In
428 Pope Celestine I reproved Honoratus the bishop of Arles
because he had introduced for his clergy the monastic dress of
tunic and belt. Hitherto priests' clothing has been just the
same as that of other men. Even in the liturgy the only
difference was that they took care to wear clean clothes as a
mark of respect for the occasion. Celestine enunciated the
principle: "We should be distinguished from others not by
our dress, but by our knowledge, our outlook on life, not by
our style of life."[18] Such protests seem to have passed
unnoticed, for as the empire declined in the West, the clergy
became more and more enmeshed in civil life and were
unmistakably a privileged class. It seems that the emperor's
money and power of patronage proved an almost irresistible
attraction. In Constantinople, the emperor Justinian (who

paid them) limited the number of clergy in the basillica of Santa Sophia to a complement of 60 priests, 100 deacons, and other minor clerics making a total of 525!

The acquisition of privilege in this fashion seems inconceivable to the modern christian because we live in a secularised age, and in this respect we seem to have understood the gospel much better than Justinian's favoured functionaries. In those days religion and civil life were so closely inter-twined that it did not seem out of place for the christian clergy to have taken over the role which the pagan priests had exercised in society. When the Roman Empire in the West collapsed, and was replaced by barbarian nations, the same religious presuppositions were taken for granted. The Church lived on as the sole survivor of the old establishment being the only surviving *ordo*. Since the clergy possessed a monopoly of education, not by design, but by accident, their position in the newly converted nations like England and Germany was even more enhanced.

When medieval society settled down to its distinctive social groupings and class distinctions, the clergy were perhaps the most prominent, wielding neither sword nor spade, but in a position of tremendous influence and privilege.

I will sketch the history up to the modern period in only the most summary terms, because the pattern of events is so clear and consistent. After the Council of Trent the clergy lost a certain amount of their political influence, but their status as a separate class was fortified by the creation of seminaries. This gave them specialised training, which was valuable, but also segregated them still further from the laity, which was regrettable. After the French Revolution the fate of the clergy varied greatly from nation to nation. In England the restoration of the hierarchy in 1850 brought the clergy out of obscurity, but local legislation soon gave them the pattern of life which was modelled on that of the Catholic nations on mainland Europe. Although the priests in England did not enjoy any special privileges in civil law, they were given, and compelled to live by, all the privileges embodied in ecclesiastical law. The pattern has remained the same up to the present day.

The only element which has changed is that of the attitude

toward privilege on the part of many priests and lay people. It has become apparent to many that a privileged status is not only useless for the apostolate, but it is also a hindrance for the evangelisation of the modern world.

The basic communities have grown up in the Church in the period since the Council, so it is useless to seek in the conciliar documents any specific advice about the kind of clergy which they might need. However, as I have shown in previous chapters the most satisfactory development of the ecclesiology of *Lumen Gentium* finds its institutionalised expression in these small groups. There are however one or two passages which indicate with remarkable clarity the kind of community and clergy which the Church now needs. In the Decree on the Life and Work of Priests we read the following remarkable statement: "No christian community, however, can be built up unless it has its basis and centre in the celebration of the most Holy Eucharist."[19] The implications of this statement, if taken seriously, are very far reaching. If we regard the basic communities as genuine christian communities, they must have the mass, and therefore the Church must remove obstacles to their being provided with priests. The most obvious obstacle is that of celibacy, which I will discuss later in this chapter, but another powerful obstacle is the privileged status of the priesthood and the financial burden which the priestly life style places upon the laity. The same decree on life and work indicates clearly that there should be no privilege. If priests live apart it is so that they can witness to the world of eternity, not so that they should be cut off from their people.[20]

In the twenty years since the Council ended, nothing has been done in England to change the clergy's status as a privileged class. The training in the seminaries has been modified only superficially. Seminarians spend some time in a presbytery, but in France in the 1950s some seminaries sent their students out to factories in what they called the "industrial stage". In all fairness to the seminaries one should bear in mind that it would be difficult to produce a radically reformed training for a basically unreformed parochial clergy. By that I mean that the parish is just the same structurally as it was before the Council, so is the presbytery, so are the clothes and the official titles. Since all this remains unchanged, in all but details, since the Council, any alterations in the training would merely cause trouble later. In fact it is distressing to see how quickly after ordination the young priests fall into the clericalised attitudes of their predecessors in the parishes. It is a significant example of how institutions mould people into their pattern.

The status of privilege which still attaches to the clergy has a seductive appeal to immature personalities. This observation became inescapable for me when I was a university chaplain and I could not help drawing comparisons between the university students, and the young men in seminaries (which I will not name). The first thing which struck me was their hard work. To secure a good degree they had to study for long hours and late into the night. The university would guarantee a room in hall for the first year, but after that they had to fend for themselves. For the most part they joined in groups of three or four to rent a flat, since only by sharing their grants could they pay the high rents of the city. The deep spiritual experience of this kind of sharing was more profound than anything which the seminarians experienced. The lay students also had to do their own shopping and cook their own food, which was also done quite often by a shared rota. In their spare time they enjoyed themselves fully, socialising in pubs, discos, visiting theatres, and cinemas, and sedulously cultivating the company of their boy friends or girl friends. They were generous with their time and energy and would work for good causes like youth clubs, or taking deprived children to the country for week-end excursions.

Compared with that pattern of life, the seminary regimes which I have known in the past, and also the present time, are exceedingly negative. Since there is no qualifying examination for ordination, or for entry to the seminary, pursuit of learning does not flourish with much evident enthusiasm. Because frivolity and materialistic pleasures are discouraged they do not spend much time in pubs or theatres. Because celibacy hangs over them they do not cultivate girl friends. But worst of all is the effortless security of the domestic regime. They do not have to search for lodgings, nor buy food, nor cook it. Everything happens automatically without their being responsible for any single item of it. In some seminaries there are nuns who do the cooking and other domestic tasks, which might well suggest to the future priest that this is the normal pattern of how nuns and priests should expect to relate to each other.

This is the environment in which an inadequate personality can so easily find a congenial refuge. If they enjoy the narrow world of the parish sacristy, the business of being an altar server, and if they have little intellectual ability and no interest in girls, they will fit into that system as to a natural habitat. It would require extraordinary imagination on the part of the seminary authorities to counteract these tendencies. They are the inbuilt hazards of the system. There is no real answer other than making a strict stipulation that a man will not be admitted to a seminary or novitiate until he has lived away from home and earned his own living. Even after that requirement has been met, six years in a thoroughly institutionalised seminary is a dangerous experience for all but the most independent personalities.

In case the reader should think I am exaggerating the danger of inadequate personalities entering the seminaries and the ranks of the clergy, I will quote the results of some psychological testing carried out on representative groups of priests. A survey conducted by Baars and Teruwe on priests in the United States and Europe, concluded that 10 to 15 per cent are psychologically mature, 60 to 70 per cent are emotionally immature, and 20 to 25 per cent present serious psychiatric difficulties. The research of Kennedy and Heckler produced similar results. Of a group of 271 American priests, they found that 7 per cent were "developed", 18 per cent were developing, 66.5 per cent were under-developed and 8.5 per cent were maldeveloped.[21] Bearing in mind all the limitations of such surveys and the measuring systems which they imply, the picture is far from reassuring.

In the twenty year period since the Council virtually nothing has been done, at the level of training or parish re-organisation, to change the clergy's role. We are still a privileged class, and maintenance men. The Church's situation in a secular society like Great Britain makes it clear that we need a missionary clergy to serve basic communities. The credibility gap between the reality, and the requirements of the mission is large, and cannot be ignored by sensitive and intelligent people. Inevitably it has its influence on the morale of the clergy. Broadly speaking there are three serious consequences for the priests. Many have left the ministry, far fewer enter the seminaries, and of those who stay, many of them cannot adapt to the new expectations and have become seriously demoralised.

Perhaps the saddest phenomenon since the Council has been the massive exodus of priests and nuns leaving the ministry. It has been so embarrassing for the authorities that very little information is published. Fortunately the diocese of Westminster has divulged some figures, and since it is a large diocese, these figures furnish an adequate sample through which to envisage the generality of the English scene.[22] Between 1968 and 1978, 49 secular priests resigned from the ministry. Since then the figure has lessened and since 1978 it has been just one a year. On average 5 priests were departing each year between 1968 and 1978, and in the same period ordinations were 8 or 9 each year. These figures speak for themselves and require little comment. Other dioceses, and religious orders have been more reticent in disclosing similar information, but from one's own experience it is clear that the situation elsewhere has been just as bad. In recent years the Vatican has published the numbers of secular and regular priests who have left the ministry, and the world-wide picture indicates that the English experience is consistent with the overall phenomenon. In 1973 a judge of the Roman Rota, Emilio Colagiovanni, published a survey of the dispensations from celibacy under the title *Crisi Vere e Falsi Nel Ruolo del Prete Oggi*. This study gave the figures from 1963 to 1969. From 1969 onwards the *Annuarium Statisticum Ecclesiae* gave figures not merely of dispensations, but of departures in general. This means the total including those who left without going through the application for a dispensation. Presumably the figures were obtained from diocesan offices, which would have accurate information. This provided one year of overlap which is valuable for comparison. In 1969, 1,780 diocesan priests left the ministry, but only 1,382 were dispensed from the obligation of celibacy. This suggests that about one quarter of those who depart do not seek dispensation. From 1975 onwards the numbers of religious priests leaving was also recorded in the *Annuarium Statisticum Ecclesiae*. Between 1978 and 1979 the total number of resignations from both branches of the priesthood dropped from 2,072 to 1,576. That is to be accounted for by Pope John Paul II's decision to withhold all dispensations for the time being. It is a measure which does not solve any of the problems, in fact it makes them worse. The numbers leaving have not been reduced significantly, but it means that all the departing priests are now in a much more complicated position spiritually. Presumably most of them have contracted civil marriages, and are denied the sacraments. It is difficult to see how the Pope or his advisors could regard this as a pastoral solution. Even if they were regarded as sinners the truly christian remedy would be to leave the other ninety nine and go and search for the lost one. By this policy they are being effectively driven away still further. An analysis of all these figures[23] indicates that in the twenty year period from 1964 to 1983, between 40,000 and 50,000 priests have left the active ministry. In 1969, which is the first year for which the real total of departures was available (including those who did not seek dispensation), the total resignations can be put at about 3,400. In that same year ordinations numbered 5,156 and deaths totalled 5,014. These three figures speak for themselves and do not require comment.

The overall world picture (with which the English experience is perfectly consistent) is serious to a degree which is difficult to express in words. Clearly it signifies a massive loss of morale among the priests, but this is merely the manifest effect of far reaching causes. It might perhaps indicate a large scale failure of leadership on the part of the bishops and religious superiors. In the next chapter I will study the bishops' qualities of leadership, or the lack of it, for the present I merely note the imperative need for more research.

Having noted with sadness the vast numbers who leave the ministry (and this applies to nuns as well), one must also reflect on the quality of the people who have resigned. Here I must limit my reflections to the area of my own experience, namely Great Britain. Thirty years ago resignations from the priesthood were regarded as moral failures. Fortunately attitudes have changed and it is now perceived that the problem is far more complex. Clearly a large number who have left were the victims of bad training, particularly the seclusion which began in junior seminaries at the age of 14 or less. As soon as they came out of the artificial seclusion into the real world where they met women, they realised that they were not suited to the celibate life. Of the others who leave it is impossible to generalise because of the secrecy which still surrounds the facts. If I may express a purely personal opinion, I have come to the conclusion that those who resign are for the most part men of intelligent and sensitive personalities. I have obtained information from one priest who is in a privileged position to assess the situation. For twenty years he was in a position to help many ex-priests individually and through their organisation, the Advent Group. He informed me that after much reflection he had come to the conclusion that the principal cause why the priests leave the ministry was the demoralisation bred of the Church's failure to implement the expectations which Vatican II gave rise to.

At the start of the last paragraph I remarked that the exodus of priests and nuns was sad. What is even worse, and frankly alarming, is the failure by the authorities to investigate the phenomenon. If the causes could be identified then it might be possible to remedy the situation. The reluctance even to examine the problem would suggest that they have less solicitude for their subjects' well-being than commercial organisations show towards their employees. A few months ago a large London firm of accountants noticed that a considerable number of their staff were leaving in order to move to other concerns, or other firms of accountants. Very quickly they set up an enquiry, investigated the matter thoroughly, published the results and then made the necessary re-organisation to cure it for the future. The investigation showed that they were recruiting the wrong people, and that after working for the company for some time the employees were not given enough responsibility. If they had problems, these were dealt with by the senior management, or the personnel department, but not by the immediate managers of their own departments. Simple organisational factors of that kind caused them to leave.

Admittedly the reasons why the clergy might resign are more complex than the frustrations in a business organisation, but this makes it all the more urgent to investigate the problem. It has more serious consequences for the Church's mission, than the inefficiencies in a commercial enterprise; here the lives of the clergy are at stake and not just their occupations. I know of two religious orders where priests committed suicide, one after a history of alcoholism. In other cases too there have been the most dreadful personal tragedies in the process of leaving the ministry. It is possible that the bishops or religious superiors have conducted secret investigations into these problems. Yet if they have not published the results they might just as well not have undertaken the enquiries. The information should be in the hands of all those involved in the training of future priests and nuns, as well as their superiors, including the parish priests who work with curates. In other words it must be made public. One is left with the uneasy feeling that such investigations would disclose problems which most of the bishops and religious superiors could not face, because they do not possess adequate qualities of leadership. In the next chapter I will deal with the problems of selecting bishops. For the present one is left with the apparent conclusion that business managers show more concern for their subordinates than religious leaders.

The second major sign of the credibility gap is the decline in the numbers of young men entering the seminaries. Figures for the novices and students of religious orders are not easily accessible, but the numbers of seminarians for the diocesan clergy are published in the *Catholic Directory*.[24] In 1983 the dioceses of England and Wales had 569 students in senior seminaries. In the same year 53 priests were ordained for the same groups of dioceses. It is not easy to speculate as to what proportion of the seminarians will eventually be ordained. If three quarters of them complete the six year course, it means that about 65 will be ordained each year in the immediate future. If the proportion is as low as a half (which is not an unreasonable assumption) then the annual average will be 48 ordinations. Neither figure is reassuring because it does not amount to replacement level. In 1983 when 53 secular priests were ordained, the total of deaths was 79. For a long time there has been a steady decline in the number of the clergy. In Westminster for instance 43 per cent of the diocesan priests are above the age of 60. In the nation as a whole the clerical body is an ageing and shrinking group.

The phenomenon is not confined to England. The United States has experienced the same decline in the last two decades. The table printed below is informative, because it looks as if the first result of the Council was to generate enthusiasm which showed itself in an increase in the number of entrants to the seminaries.[25] The figures are sufficiently clear to speak for themselves.

Year	Seminarians For Dioceses	Students For Religious Orders	Totals
1962	23,662	22,567	43,319
1965	26,762	22,230	48,992
1970	17,317	11,589	28,906
1975	11,223	6,579	17,802
1980	8,552	4,674	13,226

It has been suggested that the decline has halted and that the number of seminarians and ordinations is once again increasing. It is true that in the whole world, ordinations went up from 5,889 in 1981, to 5,957 in 1982,[26] but the increase is marginal and is incapable of catching up on the losses of the previous two decades. Morover, it is unreliable to extrapolate from such recent statistics.

The third sign of demoralisation in the clergy of Britain is the tone of the survey conducted by the National Conference of Priests as a preparation for their annual meeting in September 1984.[27] Cards were distributed through the four delegates for each of the dioceses, but one may doubt that all the five thousand or so clergy received them, because only a little over 300 were returned. This made it a self-selecting group, rather than a truly representative sample of the clergy as a whole. Even with these limitations it has some value in assessing the morale of the priests. Those who took part in the exercise sent back two cards, a pink one stating the main problem facing the priest today, and a white card on which they had been asked to write about how they would like the priesthood to be. It is a pity that this framing of the questions merely provided a negative and positive way of expressing the shortcomings. It would have given a more balanced view of reality if they had been asked to identify real progress or achievement to complement the identification of problems. The cards were then sorted into groups according to the matter which was identified. Taking the difficulties first, by far the greater number of priests spoke of loneliness as a problem. 50 cards mentioned it in one form or another. Far behind this came the worry about lack of involvement of the laity in the church's mission (16 cards). 15 identified moral problems, (notably matrimonial difficulties, which implies contraception and its unresolved debate). The same number mentioned the lack of time in a priest's life for prayer and study. 11 spoke of the difficulties created by the age gap among the clergy, particularly between parish priests who had been ordained before the Council and curates who became priests afterwards. The same number (11) spoke of people's unrealistic expectations about their priests. The other groupings of replies mustered less than ten a piece.

The white cards recording ideal aspirations did not show such numerical diversity. The topics which topped the list, but with only 35 replies, was the desire for more partnership with the laity and the same number voiced the hope that a priest would be a man of prayer. 28 expressed the wish for more support from fellow clergy. 22 opted for more availability to the people as an ideal. 15 wanted to look upon their bishop as a shepherd, not just as an administrator. 14 said that the priests should be sensitive to the requirements of the liturgy and 13 hoped that the priest would be compassionate to people in trouble. The rest which mustered ten or less cards are too diverse for the detection of any pattern.

It is difficult to summarise the results of this survey because of the negative way in which the questions were asked. Several of the disappointments and aspirations are so obvious as to make one wonder why their writers bother to put pen to paper. What could have been in the minds of those who hoped for a compassionate attitude in the clergy? Do they imply that it is absent? The priest who analysed the report declared that "The overall picture from the pink cards is one of gloom and lack of confidence". I quite agree. He then goes on to say that encouraging things are happening too, but he does not give any evidence to substantiate it.

The challenges presented by the Council, and the massive exodus of clergy in the mid-1970s, have been met by a few modest attempts to modernise the selection, training, and after-care of the priests. The limitations of these endeavours arise out of the fact that they have been conceived of in such a way that they will not involve any re-structuring of the present institutions. They aim at nothing more ambitious than the optimisation of the performance of the past methods and procedures.

In February 1983 the Bishops' Commission for Priestly Formation published a report on the discerning and fostering of vocations.[28] Neither the letter nor spirit of Vatican II is much in evidence. At some points the document merely restates well known problems, like the following:

> Celibacy: This issue can be a stumbling block. We cannot quieten fears and objections by simply repeating the established teaching. Parents simply do not understand celibacy. If they are to foster and support a son's vocation they need a far better basis to work from than is available at present. Priests too should start to explain the positive values of celibacy.

Other parts of the document rarely rise above the banal re-statement of truisms, offering no practical guidance. For instance they state that:

> An individual call to the priesthood can come at any time, and it must be met with some positive response from the community. In a young person this response may be little more initially than full involvement in the general catechetical and pastoral programmes which are, or should be, provided for all members of the community. At what state a more specialised response is required is a matter of pastoral and catechetical judgement. There is nothing inevitable about this inner call coming to fruition or the person claiming to be called being found suitable.

Careful analysis of that paragraph indicates that it tells us practically nothing. It would be cruel to quote further extracts of no greater quality, but it is a sad reflection on the sheer absence of imaginative leadership at the theological level.

At various points in this chapter I have indicated that the training in the seminaries has not shown really imaginative improvement since the end of the Council. One must

envisage clearly the kind of training which would be
desirable if basic communities became the norm, and if most
of their clergy were married. This would be considerably
different from the formation of the priests who are now
destined for celibacy and for work in the unreformed parishes
which are basically the same as in the pre-Conciliar period.
The training of married worker priests could be done by
more or less the same methods as those used in the training of
married deacons. The training of the conventional priests
destined to work in the parishes which we have known from
the past, is necessarily conditioned by the intrinsic limitations
of the system.

These limitations are principally that the clergy are still
promoted from curate to parish priest not by merit but by
seniority. It means that for the most creative period of his life
the young priest has little in the way of real responsibility. In
most dioceses of England and Wales the priest will live alone
for a substantial portion of his life, because comparatively
few parishes have curates. We have to recognise also that the
choice about celibacy dominates the whole period of formation which is regretable for many reasons, principally
because it is not intrinsic to the nature of the priesthood, nor
to the role of leadership which is required in the animator of a
eucharistic missionary community.

Bearing in mind these constraints one can take a more
tolerant view of the limitations apparent in the changes
introduced into seminary training since the Council. To their
credit the authorities have removed from the system those
aspects of past discipline which were puerile or otherwise
pointless. Students are now permitted to smoke in their own
rooms, to move from seminary to town with more freedom
(for shopping etc.) to have bicycles and wear ordinary clothes
instead of black suits or cassocks. However, in the city of
Rome, the wearing of black has recently been re-imposed.
Two English seminaries have established contact with
universities. In the diocese of Westminster the seminary has
been moved to central London and this enables the students
with the necessary A levels to attend Heythrop College for
theology, and obtain a degree from the university. The link
between Ushaw and the university of Durham has been more
integrated, and some of the lecturers at the seminary also

teach in the university. So in addition to enabling the more talented students to obtain a degree in theology, the university itself has been enriched by the participation of staff as well as students from Ushaw. Finally there has been a general willingness to encourage the students to go out of the seminary buildings to take part in what could be called social and voluntary work, and also to live for appreciable periods in presbyteries.

Unfortunately the latter experience conflicts with the inevitable limitations in the competence of the seminarians. Medical students and those destined for other professions can integrate varying amounts of practical experience into their training depending upon their usefulness to the clients before they are fully qualified. Student teachers are admitted to the class at a comparatively early stage in their studies, but for the future priests it is more difficult. In the presbytery, a parishioner will undoubtedly want to talk to a priest if he has a serious problem. In a hospital the patients are hardly likely to discuss the fear of death, or unreconciled moral problems with anyone except the priest. There is a danger that in the parish and all its points of contact they will perceive only the trivialities, and will be excluded from the serious matters of spiritual leadership or individual counselling.

The next problem which has never been faced properly is the question of objective assessment of the candidates. The memory of St John Vianney has inhibited anything like final examinations in theology before ordination because he, and others like him have proved admirable pastors though ill-equipped intellectually. It is important to keep a sense of proportion and remember that men of the stature of St John Vianney are rare exceptions. Admittedly the mysterious workings of grace in the soul cannot be measured experimentally, but that does not prevent assessment of those areas which are open to simple verification. It is quite straightforward in reality, but often overlooked, that a candidate for the priesthood should have to undergo examinations of various kinds before admission to the seminary, and before ordination, for those parts of his course which can be examined. Other aspects of his training such as his spiritual maturity will have to be gauged by less precise methods, but this does not rule out examination for the purely academic part of his formation. The same problems have been faced by other professions. For instance in the selection of officers for the armed forces the assessment of qualities of personality which are needed for real leadership cannot be ascertained by an examination. However, that does not prevent the army from having realistic tests about intelligence, intellectual achievement, physical fitness and initiative. I think that it is imperative to have recognised criteria for admission to seminaries and examinations in theology prior to ordination. In one sense it does not matter where the standard is pegged as long as there is one. Its absence casts an air of amateurishness over the whole intellectual formation.

Another item which could enrich the training of priests has been used by business corporations in training managers, and that is some form of physical endurance test. Sometimes management trainees take part in the Outward-bound courses organised at Atlantic College and similar establishments. Although little of the training is apparently of direct relevance to a business career (or to the care of souls) its indirect benefits are astonishing. For instance it is exceedingly important to see how a young man reacts under stress, and if this is induced by physical exhaustion in the course of purposefully planned exercises, it is a genuinely healthy experience. The seminarians could benefit greatly from such courses, and the assessment of character and personality which can be made as a result.

The transition from a large college to a two-priest presbytery is bound to constitute a difficult readjustment for the newly ordained priest. Some religious orders have faced this problem realistically. A few years ago I was lecturing in Australia and I met some Jesuit students in Melbourne. They were living in a street of small houses where they had connected the adjacent buildings so that a pair of houses could hold about half a dozen students and one or two priests. These small groups lived as a community, sharing domestic duties, going to the university for theology, and meeting in a chapel for mass and other spiritual exercises. This arrangement had many advantages, not least of which was that they were already living in more or less the size of community which they would live in after ordination, and for the rest of their lives.

For the secular clergy this kind of experience is more difficult to achieve, because the presbyteries with more than two priests in them are very rare. This makes it all the more urgent for the seminarians to have some kind of experience of living in a really small group. The only feasible scheme is to require them to spend at least a year in a house or flat in a group of about four. If it were necessary for them to find the dwelling on their own initiative, it would not be asking of them anything harder than the average university student has to face. Living in a small community like that for a year would enable them to face up to the personal relationships which will arise in a presbytery. It would also enable them to see whether they could sustain the practice of a serious prayer life without the time-table of a large college and the supervision of the seminary staff.

Another possibility for the training of the secular clergy also requires a considerable period of absence from the seminary. Six years of uninterrupted study is difficult even for those who enjoy intellectual pursuits for their own sake. There would be many advantages in ordaining a candidate after three years theology; let him spend three years in a parish and then return to the seminary for a further three years of theology. Their initial pastoral experience would be realistic because they would be saying mass, giving the sacraments, and fulfilling the laity's role expectations of their community leaders. During that period their relative lack of theological knowledge would not be serious since they would be curates working under the close direction of a more experienced priest. The fact of their being ordained after three years of theology would prevent the seminaries from accepting them too young. In fact it would be a fool-proof method of ensuring that they had earned their own living like other men, and probably that they had been to university, or college, and had left home. Their final three years of theology would be enriched by the motivation bred of real contact with the laity's deepest spiritual needs, and not just superficial impressions derived from living in a presbytery without any real responsibilities towards the people.

I have indicated in the previous paragraphs two systems by which the seminary training could be enriched by a serious structural re-organisation. Compared with these plans the

modernisation undertaken in most seminaries since the
Council amounts to little more than an attempt to get the
best out of the present institutions and their habitual pattern
of operation. Something much more radical is needed if we
are to produce priests capable of giving the leadership which
the post-Conciliar Church requires.

It will not have escaped the notice of the reader that this
kind of training could equally well be offered to a man who
intended to marry and serve the Church as a married worker
priest. It is only a question of how he plans his life after
leaving school, and perhaps some financial assistance from
the Church if the ordinary student grants do not quite fit the
pattern of a sandwich course spread over nine years.

The staffing of seminaries has been a problem because we
maintain too many establishments. It is desirable to move the
seminaries which are situated in Spain and Italy. They were
established there in penal days, but now the disadvantages of
training outside the society where they will work outweighs
any benefits derived from living abroad. Having brought
them back to England, we should then amalgamate them
with the existing seminaries in such a way as to give us
perhaps three major seminaries in England and Wales. They
should all be in cities, and close enough to universities so that
the seminarians could integrate their domestic studies with
what the university had to offer. The students should be
given the choice of attending which seminary they would
prefer.

The staff too should have some choice. In the past the
staffing of seminaries had depended too much upon the
bishops' initiative. Particular colleges have soldiered on for
years lacking specialist lecturers in key subjects. A few years
ago there was no English priest studying at the Biblical
Institute in Rome, nor at the *École Biblique* in Jerusalem. This
might mean that one or more seminaries will be without
qualified instructors in the future. It would seem perfectly
reasonable to allow the academically minded seminarians and
priests to study beyond ordination, and up to their own
individual ceiling. In the past it was a rare privilege, and
many talented priests have been denied the opportunity of
theological fulfilment. This would create a pool of qualified
theologians and the seminaries might well advertise for posts

when vacancies arose, as is the practice in schools and universities. The bishops should have the ultimate control over who will teach the future priests, but in the system which I envisage, the bishops would not be expected to assume all the responsibility and take all the initiatives in the process.

It will be clear from what I have said that priests for the basic communities could also study theology in that kind of seminary, although other provision could be made for their training, as I indicated above.

The third sign of malaise in the clergy is the setting up of a fairly complicated support mechanism which indicated that the old structures are inadequate to perform the kind of role which a back-up group provides for social workers, for instance. It is called the Ministry to Priests, and I can do no better than quote verbatim the description given by the director of the exercise in a diocese which shall remain nameless.

In May 1982 Father ——, the founder, was invited by the Bishop of ——, to address all the clergy of the diocese. He came to the pastoral centre and spoke to 135 of us. He spoke for an hour describing fairly vividly the state of the secular clergy both in the United States and the United Kingdom. He pointed out the great need for priests to support one another. He described how the life of the secular clergy had changed dramatically since the Vatican Council and how much we as secular clergy needed to spiritualise our lives and to acknowledge our need for support and help to enable us to withstand the pressures on the priesthood. He then gave us an outline of the programme and we were asked to hold a secret ballot there and then as to whether we wished to proceed with the matter any further by adopting the programme. The voting in our case was 95 in favour and 40 against. This was considered a sufficient majority to go ahead. On that same day our priests were asked to nominate six men in the diocese that they could trust and to write those names on a piece of paper. Those names were handed to the Bishop and from them the Bishop chose a team of 24 priests, one of whom was to be the director of the programme, in our case myself.

In October that same year the team and myself went away for two weeks rather intensive training on listening skills, confrontation, and counselling, and I can say that all of us without exception found it a very rewarding experience.

In November all the priests of the diocese were invited to take part in aptitude tests. Perhaps I ought to say that it is these tests which more than anything else alarmed many of the clergy, in fact to my mind their fears were totally groundless. The tests in fact are taken with a view to increasing one's self knowledge on the basis that no-one can move forward spiritually or humanly unless they are aware of where they stand at present. I will come back to the tests in a moment.

In February 1983 82 priests of the diocese took part in the retreats, this in itself was a remarkable achievement in a diocese where the average number of priests attending a retreat had gone down to well below 30. The retreat given by the same Father —— was certainly one of the most enlightening experiences in my own life and of others that I spoke to. At the beginning of the retreat you are presented with the results of your test and here I can only speak for myself. My profile indicated very accurately indeed where I stood intellectually, emotionally, physically, and spiritually. The retreat Father brings with him four assistants and each priest on the retreat has two interviews with an assistant with whom he discusses his profile and what is more to the point what he is going to do about it. One of Fr. ——'s points is that priests on the whole are accountable to nobody and the programme attempts in some form to remedy this. So the first interview with the assistant is assessing your profile in general, the second interview gets down to brass tacks and you make decisions as to what practical steps you are going to take about your intellectual, emotional, physical, and prayer life. At the end of the retreat each man indicates three or more names of those team members that he would feel comfortable with. I then allocate to the team members the names of two or three priests. When the retreat is over the team members will contact their particular clients, if I can use that word, and arrange to meet them within two or three months. I will comment on this later. In the following May all the priests of the diocese were called together again to be presented with a collective diocesan report based on the profiles. This report gives one a very accurate picture of the state of the diocese and indeed the needs of the diocese. On the same day the support groups are set up, they consist of eight to ten priests, who contract to meet together once a month overnight for a particular purpose. In our case we have eight of these support groups and they vary from theatre groups, to prayer groups, to walking groups, to study groups, to recreational groups. Each group is asked to be together, to pray together, to relax together, to celebrate together. That is a fairly general outline of how the programme has operated in our diocese.

Now my own comments on it. I am totally convinced that this programme is worthwhile and perhaps the most valuable aspects of it are the one to one ministry and the support groups. At first sight it may look as if the one to one ministry is rather an awkward and difficult thing to handle but in practice I have found that it is a very useful tool reminding one constantly of the need for growth and reminding one also of the great truths of the prayer life and the need for us as priests to be willingly accountable to someone else who is not a judge but a friend who walks with you. To my mind the whole value of the programme is based on this aspect of it rather than any other. That's not to say that the support groups are not valuable but they operate in a different area. The report stated most clearly that more than anything priests suffer from loneliness and the support groups go a long way to meeting this need especially with some of our more diffident brethren. The support group that I belong to is a very happy one indeed and since we have started we have brought in three other men who voted against the programme in the first place but who now recognise the benefit of being with their brother priests on a regular basis. We are fortunate in our group to have the help of an exceptional religious priest as our resource man. Each month he comes to the group and gives us a lecture on Scripture and this has proved a real benefit to all of us in the group. He himself enjoys it so much that he stays for the meal and overnight with us.

One of the features of the diocesan report was its highlighting of the needs of the priests in the diocese. We in the team had been making an intensive study of these and next week are going away with the bishop for two whole days to suggest ways and means in which these needs can be filled in the diocese.

My chief regret is that there are not more priests in the programme and my observation is that perhaps those who are not in it are those who would benefit from it most of all. Many have refrained from the programme (which thank God is entirely optional) out of fear and dismiss it as an American inspired psychology of the worst sort. I have yet to meet a priest who has been able to sustain this point of view when confronted with the facts. I would like to see the jargon done away with and the title "Ministry to Priests Programme" disappear, and just see it as a way in which the priests of the diocese can be helped to live more authentic, human and spiritual lives, and be of support to one another in so doing. The real basis of the programme is that God loves each one of us and works through our weaknesses. When we learn to accept the love of God and one another, then I confidently believe we are helped in our ministry to people where the need to put up defences is no longer necessary.

Thus far is the verbatim report on the setting up in one diocese of the programme. What is one to make of it? Clearly it is helping a large number of priests, and the scheme is being extended gradually to other dioceses. I do not wish to seem churlish, but I think that it is important to reflect upon its limitations as well. If it is moderately successful it might inhibit the bishops from facing up to far more serious reforms, such as making the basic communities the essential pastoral unit with the married priests that they will need. On the other hand the programme might almost be too successful. If it really does produce growth, the willingness to accept love, the realisation that there is no need to put up defences, and in short the attainment of a more authentic emotional life, then many priests might realise the need for a normal emotional life and seek marriage. By facing up to the inner reality of their personalities they might discover that they have been shielding themselves subconsciously from their authentic sexual needs. Real celibates who have received the grace from God will not be troubled in this manner, but the training of priests in the past contained so much repression that all too many came through to ordination with sexual repression instead of God-given celibacy.

Throughout this chapter, and indeed elsewhere in the book, I have indicated that the law of clerical celibacy is now a serious obstacle to the development of that kind of ministry which the Church's mission requires at the present time. I have left the explicit analysis of the celibacy question until this point because it is not the principal element in the reform of the priest's life and work. If the Church were to leave all the other structures as they are at the moment and insert into them priests who are married, the benefit would not be great. The first priority is the establishment of the basic communities, then comes their requirement of part-time worker priests who will share the laity's way of life, and not inhibit their contribution to the mission. Only when this much is clear, should we admit married men into that form of priestly life.

The process by which the celibates came to have a monopolistic control of the ministry in the Western Church is well known, so I will repeat briefly only the salient points.[29] The infant Church displayed pluralism in this matter as in others, and during the period of the Roman persecutions, priests, bishops and deacons were married or single according to choice. After the persecutions, there was a suggestion at the Council of Nicaea in 325 that the clergy should all be celibate. The principle opponent of this was a monk named Paphnutius who had been imprisoned in the last persecution. His words were so persuasive that the matter was dropped.

The fourth century witnessed the classical writings against sex and marriage which were destined to have great influence in the early medieval period. St Augustine and St Jerome are the best known witnesses of this attitude which when taken to its logical conclusion made normal marriage incompatible with spiritual progress. It was not simply pessimism about sex, but their view of women was such that marriage was not envisaged as a supportive relationship. St Augustine is illuminating on this point.

> The same can be said of the need for solace, if by chance the man would have become weary of solitude. For how much more suitable would it have been for association and conversation if two make friends and dwelt together instead of a man and a woman.[30]

This underlying attitude may explain another practice which is almost incomprehensible to the modern mind, namely marriage without sexual expression. St Leo the Great favoured it, stating that bishops and clergy should not send their wives away when they were ordained, "but must have them as if they had them not, so that the love which is in their unions may be preserved, but the works of marriage cease".[31]

In the early Middle Ages this current of theological thinking was joined by the powerful influence of the monastic life, and the consequences of the growing wealth of the Church. The laity were unwilling to see churches and their lands pass into family control by inheritance from priests to their sons, who would also take holy orders, thus making the church a family preserve. Finally the Gregorian reforms of the eleventh century aimed at separating the clergy to some extent from the laity for the sake of disciplining the Church into a state of greater efficiency and spiritual quality. These were the factors which produced the laws of the First and Second Lateran Councils of 1123 and 1139, by which major orders became a nullifying impediment for marriage, and marriage was a condition invalidating ordination.

Frequent reforming decrees in local Councils during the later Middle Ages, and other episcopal injunctions, suggest that it was difficult to secure the acceptance of these laws. Efforts were made to encourage the clergy to live in communities, since it was realised that a solitary existence has little to commend it. The various orders of Canons Regular resulted from this movement, but nothing could really be done for the rural clergy for whom isolation was inevitable.

The reformation polarised the matter. All the Churches sprang from the Reform adopted married clergy because it is what St Paul's letters envisaged. Unfortunately this hardened the attitude of the Catholics, who in this matter as in liturgy and other questions usually opposed what the Protestants supported. The Council of Trent's seminaries improved the education and general morale of the secular clergy, and also strengthened the practice of celibacy and the separation of the priests from everyday life.

The possibility that the law might be changed was only entertained seriously in the modern period. It is a consequence of the revolution produced by Freud in which sex is now regarded as basically good, and marriage is treated as one path to holiness and not an obstacle to it. The open discussion of the matter reflects the willingness to assess the effectiveness of every aspect of the Church's life which has been a characteristic of our debates since the 1940s. The fact that Vatican II changed the liturgy from Latin to English created a precedent which is relevant. It became clear to most people that if such a venerable practice as the use of Latin could be changed by an administrative decision, then there was nothing to prevent the same thing happening to the law of clerical celibacy which had been with the Latin Church for only half as long as the use of Latin for liturgical purposes.

The Vatican Council presented something of an anomaly on the relationship between priesthood and celibacy. The Decree on the Life and Work of Priests expressed it in these words:

> With respect to the priestly life, the Church has always held in especially high regard perfect and perpetual continence on behalf of the Kingdom of Heaven. . . . It is not indeed demanded by the very nature of the priesthood, as is evident from the practice of the primitive Church, and the tradition of the Eastern Churches. In these Churches in addition to all bishops and those others who by a gift of grace choose to observe celibacy, there also exist married priests of outstanding merit.
>
> While this most sacred Synod recommends ecclesiastical celibacy, it in no way intends to change that different discipline which lawfully prevails in Eastern Churches.[32]

Never had the matter been expressed in such "reductionist" terms. Although it supports the present law, it contains within it the seeds of future change, since no other General Council has stated plainly that the two are not intrinsically connected.

In England the twenty years since the Council can be described as the period of the breakdown in confidence about the law of compulsory celibacy. Many factors have contributed to it. Ecumenism has had its effect, the establishment of the permanent diaconate has removed the taboo separating sex and holy order, but the strongest influences have been the clear sighted study of the bible and Church history. It is

evident from the New Testament that a married clergy was
envisaged as the norm, and the Letters to Timothy and Titus
describe the qualities in a good family man which will qualify
him to lead a eucharistic community. This means that if
ecclesiastical administrators wish to exclude married men
from the ministry the onus of proof lies upon them to bring
forward very strong reasons to curtail a practice which the
Scriptures permit. Such reasons have not been forthcoming,
and this has been the root cause for the massive loss of
confidence in the present legislation. Public opinion has
become favourable to the idea as can be seen from a variety of
surveys. One of the most recent polls was published by
Gallup in July 1983. In the United States 1,326 Catholics over
the aged of 18 were asked: "Would you favour or oppose
allowing Catholic priests to marry and continue to function
as priests?" 58 per cent favoured the proposition, 33 per cent
were opposed to it, and 9 per cent offered no preference.[33]
This is a remarkable result, in view of the fact that it is the
most extreme form in which the matter can be stated.
Admission to the priesthood of men who are already
married, is much easier to accept. Since 1976 a highly
articulate pressure group has been at work in England and
Wales, known as the Movement for the Ordination of
Married Men. It conducts study days, and fosters publications, broadcasts, television interviews, and the dissemination of all relevant information on the matter. It maintains
courteous contact with all the bishops of the region. This
movement received immense encouragement from the hierarchy in 1983 when they made a decision to seek permission
to ordain married convert clergy. The text of their decision is
as follows:

From time to time the Bishops' Conference of England and
Wales has been asked to consider the possibility of petitioning
the Holy See to admit to the priesthood in the Catholic Church
individual convert married clergy. The Conference recognised
that there were precedents for such action in other parts of the
world, and notably in the time of Pius XII.
    At its meeting in April 1983 Conference resolved: "That the
Bishops' Conference with pastoral concern and ecumenical
sensitivity, considers the time is opportune for consideration of
individual applications of married convert clergy for acceptance

as candidates for the priesthood in the Catholic Church."

The Bishops wish to make it clear that:

1) Their decision concerning convert married clergy should in no way weaken the present discipline of the Catholic Church in respect of the celibacy of its clergy.

2) Individual conversions for conscience's sake do not detract in any way from that one aim of the ecumenical movement which is the unity of the Church in one visible and organic whole. The bishops are committed to that aim.

3) Individual cases, admittedly rare, will be handled in the first instance by the local Catholic bishop before consideration by the Conference of Bishops.[34]

The movement received further support in the following year from the 1984 meeting of the National Conference of Priests. A resolution was approved stating that:

> This conference recognises that the aims of the Movement for the Ordination of Married Men are of great pastoral importance for the future of the Church, and it urges that these should be discussed widely both at parish and diocesan level".

It received 57 favourable votes, 8 against, and 7 abstentions.

Because sex is so powerful a factor in human psychology, it is not surprising that the matter should be surrounded by subconscious fears and other ill defined emotional reactions. If we could imitate the pluralism of the infant Church it would put an end to many problems. The supporters of a married clergy have always made it clear that they respect celibacy if it is freely chosen, and envisage a future in which the Church will respect both married and celibate priests. Those who favour celibacy and would compel it upon all aspirants to the priesthood are in a rationally indefensible position, since their own chosen option is not going to be taken from them. Clearly it is an attitude bred of a deep subconscious fear. Such people deserve great patience and reassurance, and we must recognise that it is difficult to reason with them.

Another factor which has been clarified by recent debate is that celibacy or virginity are not sought for their own sake. A monk or nun will accept it as an integral part of the religious way of life, which together with poverty and obedience give witness to the transcendent importance of spiritual and eternal values. It has become clear to most people that community life is the only really satisfactory way in which to enshrine a life devoted to those ideals. The life of a secular priest living literally on his own in a presbytery, has little to commend it, and it can be very damaging to the personality.

The decision which faces the novice in a monastery is a relatively straightforward one. In the years of training he lives already by the pattern of life which will be his for the rest of his life, and the celibate state is an integral part of that total way of life. For the diocesan clergy there are two complications. Life in the seminary bears little resemblance to the pattern of this future work, and the exclusion of marriage has no intrinsic connection with priesthood. It is difficult to make a deliberate choice about two distinct elements which have been linked only by Church law. As a result many priests have made the wrong choice about one item in the package deal, but have discovered it only years after ordination. One simple method could be employed to forestall this dilemma. The student should be invited to reflect seriously and without haste upon this question: "If the Church were to change the law and admit married men to the priesthood as well as celibates, which form of priesthood would you adopt?" The true celibates are only those who would choose it in preference to marriage, when both would be open to them. These are the men in whom we can presume that God's grace has given them the gift of celibacy. If this gift is absent, then Church law cannot supply its absence. Undoubtedly many men have gone through to ordination making a positive choice of priesthood, and tolerating the restriction of celibacy as no more than a condition, rather like the requirement of six years study in a seminary, which has also been of little joy to some of the clergy.

All these disadvantages of compulsory celibacy are now widely appreciated by the laity. My experience as chaplain to the university of London confirmed by supposition that it is also a powerful deterrent keeping talented young men from entering the seminaries. Quite simply they are not convinced that marriage would be harmful to the priestly life, and they cannot see why the Church still excludes married men from the ministry. The maintenance of the present law is doing great harm to the Church by excluding good men from the clergy. But this is not all. In addition to excluding good men from even entering seminaries, and driving out those who discover that they do not possess the grace of celibacy, the present law inflicts considerable damage on the personalities of the priests who stay inside the ranks. To supplement my own observations in the thirty years since I was ordained, I have discussed this section of the book with two very experienced marriage guidance counsellors. I will not disclose their identities but the reader is entitled to know that they met at university, raised a large family, counselled hundreds of people in the CMAC (Catholic Marriage Advisory Council) and are now contented grandparents. We were in agreement on the following points. The isolation and loneliness of the secular clergy frequently causes a man's emotional life to shrink and wither. This has harmful effects on his spiritual life, because the natural and supernatural elements in a person's development cannot be isolated. The early years after ordination are something like a honeymoon when the young priest is buoyed up with the prospect of better things to come. This is fortified by the hope that things will definitely improve when he "gets his own parish". The death of parents, especially the mother, can be something of a crisis for a priest. In old age loneliness becomes debilitating and alcoholism can become a solace in a dangerously large number of cases. History has shown that if heterosexual contact is impossible or prohibited (as in ancient Greece or the navy in the days of long voyages under sail) homosexuality can arise easily. It has become a problem to a significant number of priests in spite of vigilance in the seminaries to exclude homosexuals from ordination. One sign of the degree of dependence upon their mothers, and the unhealthy nature of this dependence has been the nature and sentimentalism of devotion to Our Lady in the immature forms which its takes. Finally there are those cases of priests being arrested and taken to court accused of offences like soliciting in public lavatories. It is painful to mention these tragedies (admittedly rare), but they do occur. These men are undoubtedly more sinned against than sinning. They are the vicitms of a system which has wrecked them as human beings, and one can only speculate at the interior agonies of such personalities who are reduced to those forms of conduct. They deserve more than our sympathy, they deserve a change in this whole system which has eroded their personalities. On this subject I prefer to say no more.

If the priesthood and celibacy were linked on a voluntary basis, all the problems indicated in the last section could be avoided. With the law standing as it does, I have no hesitation in stating that in my opinion it harms the Church and does severe damage to a considerable number of priests who try to live within its limitations. The present Pope's policy of refusing virtually all applications for dispensation is heartless and solves none of the problems.

The atmosphere of heartlessness is manifested too in the juridical procedures of laicisation. If it should happen that a priest is suspended (that is, forbidden to say mass, preach, and administer the sacraments) he is still bound by the prohibition against marrying. In the new Code, canons 291 and 292 declare that he is free of the obligations (such as reciting the breviary each day), but bound by celibacy. The most obvious interpretation of this prescription is that the celibacy is regarded as a punishment for those misdemeanours for which he has been excluded from the active ministry. Spiritual books speak of it as a factor liberating the priest for wholehearted devotion to his parochial work. The suspension removes the positive justification and yet the law keeps him within its restrictions, for no apparent benefit, except presumably to punish him.

In the past, one frequently heard the claim that celibate priests were ideal missionaries because they could go to remote lands and live in primitive conditions without the encumberance of a wife and children. In fact the situation is much more complicated. Financially it would be very expensive to maintain families in the style to which they are accustomed, but if a priest lives alone, isolated from other men of his own culture, his personality can suffer seriously. Rather disturbing forms of eccentricity can arise. If the missionaries can live in communities they will be spared this, but the comparative fewness of priests in relation to the people to be served and the distances which must be covered make this impossible in most rural areas. Rural isolation and shortage of priests mean that the people sometimes have to walk round journeys of fifteen miles or more for Sunday mass. In times of drought and famine they are sometimes too weak, physically, to undertake such a journey, and to expect it of them would be callous. Moreover there is something artificial in requiring the people to leave their own villages which have a strong sense of community in order to assist at mass in a place where they have no natural ties. The development of a native clergy in African is retarded in many places simply because of the requirement of celibacy. Family tradition is so strong that the celibate ideal has little appeal. Zimbabwe may serve as a useful example. In one diocese there were 2 African priests in 1982, and 20 European missionaries. They were assisted by 70 catechists, and between them they cared for more than 34,000 Catholics in a region of 56,000 square kilometres. The task of the priests was almost impossible. One simple expedient could solve all the difficulties, namely to ordain the catechists, so that they can say mass, give the sacraments, and generally create christian communities in the peoples' own villages.

In the years since the Council various episcopal conferences have requested permission from the Vatican to ordain married men.[35] The Pope and the authorities in Rome generally have shown themselves unwilling and uncomprehending of the needs of the Church in general. For example when Archbishop Justinus Darmojuwono of Semarang in Indonesia returned from his *ad limina* visit to Rome in 1980 he made the following statement:

If the Eucharist is to be the centre of our lives, we must ordain married men. It is as simple as that. There is no other way we in Indonesia can have enough priests to allow people to attend mass regularly . . . Most bishops I know are in favour of married priests, but it is Rome that is not ready.[36]

Another example comes from Zambia. In 1968 the Episcopal Conference agreed to ask the Roman authorities for permission to ordain married men to the priesthood. The Roman decision was communicated to them in a letter from the Apostolic Pre-Nuncio in Lusaka which contained the following sentences:

> I have been asked to request the most reverend Ordinaries of
> Zambia to abstain from discussing in any way the priestly celibacy as
> it is observed in the Latin Church, and to weigh its value in con-
> formity with the living tradition of the Church and its constant
> teaching, as it has recently been re-affirmed by the second Vatican
> Council and declared in the Encyclical *Sacerdotalis Celibatus*. Finally
> the same ordinaries are requested to see to it, with wisdom and firm-
> ness, that any taking a stand which, in any form or under any pre-
> text, would call into question priestly celibacy, should be stopped.[37]

In addition to the condescending tone of the letter, both
incidents are deplorable. They reveal the insensitivity of the
Roman authorities to the extent of this problem, and their
inflexibility.

There are very few parts of the Church where there are
sufficient priests for an adequate maintenance of the Church's
pastoral work, and even in those places the clergy would be
enriched by having the qualities and experience which only
married men could bring to the priesthood. Elsewhere the
shortage of priests is so acute that the laity are suffering obvious
spiritual deprivation by the lack of mass, sacraments, and other
forms of pastoral care. The preservation of a merely ecclesiastical
rule has taken precedence over all other consideration. A man-
made institution which should serve the well-being of the
mission, has become an end in itself, and the needs of the laity
have become subservient to its preservation. I have no hesitation
in saying that this is extremely damaging to the Church. What is
peculiarly tragic in this instance is that the remedy would be so
simple; it would not require a lengthy programme of education,
the construction of costly buildings, or any other laborious task,
like the composition of new music to accompany the English
liturgy—it could be achieved by the stroke of a pen.

POSTSCRIPT

Much of what has been said in this chapter could apply to the
ordination of women. There seems to be no theological
objection to it. The fact that the Church has not done so in the
past is not a serious problem. Other innovations have been
made by the Church like the creation of religious orders which
are not commanded by the scriptures. The crucial consideration would have to be whether particular communities wanted
them as their eucharistic ministers.

CHAPTER NINE

Diocese As Co-ordinator

In the course of its history the Church has not found it easy to determine the optimum size of a diocese, nor has it been simple to delineate its function and decide what should be left with the parish and what should be taken over by a still larger region. By contrast the parish has settled down to a relatively clear function for more than a millenium, namely that of being the normal eucharistic community for the laity. This function has imposed some kind of uniformity on its size, and variations occur mainly on account of the different densities of population in rural or urban areas.

The diocese has not been able to define its functions with comparable clarity, and as a result its size and structure has varied. For example, in Italy, the diocese of Milan is about one hundred times as large in area and population as the small dioceses of Calabria in the south, although they are all of about the same age. Is it necessary or desirable that a diocese should train its own clergy, and should it therefore conduct its own seminary? Is it desirable that its frontiers should coincide with the administrative regions of the nation? In France the dioceses are coterminous with the nation's Departments, but that was at Napoleon's initiative.

Vatican II made important clarifications about the role of bishops, but said little about the practicalities of organisation. This fact should not worry us unduly. It would have been well within the competence of the post-Conciliar Church to have made any necessary changes. In fact neither at the theoretical nor the practical level have we seen the fulfilment of the expectations raised by the Council as far as dioceses are concerned.

For the diocese, the concept of collegiality was the most important theological contribution of the Council, but as it will not have immediate practical repercussions on the lives of the laity I will postpone the consideration of it until I have dealt with the matters of more immediate concern to the lay person.

Vatican II and the New Code of Canon Law are in agreement on one important principle, namely no effective level of command is established between the bishop and the parish. This means that all the major decisions will be referred to the bishop, and in this respect the post-Conciliar Church cannot expect more efficient dioceses than we had before Vatican II. With this implied presupposition, the Council is rather vague about the size and structure of the diocese when it says:

> For a diocese to fulfil its purpose, the nature of the Church must be clearly evident to the People of God who belong to that diocese. Likewise bishops must be able to carry out their pastoral duties effectively among their people. Finally the welfare of the People of God must be served as perfectly as possible.[1]

This is not very helpful, and the rest of that section does not become notably more specific. In severely practical terms one can say that a diocese must co-ordinate the parishes, and undertake large-scale tasks which they are too small to discharge, like, perhaps, the training of priests. This consideration yields one clear consequence. If the diocese is too large the bishop will not be able to know the priests and laity, and still less will he be able to work with them. If it is too small it will not be able to take up the kind of large scale operations that are beyond the capabilities of a parish. Personal acquaintance with the laity will always be a problem, but a realistic working relationship with the clergy is not only desirable, but strongly insisted on by the Council:

> A bishop should always welcome priests with a special love since they assume in part the bishop's duties and cares and carry the weight of them day by day so zealously. He should regard his priests as sons and friends. Thus by his readiness to listen to them and by his trusting familiarity, a bishop can work to promote the whole pastoral work of the entire diocese. He should be concerned about the spiritual, intellectual and material condition of his priests, so that they can live holy and pious lives and fulfil their ministry faithfully and fruitfully.[2]

The Code of Canon Law echoes the same sentiments:

> He (the bishop) is to have a special concern for the priests, to whom he is to listen as his helpers and counsellors. He is to defend their rights and ensure that they fulfil the obligations proper to their state. He is to see that they have the means and the institutions needed for the development of their spiritual and intellectual life. He is to ensure that they are provided with adequate means of livelihood and social welfare, in accordance with the law. (Canon 384).

To determine mathematically the number of priests whose lives and work can be co-ordinated efficiently by one bishop is notoriously difficult. Possibly about one hundred, possibly as few as fifty. Experience shows that the appointment of auxiliaries does not really help because they do not have the power of final decision. In relation to the ideal of a working partnership indicated by the Council and the Code, one can say that most of the dioceses in England are too large. If they are to be made smaller, then another consideration becomes relevant. It is necessary to avoid the sense of claustrophobia which would be depressing for the priests who would have to spend the whole of their working life in a circumscribed region. The answer to this problem is simple, because the Anglicans have practised it for a long time, namely the priests must be allowed to move from one diocese to another. Unfortunately the Code of Canon Law still envisages transfer to another diocese as an exceptional administrative measure,[3] but there is no serious theological reason against such a change. It is sometimes alleged that it would weaken the sense of team spirit in the diocese. In reply I would like to cite the rather loosely structured body of chaplains to universities. These priests are drawn from all the dioceses and many religious orders, they meet only once a year for a five day conference, yet I found in that body a stronger *esprit de corps* than I did in the two dioceses in which I worked.

In spite of the theoretical difficulties involved in trying to determine the optimum size of a diocese, one must make some attempt to arrive at a practical solution. In the first place one must be reconciled to the fact that no matter how small the diocese was made, it would not be possible for the bishop to know all the laity personally. The only feasible working partnership to aim at is that of the bishop and priests, and it is important to plan a diocese which is small enough to permit that relationship to operate efficiently.

The National Conference of Priests urged smaller dioceses and the hierarchy set up a working party to study the matter in 1966. They presented their *Groundplan* to the bishops in 1974.[4] The document shows that in 1851 there were 13 dioceses and on 30 March that year a little over 240,000 Catholics attended mass. (That survey was of particular value because it was commanded by the government, and was taken in churches of all denominations. Unfortunately it has never been repeated on a national scale.) By 1973 the mass attendance on 6 May was a little over 1,825,000 (*Groundplan*, p. 9). This is an increase of 7 to 1, and on that basis we should have 91 dioceses. In fact there were 19 in 1973, subsequently increased to 21 by the creation of East Anglia and Hallam. *Groundplan* suggests that the existing dioceses should be increased to 37, on the basis of having no fewer than 80,000 lay people and no more than 150,000 or 200,000 (*Groundplan*, p. 2). No reason is given for these figures, and they seem somewhat arbitrary, bearing no relation to the original numbers in 1851 nor to the number of dioceses which would be needed if the 1851 proportion had been adhered to up to the present.

Personally I feel that four principles must be borne in mind if we are to plan the size and number of dioceses properly. Firstly the criteria are bound to be somewhat arbitrary, secondly the natural groupings (like cities) vary considerably, flexibility will be needed whereby urban dioceses may have more people than rural ones. Thirdly, they should share central administrative offices. This is the easiest stage in the whole process. If a large diocese with 150 parishes were split into three smaller regions, then the office and staff could still deal with the same 150 parishes, since their re-grouping would introduce only minor variations into the work. Fourthly the numerical basis of division must be calculated according to the number of priests with whom one bishop could work. If I suggest 50 secular priests as an arbitrary figure, it would yield approximately 90 dioceses as there are 4,465 secular priests in England and Wales in 1984. Dioceses of this size would be much smaller than even the smallest of the existing dioceses, but it would allow for an increase in the number of married worker priests about whom I wrote in the previous chapter. Clearly these dioceses would have to be grouped into larger regions under metropolitans, and thence into the national Episcopal Conference. This system of grouping above the diocesan level would present no inherent problem. In the past the Church has developed that level of groupings more successfully than subdivisions within dioceses.

In addition to co-ordinating the priests, a diocese ought to undertake the tasks for which a parish is too small. It is instructive to examine how far this area of work has been encouraged in the last twenty years. It was presumably to stimulate work of this kind that the Vatican Council urged the creation of diocesan pastoral councils.[5] Their establisment was not commanded absolutely, but the new Code of Canon Law repeated the strong recommendation: "In each diocese, in so far as pastoral circumstances suggest, a pastoral council is to be established . . ." (Canon 511). The Code stressed especially the role of the laity therein: "A pastoral council is composed of members of Christ's faithful who are in full communion with the Catholic Church: clerics, members of institutes of consecrated life, and especially lay people." (Canon 512). In spite of this strong encouragement it is difficult to explain why only six of the dioceses of England and Wales had established them by 1984. An example of work which might best be undertaken at diocesan level is the whole area of Justice and Peace. Its ramifications are considerable, and in the course of its work the people involved might well collaborate with the race relations Councils, or national peace movements like CND. This area of activity has the advantage that it is clearly furthering the Kingdom of God, and is not simply a matter of domestic concern to Catholics. Unaccountably it remains relatively underdeveloped even after twenty years, and only nine dioceses in England and Wales have Justice and Peace commissions.

With adult education the position is somewhat better. By now nearly every diocese has a residential pastoral centre of some kind which can cater for retreats, study courses, residential training for youth groups or schools' parties also. Thousands of people have passed through them since the

Council and they have played a major part in re-educating the laity. Clearly it is a task which scarcely any parish could undertake, and even if a large parish did possess a suitable centre for it, there is an important advantage in actually going to stay in another place for a few days. The participants go through a psychological re-adjustment by which they forget about their day-to-day preoccupations, and devote greater attention to the course than they could if they were on home territory.

There has been a suggestion that adult education might vivify a whole diocese and make up for the inevitable limitations of the parish organisation. It is a scheme which has been pioneered in Australia and New Zealand, and which is envisaged as a pastoral solution to many problems, such as the drop of mass attendance to 15 per cent of known Catholics in some parishes.[6] A writer has traced the development of one such scheme in an Australian diocese whose name I will withhold in this book.[7]

> In March 1981 the archbishop set up a task force to launch a study of the people's needs and the recommendation was that the archdiocese should undertake a programme of pastoral renewal. In June 1982 a combined meeting of the Senate of Priests and the Diocesan Pastoral Council supported this. The archbishop formally accepted the recommendations. His two goals were:
>   a) Renewal in faith for the people of the diocese.
>   b) A creative review of the diocesan structures and use of resources.
> In January 1983 he appointed a director of the programme (a layman with much experience in this field in the diocese) whose basic aim is to help people to integrate their faith into their life. In August 1983 they published a pamphlet entitled *Towards a Vision of Renewal*. In January 1984, 36 people undertook a leadership course lasting for a long week-end, and subsequently gave the same course to 450 people. Between June and December 1984 it was planned to explore the needs, concerns, questions, hopes, etc., of the people; and in this way to deepen the diocese's understanding of society. And after that what? Some at least see themselves in a no man's land at present.[8]

I am not surprised that they find themselves in no man's land. Without wishing to belittle their sincerity and hard work, I cannot refrain from observing that their whole methodology is mis-directed. They should first have examined the Church's objectives in relation to their society, then measured the attainment of them by the existing structures. If the existing apparatus was found to be inadequate they should have devised alternative experimental institutions and only then start to educate the laity within the new structures and when they were clear about the goals to be pursued. As it is the statements of intention amount to little more than platitudes, or else they were the kind of appeals for spiritual renewal which might have been made even if the Vatican Council had not taken place. But above all, one detects the reluctance to recast the structures radically. There is the implied desire to optimise the performance of the existing structures.

The writer in the *Clergy Review* indicated rightly that for adult education the parish was probably too small, and in other ways an unsuitable unit to serve as a base for the operation. There are other activities too in the Church's mission for which the parish is either too small or wrongly structured. I suggest that a successful activity on a scale larger than that of a parish needs some careful structuring, it will need to utilise the skills and personnel at parish level, yet somehow take them out of the limitations of the parish. Let us keep to the example of adult education. The staging of a large scale programme and the required lecturers would be beyond the capability of a parish. What about the deanery then? It would work if it had the consent of all the parish priests. Under present law, the parish priest could forbid it in his own parish. If one priest or layman in the deanery had been seconded with special responsibility for this work, he would still be powerless against the veto of an unco-operative parish priest.

The only satisfactory way to circumvent this problem is to overhaul the parish structure completely. Towns of the size of Cambridge, Bedford or Ipswich could be treated as one pastoral unit, in which the priests would be of equal rank regardless of seniority. They could be given special responsibilities within the town, one for adult education for example, another priest for ecumenism, another priest for youth work and so on. This means that in response to an initiative from the bishop the priest for adult education could organise the whole town without having to obtain the consent of the various territorial parish priests (since they would no longer be functioning in that manner and with those powers). In rural areas something similar could be organised. The principles would be the same; the only difference would be the geographical distribution, which would impose its own limitations on the work. This kind of scheme would also have the advantage that if the bishop wished to plan youth work, for example, for the whole diocese he would have to summon only those priests who held this specialist responsibility. It would be a vast improvement on the present system which requires that all parish priests are competent in all spheres, and have the power to block activities of which they disapprove.

One of the most important theological achievements of the Council was the re-affirmation of collegiality. Basically it means that the bishops collectively have a measure of joint responsibility for the whole Church. In the Decree on the Church it was expressed in the following words:

> Just as by the Lord's will, St Peter and the other apostles constituted one apostolic college, so in a similar way the Roman Pontiff as the successor of Peter, and the bishops as the successors of the apostles are joined together. The collegial nature and meaning of the episcopal order found expression in the very ancient practice by which bishops appointed the world over were linked with one another and with the Bishop of Rome by the bonds of unity, charity, and peace; also in the conciliar assemblies which made common judgements about more profound matters in decisions reflecting the views of many. The ecumenical councils held through the centuries clearly attest this collegial aspect. And it is suggested also in the practice, introduced in ancient times of summoning several bishops to take part in the elevation of someone newly elected to the ministry of the high priesthood. Hence one is constituted a member of the episcopal body by virtue of sacramental consecration and by hierarchical communion with the head and members of the body . . . The order of bishops is the successor to the college of the apostles in teaching authority and pastoral rule; or, rather, in the episcopal order the apostolic body continues without a break.[9]

An interesting example of this consciousness of being responsible for the whole Church can be seen in the second century. When the heresy of Gnosticism threatened the Church the bishops exchanged letters, several of which have survived, to check with one another about the traditional teaching of the Church. It was a fairly slow process, but they established a world-wide consensus, on the basis of which they repudiated the theories of the Gnostics. In the fourth and fifth centuries the heresies were more dangerous and something swifter was needed; hence the General Councils. However it is useful to reflect that the doctrinal competence and the responsibility which goes with it, are not specifically different in the two methods of operation.

The Decree on Bishops repeat what was stated by *Lumen Gentium* concerning the insertion of a new bishop into that college: "By virtue of sacramental consecration, and hierarchical communion with the head and other members of the college, a bishop becomes a part of the episcopal body."[10] It was important to spell it out, because prior to the Council, some theologians taught that jurisdiction came to the bishops directly from the Pope as if they were something like his deputies.

It is agreed by all that collegiality expresses itself in the Church's General Councils, but apart from those gatherings, is there any institutionalised form for this activity to assume? Unless collegiality can be expressed in some practical form there is a danger that it will lie dormant, or be superseded by something else. Many people hoped that the Synods of Bishops would fulfil this role. The plan was announced in 1965, and provided for meetings of a small but representative number of bishops deliberating with the Pope on Church matters. In practice the crucial factor is whether or not they have a deliberative vote as in General Councils. The official document which inaugurated the Synods left the matter open.[11]

> By its very nature it is the task of the Synod of Bishops to inform and give advice. It may also have deliberate power when such power is conferred by the Sovereign Pontiff, who will in such cases confirm the decisions of the Synod.

So it depends upon the Pope whether or not their meetings will rise above the level of advice, and in practice it is a

question of how seriously he listens to them. It is the opinion
of one commentator on Vatican affairs that this is not real
collegiality.[12]

However the notion of collegiality is not excluded from
their deliberations. When Pope Paul VI was opening the
Synod of 1969 he said:

> Remembering that the episcopate is the true successor of the
> apostles and that they for their part formed a particular group,
> chosen and willed by Christ, it has seemed a happy thing to take
> up once more the concept and term collegiality, applying it to
> the order of Bishops.[13]

Possibly we will have to wait some more years for the idea of
collegiality to find its appropriate expression and organs of
operation. The publication of the new Code of Canon Law in
1983 stressed that the real power rested with the Pope, and
did not indicate any more flexibility by which it might better
epitomise the concept of collegiality. Canon 343 expressed it
in these words:

> It pertains to the synods of bishops to discuss the questions
> under examination and to express their wishes, not however to
> decide the matters, nor to pass laws about them, unless the
> Roman Pontiff should confer deliberate power in certain cases,
> in which case it would be for him to ratify the decisions of the
> Synod.

Meanwhile the theologian J. Tillard has summed up the
situation in these words: "The structures of collegiality and
ministerial subsidiarity have not yet been set up with the
clarity required by the fundamental insights of *Lumen
Gentium*."[14]

So far there have been five international Synods in Rome,
the last being in 1980. They have been of uneven quality.
That of 1971 dealt with international justice and eventually
published an interesting document.[15] The Synod in 1980 on
marriage and the family was something of a disappointment,
since it offered no substantial theological elucidation of the
birth-control dispute. Nothing was offered which could
engender serious conviction that contraception should be
regarded as morally wrong.

If the Roman Synods have been something of a disappointment in the wake of the revalidation of the concept of collegiality, regional developments have been very encouraging. The episcopal conference of the United States has published its remarkable doctrinal statement about war and peace, and two more such statements are in the course of preparation. In Latin America, still larger meetings, namely of the whole episcopal body of that sub-continent, have held the well-known plenary meetings at Medellin and Puebla which produced the documents which I have referred to earlier in this book. There can be no doubt of the value which those two declarations have contributed to the apostolate in Latin America, particularly in the development of liberation theology and basic communities. So although the Roman Synods have not yet fulfilled the hopes which have been focused on the concept of collegiality, elsewhere there are signs of optimism for the future.

When writing about collegiality, Jean Tillard mentioned another important concept, that of subsidiarity. He lamented that the appropriate structures had not yet been set up. As far as Great Britain is concerned there are indications of a reverse tendency. Not only is the exercise of subsidiarity conspicuously absent, but small matters of Church business which are clearly within the competence of the local bishops are unaccountably referred to Rome for decisions. The simplest example concerns Friday penance. *The Tablet* for 8 December 1984 contained the following extraordinary announcement:

> Catholics in England Wales will not have to abstain from meat on Fridays under new rules laid down by the Bishops' Conference. When official approval has been received from the Vatican, the English and Welsh bishops are expected to announce requirements similar to those recently introduced in Scotland.

A previous public notice earlier in the year indicated that the hierarchy had discussed the matter of Friday self-denial at the Low week meeting in April 1984, and had sought permission from Rome to implement their decisions. From the standpoint of business management it is extraordinary that so

small a matter should have to be referred to the Church's
highest authority for confirmation, or simple permission
From the theological point of view it is a serious diminutior
of bishops' normal responsibilities if the officials at the
Vatican consider them incompetent to make these relatively
small decisions, or worse still if they choose to reserve such
matters to themselves, regardless of the bishops' competence. The same pattern of quite unnecessary centralisation is
to be seen in the process by which a convert married
clergyman can be admitted to ordination in the Catholic
Church. Once again I will quote a letter published in *The
Tablet* because a letter there expresses the matter succinctly.'
It was written in answer to another letter on the same subject

> Sir, I read with interest Archbishop Law's letter explaining the
> process to which a married convert seeking the priesthood must
> admit. Searching scrutiny of the diocesan bishop's detailed
> examination by the Congregation for the Doctrine of the Faith
> then, if it gets past them, further scrutiny by the Holy Father.
> with whom the decision lies.
> I wish, however, that the archbishop had also explained why
> the man, already chosen and appointed by the Pope to rule the
> diocese, cannot be trusted to act upon his own judgement in
> such a matter. (The name and address were published.)

Once again a straightforward matter of pastoral responsibility
has been taken out of the hands of the local bishops. There is
no good reason why this should happen, it simply weakens
the position of the bishops, and removes the decision-making
to superiors who have probably no experience of the region
The practice is also bad for ecumenical relations. It is a
powerful disincentive for episcopally governed Churches
who are justifiably apprehensive that if they were united with
the Catholic Church their bishops would lose a substantia
part of their rightful responsibilities.

The most recent and saddest example of the Vatican's
direct involvement of matters which would better have been
left to the local bishops to decide, is the fate of the four priest
working in the government of Nicaragua. Four priests have
held office in that government: Fr Ernesto Cardenal and hi
brother Fr Fernando, Fr Edgar Parrales, and Fr Migue

d'Escoto. All have have been ordered to give up their political positions. Although this may be a laudable rule for normal circumstances it is arguable that the situation in Nicaragua is so exceptional that an exception should have been made for them. The real difficulty for those who take seriously the concept of the episcopate is that once again Rome has intervened in what ought to be within the competence of the local hierarchy. Fr Fernando Cardenal has expressed his own opinion forcefully, but without bitterness:

> The one who has categorically refused to grant an exception to the priests in Nicaragua so that they might continue working in the revolutionary Government has been Pope John Paul II. It hurts me to say this, but as a Christian I cannot keep quiet. [17]

The reaffirmation of the importance of the episcopate in Vatican II might have led one to hope that a more imaginative method might have been found for the appointment of bishops. The Conciliar statement on the matter did not reserve it to the Popes, but to the Church, in these words:

> Since the apostolic office of bishops was instituted by Christ the Lord and serves a spiritual and supernatural purpose, this most sacred Ecumenical Synod declares that the right of nomination and appointing bishops belongs properly, peculiarly, and of itself exclusively to the competent ecclesiastical authority. [18]

The rest of the paragraph indicates that the Church wished to bring to an end those concordats with governments which had conceded to them the right of nominating bishops. In the last twenty years a number of such concordats, notably that with Spain, have been altered to give the Church the competence to nominate bishops.

The fact that the Conciliar statement did not stipulate the Pope but said simply "competent ecclesiastical authority" is significant. The Code of Canon Law in 1918 had reserved all such appointments, in principle to the Pope, and practically every bishop at the Second Vatican Council would have been appointed under that system. Was the Church being prepared for a new method which was less centralised? Whatever may have been in the minds of the bishops, the new Code of Canon Law gave little encouragement, because it states simply: "The supreme Pontiff shall freely nominate bishops, or confirm those who have been legitimately elected." (Canon 377, section 1).

For the last half century the appointment of bishops has displayed the characteristics of all large bureaucracies, namely the selection of men whose principal characteristics would be predictable conformity to the wishes of the Vatican, regardless of other qualities of leadership. In 1972 the Curia showed that it was aware of some disquiet, and they published the document *Norms for the Appointment of Bishops*, after which there has been a measure of consultation before the nomination of a new bishop. When the See falls vacant, both laity and clergy are invited to express their wishes about the kind of candidate who would be suitable, or about names which they might wish to put forward. However, since the whole process takes place in secret, there is no guarantee that the views of clergy and laity are taken into consideration, and in recent years there has been mounting cynicism about the usefulness of the exercise.

The conscious quest for safe men has taken a turn for the worse in recent years, since it appears that for the most important bishoprics in the Church, the most conservative candidates are being selected, regardless of local wishes. The recent appointment of an archbishop in Dublin illustrates the tensions, and the process has been well documented. By September 1984 it was apparent that the selection of an archbishop had come up against some difficulties. *The Tablet* reported it thus:

> A number of priests in Dublin have written to the Papal Nuncio, Archbishop Aldobrandini, to express their concern over the appointment of a successor to Archbishop Ryan. Archbishop Ryan left Dublin earlier this month to take up his duties as pro-prefect of the Congregation for the Evangelisation of Peoples. His message of farewell has been read in all the parishes, his name has been dropped from the canon and an administrator has taken charge of the diocese. The archbishop has therefore conclusively gone, notwithstanding the intention which he stated last April of remaining at his post until he had been replaced. The widespread suspicion that the appointment is deadlocked would therefore appear to be confirmed. Anxiety has been growing among the clergy. Some believe that the delay and the impenetrable secrecy

must conceal procedures very much at variance with what they thought was the norm. They have accordingly requested Rome through the nunciature to initiate a fresh poll of the priests of the diocese so that the Holy See may be left in no doubt regarding at least one important element of local opinion. They consider their suggestion to be reasonable because it stresses procedure rather than personalities. Its only purpose they argue, is to ensure that a prudent due process is seen to be implemented and its outcome weighed in the balance.[19]

Two months later it was announced that Dr Kevin McNamara, the bishop of Derry had been nominated as archbishop of Dublin. Of him *The Tablet* (24 November) made the preliminary observation:

Bishop McNamara, 58 years of age, is a native of County Clare in the west of Ireland and is noted for the conservatism of his theological opinions. Initial reaction in Ireland to the appointment sees it as a rebuff to the clergy of Dublin, whose wishes appear to have been overruled.

A week later *The Tablet* contained a detailed analysis of the process[20] of which I reproduce some extracts:

Archbishop McNamara takes up his new office in the certain knowledge that most of his clergy did not want an "outsider" appointed and that quite a number specifically did not want this outsider . . . While Archbishop McNamara may be judged to be a victim of the process as much as any one else, it has to be said that the appointment and the manner in which it was arrived at give cause for serious alarm. The Church in Dublin is a Church in crisis, marked by all the urban ills of inner-city squalor, a generation-gap, tensions in the suburbs, unemployment, drug addiction, permissive materialism and lapsing from religious practice. With 800 priests and 4 auxiliary bishops serving its million Catholics, it seems extraordinary that a pastor acquainted with the special problems and needs of the city, and responsive to them, could not have been chosen from within the clergy of the diocese . . . The question immediately arises: what particular qualities does Kevin McNamara display which might not readily be duplicated within the existing body of priests in Dublin? The answer is that he represents the extreme right wing of conservatism in the Irish hierarchy . . . Since his commitment to a rigid orthodoxy restrictively interpreted is Archbishop

McNamara's distinctive characteristic, it has to be assumed that it was for this that the Pope appointed him to Dublin . . . What it implies for Dublin, is, sadly that the opinions of the dedicated clergy of the Irish metropolis were set aside in favour of a few very different voices of a small group of well-placed churchmen and reactionary laity whose identities we can only guess at—but with fair accuracy. It is deplorable and bodes ill for the credibility of the Church, especially among the youth of Dublin and Ireland.

Recent appointments of this kind are merely a more extreme form of what has gone before, namely the selection of safe men whose conservatism has apparently been their chief qualification. It is depressing to contemplate the possibilities of such a method of filling the Church's vacant dioceses. However it carries with it a measure of frankly crude self rectification. It is said, in another context, that nature cannot be abused indefinitely for it will take its own revenge. Something similar applies to truth, and can be seen when objective criteria are not observed in the selection of bishops. The situation has arisen where more and more bishops have been appointed for their predictable conformity to the Vatican's wishes and other qualities of leadership have been neglected. (For instance a glance at the *Catholic Directory* for England and Wales will indicate that half the bishops have not had a university education.) When the Holy See needed very positive qualities of leadership from these men, they were unable to rise to the demands of the situation. I refer to the birth-control controversy which arose in the wake of the encyclical *Humanae Vitae* in 1968. In most countries, certainly in those where surveys have been conducted, the bishops proved incapable of enforcing the Pope's wishes. They were unable to inspire the necessary confidence, and carry conviction among the laity and priests, with the result that the encyclical has been defied blatantly, as no other Papal document had been in the past. In a situation like this which required positive qualities of leadership, the safe men proved inadequate to the task, and the Vatican officials had none but themselves to blame.

The quest for a satisfactory method of appointing bishops has been a perpetual problem in the history of the Church. The situation at the present is as favourable as the Church could wish for, since we are more free of political interference than at any other time in the last millenium. The present pattern of selection of bishops goes back about 150 years and has been shaped by the situation when the Church was rebuilding its shattered organisation after the French revolutionary wars. In 1832 Rosmini published his book which was translated as *The Five Wounds of the Church*.[21] Half the book was devoted to "The Wound in the Right Foot", which he took to be the symbol of harmful methods for the appointment of bishops. At that time there were in the Church 646 ordinary bishops of whom 555 were appointed by civil governments, kings, noble families or some form of lay patronage, 67 were selected by Cathedral chapters, and 24 were nominated directly by the Pope.[22] Rosmini was adamant that the Church should regain control of episcopal appointments, but he did not wish the Pope to take it over from the civil powers. He favoured local elections, but the trend of theology combined with the accidents of history thrust it all into the control of the Pope. The reunification of Italy in 1870 gathered into the hands of King Victor Emmanuel's government the patronage of all the Italian Sees which had hitherto been divided among more than half a dozen royal houses. That government had no wish to control the episcopal nominations and literally dumped the responsibility on the Pope who tacitly accepted it in the arrangement of 1871, known as "the unspoken compromise". This put into the control of the Pope the filling of 237 dioceses. It also served as a precedent for France. In 1905 the separation of Church and State was decreed and the French government relinquished the right of episcopal appointments which it had acquired in the concordat with Napoleon. It is conceivable that the process could have been entrusted to election by cathedral chapters, but the current of theology was then running in a strongly centralising direction. The first Vatican Council in 1870 had defined that the Pope had supreme jurisdiction over the whole Church, and it was in conformity with the spirit of that decree that Pope Pius X took it upon himself thenceforward to nominate bishops in France as the dioceses fell vacant. In view of the immediate past, it is not surprising that the Code of Canon Law promulgated in 1918 gave to the Pope the competence to nominate bishops throughout the universal Church.

Having lived with this system of episcopal appointments for more than half a century, and considering the most recent extremes of augmenting the Papal power by selecting really conservative men, one is entitled to ask whether the best interests of the Church are really served by this method. It seems reasonable to look for a method which will ensure that a bishop will be thoroughly cognisant of local needs. Obviously this qualification is not in conflict with his loyalty to the universal Church and to the Pope, but it does mean that the pastoral problems of the local diocese will be the first consideration in the selection of a bishop. For this kind of selection to work properly it seems inevitable that it must be based on some sort of local election. It would be desirable to associate the laity with the process, but the sheer numbers might make it difficult. Certainly the priests of the diocese should all have a vote. I will not go into exact details of how an elective process might be worked out. It is bound to have some disadvantages, but in principle it would seem to be the most satisfactory method. It is also the method which was universally employed in antiquity before the Church came under the influence of the christian Roman emperors, and later of other christian kings.

One further refinement could be envisaged from the modern world which the ancients would not have approved of. In antiquity the process of transferring bishops from one diocese to another was strongly discouraged, if not forbidden. With the passage of time that concept of permanence has been discarded and translations are now comparatively common. The principle could therefore be extended so that a bishop would be appointed for a limited period, say ten years, for example. I suggest that figure because experience indicates that what a man has not achieved in ten years he never will achieve, and it is a period of time long enough for him to bring to fruition a constructive policy even if it entailed considerable organisational innovations. At the end of ten years he could resume other work with as little fuss as do the provincial superiors of religious orders at the end of their pre-determined period of office. It is edifying to note that the former Bishop of Brentwood is once again a parish priest in London after completing ten years in that diocese.

Epilogue

As I was nearing the end of the text of this book, it was
announced from Rome that in November 1985 the Pope will
hold a Synod of bishops to reflect upon the implementation
of the Council's Decrees, and to survey the twenty years
since the end of Vatican II. This seems therefore an
appropriate time to offer to the laity and clergy of Great
Britain this modest volume to stimulate discussion on the
results which have so far accrued from the Council, and to
encourage those who have the authority to ensure that yet
more of its great promise may be translated into practice to
improve still more the mission of the Church.

Notes

INTRODUCTION

1. John Adair, *The Becoming Church*, London 1977, pages 36–38.
2. Adair, page 36; and *Whitaker's Almanack*, 1974, page 486.
3. M. Hornsby-Smith and R. M. Lee, *Roman Catholic Opinion*, University of Surrey 1979, page 33.
4. *The Tablet*, 13 October 1984, page 1010.
5. *Whitaker's Almanack*, 1984, page 469 ff.
6. M. Hornsby-Smith and R. M. Lee, *op. cit.*, page 106.
7. The literature on this subject is too vast to quote in full. One of the most important works is the Brandt Report, pubished as *North, South*, London 1980. See especially pages 32 and 103.
8. P. Arrupe, as reported by the Swiss news agency KIPA, 27 September 1965. (Author italics.)
9. E. P. Thompson, *The Making of the English Working Class*, London 1980, page 375.
10. M. J. Congar, *Vraie et Fausse Réforme dans l'Eglise*, Paris 1950.
11. *Bishops' Conference of England and Wales: The Review of Its Structures and Procedures*, Catholic Information Services, 1983. This designates them as "Bodies", paragraph 18, page 18, and supplies no other title.
12. The account of these events is recorded in D. A. Winstanley, *Early Victorian Cambridge*, Cambridge 1955, pages 218 and 220.

CHAPTER ONE *The Church's Mission*

1. B. C. Butler, *Searchings*, London 1974, page 260.
2. A. Dulles, *Models of the Church*, Dublin 1976. I have drawn extensively from this book in this section.
3. Denziger-Schönmetzer, *Enchiridion Symbolorum*, Edition 33, 1965, numbers 3050–3075.
4. Dulles, page 35.
5. Extracts from the encyclical *Casti Connubii* of Pope Pius XI,

Catholic Truth Society, translation, London 1930, sections 1 and 56.

6. The title is unfortunate because it fails to capture the positive overtones of the original *France Pays de Mission*.

7. Vatican II, Decree on Priests, *Presbyterorum Ordinis*. From Section 8, page 550 in the edition of W. A. Abbott, *The Documents of Vatican II*. Published in 1966 by The America Press, New York.

8. Vatican II, *Lumen Gentium*, Chapter 2. Sections 9–17, pages 24–37 in Abbott.

9. L. Cerfaux, *The Church in the Theology of St Paul*, New York 1959. I have drawn extensively from this book in this section.

10. *Lumen Gentium*, Chapter 1. Section 1, page 15 in Abbott.

11. *Lumen Gentium*, Chapter 3. Sections 18–29, pages 37–58 in Abbott.

12. *Lumen Gentium*, Chapter 3. Section 24, page 47 in Abbott.

13. *Lumen Gentium*, Chapter 4. Especially Section 31, page 57 in Abbott.

14. Countless books have been written on the subject. Useful summaries can be found in J. L. McKenzie, *Dictionary of the Bible*, London 1972, pages 479–82; and X. Leon-Dufour, *Vocabulaire de Théologie Biblique*, Paris 1966, Cols. 951–956.

15. *cf.* Matthew 7:21, as elucidated by X. Leon-Dufour, Col. 955.

16. Matthew 25:37, *cf.* J. Fenton, *St Matthew* (Penguin Commentaries), London 1963, page 402.

17. *Lumen Gentium*, Chapter 1. Section 5, page 18 in Abbott.

CHAPTER TWO *Ecumenical Standstill*

1. M. J. Congar, *Divided Christendom*, London 1939.

2. I am quoting from the 1958 edition of the *Catechism of Christian Doctrine*, Catholic Truth Society, London.

3. Vatican II, *Unitatis Redintigratio*, Chapter 1. Section 4, page 349 in the edition of W. A. Abbott, *The Documents of Vatican II*.

4. Page references in this section refer to *Anglican–Roman Catholic International Commission: The Final Report*, Catholic Truth Society/Society for Promoting Christian Knowledge, London 1982.

5. *Unitatis Redintigratio*, Chapter 1. Section 4, page 348 in Abbott.

6. *Papal Primacy and the Universal Church: Lutherans and Catholics in Dialogue*, Volume 5, edited by Paul C. Empie and T. Austin Murphy, Minneapolis 1974.

7. Empie and Murphy, page 20.

8. *Quadragesimo Anno, Acta Apostolicae Sedis*, 1931, page 203; and

Mater et Magistra, A.A.S., 1961, page 414; and Vatican II, *Gaudium et Spes*, Chapter 5. Section 86, page 300 in Abbott.
9. Empie and Murphy, page 32.

CHAPTER THREE *The Clergy React*
1. Resolution 7, page 9 of the official report.
2. *Co-responsibility in the Church*, paragraph 11.
3. *ibid*, paragraph 20.
4. *ibid*, paragraph 34.
5. *ibid*, paragraphs 47 and 48.

CHAPTER FOUR *The Laity Assimilate The Council*

1. C. H. Lawrence, *Mediaeval Monasticism*, London 1984, page 78.
2. The most accessible presentation of his views is perhaps in K. Rahner, *Mission and Grace*, Volume II, London 1964, pages 95–98.
3. Vatican II, *Lumen Gentium*, Chapter 5. Section 40, page 67 in the edition of W. A. Abbott, *The Documents of Vatican II*.
4. A concise statement of the principles is to be found in the Decree on the Laity, Section 3, page 492.
5. *ibid*, Section 19, page 510; and Section 24, page 513.
6. *Lumen Gentium*, Chapter 4. Section 37, page 64; and *Gaudium et Spes*, Section 62, page 270.
7. M. Hornsby-Smith and R. M. Lee, *Roman Catholic Opinion*, page 192. Similar results have been published for other nations where sociological investigation is accepted as normal.
8. The final article in the series, by Dr J. Dominian, was published in the issue of 17 November 1984.
9. Specifically requested in *A Time for Building*, 1976, page 41.
10. "The Easter People", Section 85, states: "We have no adequate analysis of lapsation, and an insufficient analysis of the world we need to evangelise."
11. Catholic Truth Society, London 1980, reference number Do 521. I will designate it as CR for the rest of this section.
12. St Paul's Publications, Slough 1980. I will designate it as EP for the rest of this section and I will refer to it, not by page numbers, but by the numbers of the paragraphs.
13. *A Time for Building*, Section F, page 41.
14. M. Hornsby-Smith and R. M. Lee, *Roman Catholic Opinion*.
15. *Catholic Voice*, Catholic Voice Publications, September 1984. (I hasten to add that *Catholic Voice* is not the journal of the diocese of Lancaster.)

16. J. F. Coventry, *Problems of Authority*, edited by J. M. Todd, London 1961. Also published in French by the Editions du Cerf, Paris.

17. Much of the remaining part of this chapter was published in an article entitled "Catholic Theology in the U.K.", in *The Month*, September 1984. I am grateful to the editor for permission to reproduce it here.

18. One of the most accessible studies in English is the symposium *Authority in the Church*, edited by J. M. Todd, London 1961; also M. J. Congar, *Power and Poverty in the Church*, London 1964.

19. *Lumen Gentium*, Section 24, page 47 in Abbott.

20. O. Chadwick, *The Popes and the European Revolution*, Oxford 1981, page 104.

CHAPTER FIVE *Handing It On To The Next Generation*

1. Analysed by M. Wordsworth and S. Freeman, "Generation Differences in Beliefs", *The British Journal of Sociology*, Volume XXXIV, number 3, 1983, pages 416–437.

2. Wordsworth and Freeman, page 424.

3. Wordsworth and Freeman, page 422.

4. M. Hornsby-Smith, *Catholic Education: The Unobtrusive Partner*, London 1978.

5. *ibid*, page 66.

6. *ibid*, page 67.

7. *ibid*, page 180.

8. *ibid*, page 180.

9. *ibid*, pages 137–138.

10. M. Hornsby-Smith and R. M. Lee, *Roman Catholic Opinion*.

11. *ibid*, page 214.

12. *ibid*, page 215.

13. *ibid*, page 104.

14. *ibid*, pages 90–91.

15. *ibid*, pages 88, 89 and 104.

16. *ibid*, pages 104 and 131.

17. Published in the Fisher House Newsletter, Cambridge 1983; and also in *The Universe*, 11 November 1983.

18. Ronald Pluck, *Religious Beliefs and Attitudes of Young People raised in the Catholic Faith*, Bedford College, 1983. Shortened version by Georgette Carver.

19. *ibid*, page 2.

20. *ibid*, page 3; and G. Carver, page 2.

21. G. Carver, page 2.

22. E. Guy, *The Synods in English*, Stratford-on-Avon, 1886, page 268.
23. Edited by Kevin Nichols, and published in London by the Association of Teaching Religious.
24. *Theology and Education*, page xiii.
25. Jean Wicks, *Theology and Education*, page 2.
26. Patrick Walsh, *Theology and Education*, pages 63–64.
27. K. Nichols, *Theology and Education*, page 116.
28. Mervyn Davies, *Theology and Education*, page 93.
29. W. T. Glynn, *Aims and Objectives in Catholic Education*, Stoke-on-Trent, 1980.
30. *ibid*, pages 1, 2 and 3.
31. *Signposts and Homecomings*, edited by Bishop D. Konstant, London 1981, page 1.
32. *ibid*, page 105.
33. *ibid*, page 116.
34. *ibid*, page 143.
35. Commented on in *The Month*, June 1984, pages 222–225.
36. Vatican II, Decree on Religious Freedom, *Dignitas Humanae*, Chapter 2, Section 9, page 689 in Abbott.
37. Much of this final section was published in *The Month*, October 1980, and I am grateful to the editor for permission to reproduce it here.

CHAPTER SIX *The Nerve Centre*

1. M. Hornsby-Smith and R. M. Lee, *Roman Catholic Opinion*.
2. E. P. Thompson, *The Making of the English Working Class*, London 1980, page 384.
3. Quoted in Thompson, page 434.
4. Reported in *The Month*, September 1981, pages 293–300.
5. *The Month*, page 294.
6. *The Month*, page 295.
7. Vatican II, Decree on the Laity. Sections 5 and 10, page 495 in the edition of W. A. Abbott, *The Documents of Vatican II*.
8. Christopher Brooker, *The Observer*, 6 January 1980.
9. *The Sower*, August 1980, "Small Groups in a Parish".
10. This in essence is the widely accepted theory of Ulrich Stultz, "Die Eigenkirche als Element des mittelalterishgermanischen Kirchenrechtes", Basle, 1895.
11. G. Bardy, *Pretres d'hier et d'aujourd'hui*, Paris 1945, page 53.
12. *Codex Iuris Canonici*, Vatican Press, Rome 1983.

CHAPTER SEVEN *Basic Communities*

1. *Pro Mundi Vita*, Bulletin Number 62, September 1976. Edited by Michael Bergman, page 7. I am indebted to that bulletin for much of the information in this chapter.
2. *Pro Mundi Vita*, page 12; and *The Month*, June 1980, page 184.
3. Medellin Declaration, Chapter 15, Section 10, in "The Church in the Present Day Transformation of Latin America in the Light of the Council", Washington 1979, page 185.
4. Puebla Declaration, Section 96, in "Evangelisation at Present and in the Future of Latin America". Published by Catholic Institute for International Relations, London 1980, page 499.
5. *Pro Mundi Vita*, page 13.
6. *ibid*, page 15.
7. *ibid*, page 15.
8. *ibid*, page 17.
9. *ibid*, page 20.
10. *ibid*, page 22.
11. *ibid*, page 22.
12. Author of *France: Pays de Mission*, 1943, translated into English as *France Pagan*.
13. Author of *Paroisse Communaute Missionaire*, 1945. Translated into English as *Revolution in a City Parish*, Blackfriars, Oxford 1949.
14. *Pro Mundi Vita*, page 4.
15. *ibid*, page 5.

CHAPTER EIGHT *Basic Priests*

1. Bernard Cooke, *Ministry to Word and Sacraments*, Philadelphia 1976, page 63.
2. *ibid*, page 544.
3. *cf.* J. P. Audet, *Structures of Christian Priesthood*, London 1967, page 159.
4. Printed in H. T. Bruns, *Canones Apostolorum et Concililorum Veterum Selecti*, Berlin 1983, Volume 2, page 5.
5. *ibid*.
6. Council of Arles, Canon 12. From Bruns, Volume 2, page 108.
7. *Eusebius Historia Ecclesiastica*, X, 6, 1–3. *Codex Theodosianus*, 16, 2, 8; 16, 2, 10; (346 AD), 13, 1, 1, (356 AD), 16, 2, 14. All quoted in J. Gaudment, *L'Église dans l'Empire Roman*, Paris 1958, pages 167 and 170.
8. Sozomen, *Historia Ecclesiastica*, VI, 3; and Theodoret, *Historia Ecclesiastica*, IV, 4.

9. Jerome, Letter 52, 5.

10. Jerome, *Commentary on Titus*, Chapter 3, *ad vers.* 14; ed. P. L. Migne, Volume 26, Col. 599.

11. Both noted in Bruns, *op. cit.*, Volume 2, page 146.

12. *cf.* Sulpicius Severus, *Chronicle*, I, 23. in C.S.E.L. I, 26.

13. Canon 6 of the Council of Carthage, 348 AD, echoes again in the Councils of 397 and 419. Bruns, *op. cit.*, Volume 1, pages 125, 137 and 162.

14. Letter 14 to the Bishops of Lucania, Chapter 15, quoted in A. Thiel, *Epistolae Romanorum Pontificum Genuinae*, Brunswick 1867, Volume 1, page 371.

15. Vatican II, *Presbyterorum Ordinis*. From Section 8, page 550 in the edition of W. A. Abbott.

16. *Codex Theodosianus* 16, 22.

17. They have been collected in J. Palanque, *Histoire de l'Église*, edited by Fliche and Martin, Volume III, pages 61 and 519, to which I refer the reader, instead of burdening this section with too many text notes.

18. Quoted by M. J. Congar in *Problems of Authority*, ed. J. M. Todd, page 135.

19. *Presbyterorum Ordinis*. Section 6, page 545 of Abbott.

20. *ibid*, Section 3, page 536.

21. Both surveys are printed in L. Rulla, Immola and Riddick, *Psychological Structure and Vocation*, Rome 1973, page 15.

22. Colin Davies, *The Ageing Clergy*, Allen Hall Review, London May 1983.

23. Studies in the Bulletin of the Movement for the Ordination of Married Men, Liverpool 1984, pages 40–41.

24. Figures in this section come from the *Catholic Directory* 1984, Statistical Section.

25. *The Catholic Almanac*, Huntington, Indiana, 1981.

26. *The Tablet*, 22 September 1984, page 919.

27. *The Priest Today*, Standing Conference of the National Conference of Priests, 1983.

28. *Briefing*, 11 February 1983.

29. The standard sources are: E. Vacanard, *Célibat Écclesiastique, Dictionnaire de Théologie Catholique*, 11, Cols. 2968–2988; L. H. Weber, *Celibacy, in Sacramentum Mundi*, I, pages 275–280; J. Coppens, *Sacerdoce et Célibat*, Louvain 1971; R. Gryson, *Les Origines du Célibat Écclesiastique*, Paris 1970; Pope Paul VI, Encyclical Letter, *Sacerdotalis Coelibatus*; C. H. Lawrence, "The Origins and Development of Ecclesiastical Celibacy", *Clergy Review*, 1975, pages 138–146; O. P. Paul Parvis, "History of Celibacy", *Clergy Review*, September and October 1981, pages 322 ff and 354 ff; *Concilium*, March 1980, "A

Parish's Right to a Priest", edited by J. B. Metz and E
Schillebeeckx.

30. Augustine, *de Genesi ad litteram*, X, 5; and P. L. Migne, 34, 396

31. Letter 167, Section 3.

32. *Presbyterorum Ordinis*, Section 16, page 565 of Abbott.

33. *Pro Mundi Vita*, "Ministry and Community", 3, 1983, page
166.

34. Text in the Bulletin of the Movement for the Ordination of
Married Men, Liverpool April 1984, page 11.

35. The details can be found in *Mission Resumed?* by the author
page 107.

36. Quoted in *The Tablet*, 13 September 1980.

37. Quoted in *The Tablet*, 18 July 1981.

CHAPTER NINE *Diocese as Co-ordinator*

1. *Christus Dominus*, The Decree on the Bishops' Pastoral Office
in the Church, Section 22, page 412.

2. *ibid*, Section 16, page 408.

3. Canons 265–267.

4. *Groundplan*, Catholic Information Office, 1974.

5. *Christus Dominus*, Section 27, page 416. Decree on the Laity
Section 26, page 515.

6. E. Flood, "Will the Sheep be Fed?", *Clergy Review*, December
1984, page 423 ff.

7. E. Flood, "Will the Sheep be Fed?", Part 2, *Clergy Review*
January 1985, page 10 ff.

8. *ibid*, page 11.

9. *Lumen Gentium*, Section 22, pages 42 and 43.

10. *Christus Dominus*, Section 4, page 398.

11. Motu Proprio of Paul VI, "Apostolica Sollicitudo" section 2
page 721, of *Documents of Vatican II*, ed. W. Abbott.

12. P. Hebblethwaite, *Understanding the Synod*, Dublin 1968, page
13.

13. Quoted in J. Tillard, *The Bishop of Rome*, London 1983, page
44.

14. *ibid*, page xii.

15. Catholic Truth Society, London 1972, reference number D
49.

16. *The Tablet*, 26 January 1985, page 98.

17. Quoted in *The Tablet*, 19 January 1985, page 61.

18. *Christus Dominus*, Section 20, page 411.

19. *The Tablet*, 20 September 1984.

20. *The Tablet*, 1 December 1984, page 1205 in an article by Louis McRedmond.
21. Translated into English, by H. P. Liddon, and published in London, 1883.
22. G. Sweeney, "The Wound in the Right Foot: Unhealed?", page 207 of *Bishops and Writers*, edited by A. Hastings, Hertfordshire 1977.